Anne
Campbell

GIRL
DELINQUENTS

BASIL BLACKWELL · OXFORD

© Anne Campbell 1981

First published 1981
Basil Blackwell Publisher Ltd
108 Cowley Road
Oxford OX4 1JF
England

British Library Cataloguing in Publication Data

Campbell, Anne
   Girl delinquents.
   1. Delinquent girls
   I. Title
   364.36'4   HV6046

   ISBN 0-631-12741-0
   ISBN 0-631-12575-2 Pbk

Typesetting by Pintail Studios Limited, Ringwood, Hampshire
Printed in Great Britain by Billing and Sons Ltd
Guildford, London, Oxford, Worcester

Contents

Acknowledgements

I would like to thank all those people beside whom I have worked over the last few years and who have contributed, often unwittingly, to the ideas expressed in this book. In particular I thank Steven Muncer, Peter Marsh, Michael Argyle and Ann McKendry. I owe particular gratitude to all the girls who participated in my research, especially those who talked to me about fighting. I hope that I have done justice to the ideas that they expressed to me. I am also grateful to the Home Office, which granted permission for me to work inside two of its Borstals, and to all the schools, assessment centres and youth projects that co-operated so fully.

I would also like to thank those people, some of whom I never met, whose work gave me a lot to think about: Freda Adler, Phil Cohen, Angela McRobbie, Walter Miller, Carol Smart and Ian Taylor and his associates.

The manuscript was typed by Ann Tomlinson and Debbie Smith.

CHAPTER 1

Girl Delinquents: the Problem of Definition

Unfortunately, but not altogether surprisingly, the serious study of female crime emerged hand in hand with the popularization of the women's movement, before which women had been little more than a footnote in the world of sociology. As women gained visibility, they became more inviting targets of research. As middle-class women flooded into academia, they had a natural desire to study their own sex. But this conjunction was also unfortunate in its consequences. The rush of enthusiasm galloped straight past even the most fundamental need to define its own subject matter. It sped past the massive body of available data on males, blinkered to the possibility of its relevance to females. Dizzy with monomania, women became obsessed with their total uniqueness – *their* alienation, *their* frustration, *their* powerlessness. Breathlessly, this enthusiasm careered into a single arena of politico-social debate: did liberation cause the increase in women's crime? With the din of sometimes ill-informed intellectual battle raging in the background, the time is right to pause, reassess and review some of the assumptions that have been made to date. To do this, it is necessary to begin with the most central question of all: what is female delinquency?

If you walked out in the street today, stopped ten people at random and asked them, 'What is a delinquent?', almost certainly you would get ten different replies. The problem seems to arise because people look for different things as the defining features of delinquency. Some people believe it can be assessed simply by appearance – delinquent kids are those who wear braces or big boots or who sport tattoos; others believe that it is to do with the attitudes they hold – anti-disciplinarian or anarchist. Some would say that it is to do with where they are – in Borstals or community homes or prisons; others might argue

1

that it is to do with their lifestyle – delinquents are kids who skip school or go to punk clubs or support Manchester United. Some would say delinquency is about breaking the law – the definition includes any young person who mugs an old lady or rides a bicycle without lights; other people argue that the issue has to do not with law-breaking but with detection.

If you went on to inquire whether there were important differences between male and female delinquents, the confusion would almost certainly worsen. Some would tell you of the shocking decline in girls' sexual standards today. Others would claim that girls are far more vicious than boys, or that all these new walk-through stores encourage girls to steal. Others firmly maintain that boys will be boys and that getting into trouble is part and parcel of male development. Yet others would say that there is nothing to choose between the sexes. Girls don't get enough love, and boys don't get enough beatings. Give them sympathy; give them the birch. Bring back National Service; stop all this feminist nonsense. Different solutions for different sexes.

In the public mind confusion exists at all levels, from the definition of delinquency, through its public expression and on to its treatment. It is tempting to imagine that this public view doesn't matter. After all, it is the police, the magistrates and judges, the professionals who control delinquency. But are these official bodies any more unanimous than the people in the street? Are they not just as responsive to the climate of opinion percolating through society from radical movements, newspapers, legislation and education? The implementation of the law changes faster than legislation and is far more real in its effects on people's lives. Public services and the people in the community live side by side and can affect one another. Amid the confusion, surely there is some absolute standard of delinquency for girls and boys? For many years criminologists have struggled with this central problem, often within the illusory order of the ivory tower. Before considering what adolescent girls do when they break the law, it is important to understand the backdrop of definitions and theories that have affected public policy and public understanding.

Sociologists in the 1930s wanted to arrive at a very precise definition of what criminality or delinquency might be.

Fortunately, criminal law itself provided them with a ready-made answer to their problems. Laid out in black and white were the rules of society, and the term 'criminal' was thought to refer, quite simply, to those people who broke them. But a second glance at this solution revealed problems. New laws were generated and old ones repealed. Different countries (even different states within the same country) failed to agree on what should be considered a crime. The universal definition of criminality kept slipping and sliding as social attitudes all over the world changed.

Statistics were then invoked to formalize the notion of deviance and, by implication, criminality. For many traits or behaviours it was found that the population ranged itself along a frequency axis in a bell-shaped curve, with by far the majority of people falling solidly in the middle. Lemert (1951) argued that the small number of people who were at either end of the continuum should be considered, in a mathematical sense, deviant. So where intelligence was concerned, deviants were geniuses and subnormals; in the context of height, dwarfs and giants were deviants. This principle was applied to law-breaking also. But in most people's minds the very word 'deviant' was (and is) a value-laden one with very pejorative overtones, and it was still unclear what the criterion should be by which one could decide who was abnormally pro-social and anti-social – let alone how such traits could ever be measured.

Becker (1973) proposed that the idea of an objective, value-free definition of delinquency was impossible, and that the definition must take into account the fact that society singles out certain individuals for blame and punishment. A deviant, then, is someone who society has labelled as such. According to this definition, of course, the murderer who remains undetected and lives out his life peacefully in suburbia is not a deviant at all. Becker's definition hinges very strongly on other people's judgements of the individual and fails to stress that the individual holds views of his own, which may or may not be affected by society's judgement of him. The undetected murderer may experience lifelong guilt and may believe himself to be a criminal or a psychopath even though he has never been labelled as such. However, Becker certainly succeeded in making one point strongly and correctly: laws and norms are not arbitrary. They are the products of the values and attitudes of those in power, who are trying either to maintain the *status quo* or to change it in a way that is favourable to their goals. Politicians, not gods, make laws, and politicians are usually in league with those who wield power in any society. The laws are supported by the media (similarly, the instruments of the powerful) which assume postures of moral outrage towards particular forms of mis-behaviour or crimes. Socialist newspapers decry the crimes of industry – tax frauds and investment crimes. Tory papers attack the teenage mugger and football hooligan. The attitude that the law adopts towards the female offender has to be seen in terms of the general position of women, which those in power wish to maintain or change.

Having considered the way in which criminologists have attempted to arrive at some acceptable definition of their subject matter, we can now see how these three approaches have manifested themselves in the study of that little-understood 'deviant' the *female* delinquent, and to what mistaken assump-tions they have sometimes led in understanding the real nature of female crime.

Behind institution walls

It is the Italian Lombroso (with W. Ferrero) who must be credited with the first systematic attempt to study female law-breakers, undertaken in 1895. His choice of criminal criterion was unproblematic – he simply went into prisons and took measurements from the inmates. Studies up to the present day have been content to share this early methodology. However, there is good reason to believe that Lombroso studied a very restricted, and perhaps untypical, sample of women criminals.

First, it is obvious that not everyone who commits a criminal offence ends up in prison, and this is not merely a practical matter associated with the size and efficiency of the police force. Sometimes the courts give suspended sentences, conditional discharges and fines in order positively to prevent someone who is not a 'criminal type' from going to prison. Second, in the main it is true to say that the more serious the crime, the more likely it is that the perpetrator will be arrested and finally institutionalized. So it is probable that there were a disproportionate number of murderers and violent criminals among Lombroso's women. Third, in a strongly religious country, as Italy was at that time, acts of immorality were particularly likely to be heavily punished. The Roman Catholic religion's exaltation of women to the status of earthly Madonnas strongly sanctioned those who failed to adhere to the prevailing view of sex as designed for the lawful procreation of children and as an act of submission by the woman. This must have led to a particularly stern view being taken of prostitution.

Because of the position of women at that time, it would be wrong to view these female criminals as early liberationists struggling consciously to reject their female role. Changes in women's rights have been problematic in Catholic countries even in this decade, let alone a hundred years ago. It seems more likely that imprisoned women were made up of three types: women whose prostitution or theft offences were motivated quite simply by poverty; others who had failed to become socialized into the 'appropriate' female role because of low IQ or severely disturbed family relationships; and those whose violent behaviour was symptomatic of some clinical disorder. Poverty was not invoked by Lombroso as a plausible motive for crime, since women were seen as marginal to society and were deemed to be the financial responsibility of their families or their husbands. To have neither of these sources of support represented more a failure than a misfortune. A man's sphere of influence was in society, and therefore in men poverty might be considered an understandable motive for theft. But a woman's arena was the domestic hearth, and crimes committed beyond the boundary of the home represented real deviance not only from morality but from the role of womanhood.

It was this supposition – that the domestic nature of women was ordained by God and nature – that prompted Lombroso to assert that female criminals were not women at all but hermaphrodites. Lombroso's theory of female criminality certainly accommodated the idea that crime was associated with a low IQ and, indeed, with a general deficiency in most spheres of mental activity. Similarly, the psychopath or schizophrenic provided him with the perfect evidence on which to base his view that these women were at an earlier, less evolved stage of development than either normal women or males. They could easily be likened to unthinking savages. It is unfortunate that this strongly deterministic view of women criminals did not lead to more humane treatment of them but, as Lombroso pointed out, like animals, they had a greater capacity to survive harsh conditions than the more refined and cognitive male.

Many of the major works written in this century on the subject of female delinquency have similarly looked at institutional inmates (Cowie et al., 1968; Konopka, 1966; Richardson, 1969). However, the advent of the juvenile court, set up to deal specifically with young people's offences, has changed the nature of the bias in selection for institutionalization. In Britain the Children and Young Persons Acts of this century represented landmarks in the gradual modification of society's attitude towards the young offender. No longer seen as simply bad, youthful misbehaviour was regarded in a more humanitarian light: 'When in any proceedings before any court ... the custody or upbringing of an infant ... is in question the court, in deciding the question, shall regard the welfare of the infant as the first and paramount consideration' (Guardianship of Infants Act 1925). This principle was taken further in 1969, when a new Act was passed that specified the conditions under which a young person should be taken away from the care of his parents and entrusted instead to the local authority, which should stand *in loco parentis*. The court must be satisfied that the child's development or health is being neglected, that he is exposed to moral danger, that he is beyond the control of his parents, that he is truanting from school or that he is guilty of a criminal offence. In addition, the court must also decide that he is in need of care and control, which he is unlikely to receive unless the court makes an order on him.

One of the most important effects of this Act was to destroy the previous demarcation between criminality and deprivation. Up until 1969 young people were put into care either because they had been found guilty of criminal offences or because they were found to be in need of care and protection. A clear distinction was made between these cases in the workings of the court and in the files that would follow the young people through their career in the hands of the social services. In 1969 the distinction was swept away, reflecting the more liberal view that young people are not by nature bad or depraved but are rendered so by the influence of their family or of society. The major writers in the field of female delinquency based their conclusions on children admitted to approved schools and reformatories *before* the 1969 Act was passed. According to the Ingleby Report of 1960, the Home Office noted that while 95 per cent of boys were sent to approved schools by reason of having committed imprisonable offences, the same was true of only 36 per cent of girls. Indeed, Richardson, writing nine years later, finds that in her sample of girls only 24 per cent were guilty of an offence. Chesney-Lind (1973, 1977), writing on the juvenile justice system in America, makes the same observation: between 70 and 75 per cent of girls before the courts in America were charged with 'juvenile offences' (offences that, if committed by an adult, would not be regarded as criminal at all), whereas the same was true for only 31 per cent of boys. The implications of these figures are very important indeed. Regardless of whether girls commit as many illegal acts as boys, the courts prefer to judge girls in terms of their *moral* welfare rather than in terms of their status as delinquents.

When a court makes a decision to remove a girl from the custody of her parents and she is not charged with any criminal offence, what evidence does it take into consideration? It is informed by the statements of social workers, psychologists, psychiatrists and educationalists, whose testimony makes reference to the girl's current lifestyle. The court then attempts to assess whether or not the girl is in a state of 'moral danger' or 'beyond the control of her parents'. In certain states in America the legislation is even more archaically worded. In Alaska, for example, a delinquent is 'any child under the age of 18 years . . . who is in danger of becoming or remaining a person who leads an idle, dissolute, lewd or immoral life . . . or who is guilty of or takes part in or submits to any immoral act or conduct'. Until 1972 girls in Connecticut were subject to this ruling: 'Any unmarried female between the ages of 16 and 21 . . . who is in manifest danger of falling into habits of vice, or who is leading a vicious life, or who has committed any crime . . . may be committed to . . . an institution.'

It is apparent that the juvenile court faces two major

difficulties with this kind of decision. First, who is to decide what constitutes lewdness or vice or viciousness or moral danger? In concrete terms, the magistrates, who are lay people recruited from the community with a 'special aptitude' for this kind of work. Their judgement will be based on the report of the social worker assigned to the case, so that a great deal rests on the information that he selects and the way in which he words his final conclusions. The magistrates may ask for further information to be provided and, for girls only, this information can take the form of a virginity test performed by a doctor or a vaginal smear to test for venereal disease. This is true in both the United States and Britain. Girls are quite routinely asked in court about their sexual experiences, in a way that reduces the question of immorality quite clearly to sexuality. The double standard is alive and well. While boys are expected to experiment sexually (and, indeed, a failure to do so may be taken as abnormal), among girls such behaviour is sufficient grounds for legal action. So the fate of a girl appearing before the juvenile court may well hinge on the magistrates' attitudes to sexuality or drugs or the girl's choice of companions. It should be noted also that in Britain while guilt of a criminal charge must be proved to the magistrates 'beyond reasonable doubt', for issues of a non-criminal nature guilt must be demonstrated only on the 'balance of probabilities'. Unlike in criminal proceedings, hearsay evidence is considered admissible. In the United States the wording of juvenile legislation has recently been challenged as unconstitutionally vague, over-broad and unacceptable, since it punishes a status (see Armstrong, 1977).

The second difficulty in this kind of case is that the juvenile court is being asked to do something that no fully trained social scientist would ever dream of attempting. It must predict the future of the young person. From the information that it hears it must try to assess what will become of the girl if the courts were not to intervene. In the last decade intense debate among psychologists has led to the virtual rejection of the notion of measurable and enduring personality dispositions. It has become more and more clear that situational factors have a very marked effect on behaviour, and that these variables are well-nigh impossible to predict in advance. In spite of this, in magistrates' courts three laymen from the community attempt the impossible, assisted only by a mixture of common sense and faith. On the basis of their decision the girl may be removed from her home, parents and schooling and subjected to a reformatory system that has received little support from outcome studies designed to assess its success.

Since 1969 the distinction between the criminal girl and the girl 'in need of care and protection' has been removed. Both may be assigned to similar institutions and may receive similar treatment. But has the double standard applied to boys and girls really been removed? In 1977, of all young people placed on care orders in Britain because of moral danger, 85.3 per cent were female and 14.7 per cent male. Although similar numbers of males and females received court orders, seven times as many girls as boys did so as a result of being 'in moral danger'. Cowie et al. and Richardson were prepared to assume that there were no important conceptual or practical differences in their samples between girls who had committed offences and those who had not. They were all taken together as one homogeneous group. In justification of this Cowie et al. state: 'In three-quarters of the cases, the delinquency was in the nature of misbehaviour, mainly sexual, of a kind not subject to legal sanction after the age of 17; in the remainder there was an indictable offence.' Authorities are agreed that not too much should be made of this difference. Gibbens (1959) has commented on the close association between waywardness and anti-social behaviour, noting that 'girls who before puberty steal from home . . . later turn to . . . making undesirable sexual relationships' (p. 67).

The Association of Headmasters, Headmistresses and Matrons of Approved Schools reported to the Ingleby Committee that:

> In our view this term [in need of care and protection] is wrongly used, as they are not usually innocent victims of circumstances, but girls of shallow personality to whom promiscuous living appears attractive. They are often completely anti-social, absconding, refusing training and committing *further offences*, (Richardson, 1969, p. 84; present author's emphasis).

(Note that they have never been charged with any offence to date.) Richardson also quotes the 1960 Home Office Ingleby

Report in support of her contention that her sample is homogeneous:

> Almost all adolescent girls sent to approved schools (whether as offenders or not) have a history of sexual immorality, and many of those sent as being in need of care and protection or beyond control are known to have committed offences. (p. 84)

If this is indeed the case, why are the girls never formally charged with them and given the opportunity to defend themselves? Further, even if this association between promiscuity and crime has been shown to be empirically true of *some* girls, it is surely quite wrong to extrapolate this finding and apply it to all girls in institutions.

This equation that writers have made between institutionalization and behavioural delinquency (in terms of committing criminal offences) has further confused the issue of defining female delinquency. The over-concern with sexuality in the case of girls as distinct from boys had led to the popular assumption that the greater part of female delinquency is sexual in nature. The popular belief is that girls mature faster than boys and that they are often emotionally unready for sexual relationships, although physically capable and desirous of them. Society believes it must protect them from themselves. This is obviously a matter for debate. A fact that seems beyond dispute is that society has no right to penalize girls for behaviour that it excuses, and even encourages, in boys. This preoccupation with sexual precocity in girl delinquents has had powerful effects on the theoretical formulations that have been offered to account for their behaviour, as well as on popular views about the legislation and treatment of female offenders.

Official crime figures

Some writers have based their explanations of female criminality not on institutionalization but on official criminal statistics — more specifically, on the number of females found guilty of indictable offences. If there were a perfect correspondence between the commission of a criminal act and the proof of guilt in court, this approach would be unproblematic. However, many criminologists have pointed out the ways in which police and court procedures systematically militate against the apprehension and conviction of certain crimes and certain criminals. These procedural biases are particularly relevant when we consider the position of women in the legal system. Even if girls committed the same gross number of offences as boys, there are many factors that might conspire to make them less likely ever to appear in the official statistics.

At the level of the act itself, it is known that the likelihood of a final conviction is directly and positively related to the gravity of the offence. Very few murderers remain undetected, but estimates show that with respect to more minor crimes the criminal has the odds in her favour. One American study (United States President's Commission, 1967) found that 98.2 per cent of traffic violations, 97.1 per cent of petty theft offences and 99.7 per cent of fist fights went undetected. This means that if girls confined themselves to more minor crimes, they would have a much better chance of evading detection. Similarly, some sorts of offences are much less visible to the police than are others. Domestic fighting and theft, violence within schools and other autonomous institutions are unlikely to be witnessed by the police. Certain kinds of offences, particularly relating to prostitution, theft by prostitutes, illegal abortion and infanticide, are also unlikely to be detected by the police, since the victims are usually unwilling or unable to report them, and other witnesses may conspire to keep them secret. It is also true that within some classes and subcultures many technically illegal offences are not considered wrong. In many jobs petty theft from the employer may be a 'perk' of the job, and men who use prostitutes accept the possibility of being 'rolled' as part of the game. Playground fights or wife beatings, while technically cases of assault, are often thought to be part and parcel of daily life. The mode of commission and location of offences also affect the likelihood of detection. Hindelang (1976) has shown that youngsters who commit crimes in groups rather than alone are more likely to be apprehended, and in rural districts more crime is detected than in cities.

Even when a crime comes to the attention of the police the

individual officer will exercise his discretion in deciding whether to book the offence or dismiss the suspect with an informal or formal caution. This decision does not rest wholly on the whim of the individual policeman, and there are good reasons why a caution may be preferred. In the case of a first offence, a relatively petty misdemeanour or insufficient evidence for conviction, the suspect will usually be cautioned. However, some studies have shown that other, more personal factors are often involved in this decision (Hindelang, 1976; Piliavin and Briar, 1964). These factors include the suspect's age, race, mode of dress, his parents' willingness to take responsibility for him, his class, accent and attitude to the officer. In some cases where a caution might be preferable an officer may find himself provoked by verbal bravado of a group of boys into booking them. It is at this point that girls clearly have an advantage. Their interpersonal style and attitude to the policeman are likely to be much less aggressive and provocative. While a boy may have to prove to his friends that he is not intimidated by this rival male merely because he is in uniform, girls are not subject to the same pressure. If anything, girls may take pride in their ability to disarm police officers and may diffuse the situation by a show of feminine remorse or flirtation.

The policeman feels less threatened by a girl than by boys. He also is aware that the crime rate among girls is about one-eighth as high as it is among boys. He may therefore feel that girls by nature are not 'criminal types' and so seek some explanation to account for this statistical rarity, a young female delinquent, whom he finds himself facing: perhaps she has been led on by boys or older girls? Perhaps her parents are guilty of not exercising proper control over her whereabouts? In any case, a booking and the consequent trial would only serve to turn an innocent piece of misbehaviour into a full-scale crime, for which the girl would be stigmatized for years. In order to protect her from the legal machinery, he may leave the whole affair at the stage of caution. In this way one fewer girl appears in official statistics, and the self-fulfilling belief that women are not 'criminal types' has turned through one more cycle.

Many people, including policemen, take the view that female delinquency results from factors beyond the girls' control. While boys must stand up and take responsibility for their actions in the face of society, girls are seen as helpless victims of circumstance, in need of understanding, not punishment. How does this differential attitude arise? Fundamentally, girls are still seen as relatively passive and tractable. They are affected not so much by societal pressures as by the attitudes and values of their families. They are *tabulae rasae*, blank slates waiting to be inscribed with the moral dictates of life as taught by parents and schools. Boys, on the other hand, are seen as having a 'bad streak', a view that is similar to the notion of original sin. It is only by the restraining and repressing *mores* of society that their natural, headstrong impulsiveness can be contained. When it breaks through in the form of delinquency the parents may be charged, if at all, with a sin of omission, not commission. Since so few girls commit crimes, the explanation for delinquency is sought in individual pathology, and a young female criminal is more likely to be labelled as maladjusted or afflicted with behavioural or emotional problems than as simply delinquent. These assumptions are as much in the head of the policeman as in that of anyone else. Up to a much later age than boys, girls are seen as the responsibility of their parents. So the policeman may take a young girl home and hand the problem over to them, rather than to the courts.

In 1978 in Britain of all girls aged 14–17 suspected of having committed an indictable offence, 56 per cent were let off with a caution as compared with 33 per cent of boys. With respect to sexual offences, 78 per cent of girls but only 67 per cent of boys were simply cautioned. For theft offences, 62 per cent of girls and only 41 per cent of boys were cautioned. For violent crimes against the person, 36 per cent of girls were not prosecuted, but only 23 per cent of boys were that lucky. In the face of these figures, it is clear that girls are much less likely to figure in official statistics than boys, particularly in relation to the less serious offences.

Even when a girl reaches the court because of a criminal offence she may still have factors working in her favour. In the United States there has been a wealth of simulated jury studies attempting to investigate the psychology of the establishment of guilt in courts. Efran (1974) has shown that attractive defendants are much less frequently found guilty than ugly ones, and that this bias reaches its peak when males judge the culpability of females. However, when an attractive woman has been accused of using her attractiveness to illegal ends there is a reversal of judgement, so that she is *more* likely to be thought guilty than a less attractive woman. Now, Morris (1964) claims that girls in institutions are much less attractive than control groups of girls. She suggests that physical appearance may be of direct etiological significance among girls. However, two much more plausible explanations present themselves. First, institutional food is designed to promote neither slim figures nor clear complexions; much of it is stodgy and greasy. Also there is little incentive in an all-female punitive institution to look stylish – girls are issued with second-hand clothing and are not allowed to use cosmetics. A second explanation is that physically unattractive girls may be more likely to be found guilty of offences and subsequently to find themselves in reformatories. If Efran is right, then we might expect male magistrates to be harsher on attractive girls who, as a result of their looks, may have engaged in precocious sex or associated with older males. However, magistrates, like policemen, also harbour protective feelings towards girls as opposed to boys. This may affect their decision about guilt where the evidence is ambiguous or insufficient. They may feel that where there is room for doubt, a girl should not be subjected to the harsh conditions of an institution and the stigma of a criminal label.

Another important factor is the nature of the court case faced by girls as opposed to boys. Even if a girl is suspected of having committed an illegal act, she may well find herself facing a charge of being beyond parental control or in moral danger. Chesney-Lind (1974) argues that in the United States many female crimes are 'sexualized'; that is, the criminality is excused but the sexual aspect is not. A girl who is found soliciting or using a house for immoral purposes may well have the criminal charge dropped but may still appear in a juvenile court on a 'moral danger' case. Similarly, even non-sexual acts, such as shoplifting and fighting, may be dealt with not as crimes but as indicators of the fact that a girl is 'beyond parental control'. In 1973, of all youngsters charged with offences in juvenile court (as opposed to non-criminal proceedings) 63 per cent were boys and only 37 per cent girls (Smart, 1977). By 1977 no girls at all were given court orders as a result of a criminal act. This may reflect the true rate of commission of criminal offences, or it may reflect a bias in the sorts of proceedings brought against girls.

If we look at official statistics relating to the way in which the courts deal with boys and girls, these suspicions of a double standard are endorsed. In Britain in 1975, of all girls between 14 and 17 who came before the courts 53.4 per cent were given a non-custodial sentence, compared with 36.5 per cent of boys of the same age. (A non-custodial sentence is any disposal which does not immediately consign the individual to an institution.) At age 17–21 the same imbalance was evident: 63 per cent of girls but only 42.7 per cent of boys received non-custodial sentences.

Self-reported delinquency

The self-reported delinquency technique has been developed in order to avoid these biases in official figures and to gain a better picture of the true rate of undetected crime in the community. Basically, it consists of asking a selected group of individuals to admit to any illegal acts in which they have taken part. Sometimes the questioning takes the form of an interview, at which the interviewees are asked to sort cards, each bearing a description of an offence, into boxes marked 'yes' and 'never'. They are then questioned about the circumstances and details of each admitted offence. More usually, subjects are given a checklist of offences and asked, under conditions of anonymity, to tick those acts that they have performed at least once. In terms of the results produced by these two techniques, Krohn et al. (1975) have shown that it makes very little difference which one is used.

The biggest difficulty is, of course, the validity of the individual's report. How can we be sure people are not exaggerating or concealing their own delinquency? Many studies have shown that there is a strong positive association between an individual's report of his own delinquency and his official police record (Gibson et al., 1970; Hardt and Peterson-Hardt, 1977; Kulik et al., 1968). Shapland (1975) in Britain showed a clear relationship between the degree of reported contact with police and self-reported delinquency. Boys with no contacts admitted 8.94 offences; those with informal contact, 13.56; those with formal cautions, 15.33; and those with convictions, 20.25. So there is some correspondence between official and unofficial delinquency. But it could be argued that boys who have been in contact with the police admit to more offences because they have already been labelled as delinquent and feel that they must live up to that image. Clark and Tifft (1966) used a polygraph lie detector to check the truth of what individuals said in interviews and concluded that 92 per cent of responses were honest. However, the apparatus measures fluctuations in general autonomic excitation, which may occur not only because the subject is lying – it may be a natural response to the shock of being asked incriminating questions. Gold (1966) checked his informants' admissions against statements by friends about the subjects' delinquent involvements. He found substantial agreement. Overall, the evidence suggests that while exaggeration and concealment may occur, self-report measures are likely to be a more reliable index than official figures.

Many American self-report studies have shown that girls admit to far more criminal activity than official figures would indicate (Gold, 1966; Short and Nye, 1958; Wise, 1967). Hindelang (1971), for example, conducted an extensive self-report study in a co-educational high school in Oakland, California, giving checklists to 319 boys and 444 girls (see table 1.1). More males than females admitted to every offence. Offences that showed the greatest sex differences were gambling, theft over $10, gang fighting and promiscuous sexual behaviour. This last item is particularly interesting, since girls are frequently removed from home because of it, yet it was admitted by 58.2 per cent of boys and only 11.9 per cent of girls. The smallest sex differences emerged with respect to drug items (using LSD, heroin, sniffing glue and drinking alcohol) and minor school misdemeanours (skipping school, cheating on exams and using false identity cards). Although more boys admitted offences than girls, the overall ratio was 2.56 to 1; considerably lower than official figures, which put it at about 8 to 1. If boys and girls admitted to very different sorts of offences, then a correlation between them would give a value of around −1.0. In fact, Hindelang reports a correlation of +0.925 between admission patterns of boys and girls. Now this is very important indeed. In

TABLE 1.1   *Self-reported delinquency among schoolchildren*

| | Those engaging in acts one or more times | | |
Acts of delinquency	Male (N = 319) %	Female (N = 444) %	Ratio male:female
Theft less than $10	53.45	26.27	2.03
Theft greater than $10	19.02	4.58	4.15
Property destruction (<$10)	51.31	16.35	3.13
Property destruction (>$10)	23.78	7.72	3.08
Drinking alcohol	63.61	42.79	1.48
Getting drunk	39.42	17.44	2.26
Individual fist-fights	56.03	21.64	2.58
Gang fist-fights	25.82	6.27	4.11
Carrying a concealed weapon	33.23	10.13	3.28
Individual weapon fights	11.08	4.10	2.70
Gang weapon fights	8.47	2.90	2.92
Gambling	16.34	3.86	4.23
Using marijuana	26.15	14.50	1.80
Sniffing glue	10.75	6.75	1.58
Using LSD, methedrine or mescaline	7.50	4.86	1.54
Using heroin	4.27	2.90	1.47
Shaking down others for money	9.45	3.15	3.00
Promiscuous sexual behaviour	58.22	11.96	4.86
Drag racing on street	45.17	22.49	2.01
Driving under the influence	21.20	6.36	3.33
Hit-and-run accidents	9.73	7.00	1.39
Cheating on exams	71.76	59.67	1.20
Using false ID	23.86	15.29	1.56
Cutting school	40.56	24.75	1.63

SOURCE: Hindelang, 1971, p. 525.

1968 Cowie et al. wrote:

> The nature of delinquent offences among girls is *completely different* to the delinquent offences committed by boys. A large part of the delinquencies of girls consist in sexually ill-regulated behaviour of a type not to demand social sanctions in the case of an adult. A large part of the indictable offences committed by girls is of a relatively trivial kind, e.g. larceny. The spectrum of offences committed by boys is much more

TABLE 1.2 Results of three British self-report delinquency studies

Acts of delinquency	West and Farrington (1973) Boys (N = 397) per cent admit	Significance level of 2-tailed comparison between boys and girls	Campbell (1976) (N = 66) per cent admit	Jamison (1977) Boys (N = 781) per cent admit	Jamison (1977) Girls (N = 501) per cent admit
1 I have ridden a bicycle without lights after dark.	78.8		68.3	84.6	53.9
2 I have driven a car or motor bike/scooter under 16.	40.1		31.8	28.4	9.8
3 I have been with a group who go round together making a row and sometimes getting into fights and causing disturbance.	23.4		15.2	25.5	23.2
4 I have played truant from school.	80.9		71.2	26.4	34.5
5 I have travelled on a train or bus without a ticket or deliberately paid the wrong fare.	84.4	.001	62.1	59.9	59.5
6 I have let off fireworks in the street.	86.7	.001	18.2	52.8	6.6
7 I have taken money from home without returning it.	11.3	.001	36.4	29.2	24.4
8 I have taken someone else's car or motor bike for a joy ride then taken it back afterwards.	15.6	.01	3.0		

9	I have broken or smashed things in public places like on the streets, cinemas, dance halls, trains or buses.	18.1	.05	12.6	38.9	15.0
10	I have insulted people on the street or got them angry and fought with them.	23.4		15.2		
11	I have broken into a big store or garage or warehouse.	7.3		1.5		
12	I have broken into a little shop even though I may not have taken anything.	8.6		1.5		
13	I have taken something out of a car.	9.6		3.0		
14	I have taken a weapon (like a knife) out with me in case I needed it in a fight.	25.4	.01	7.6	27.0	9.6
15	I have fought with someone in a public place like in the street or a dance.	24.4	.001	19.7	35.7	17.8
16	I have broken the window of an empty house.	66.8	.01	28.8	46.5	8.2
17	I have used a weapon in a fight, like a knife or a razor or a broken bottle.	17.1	.05	3.0	21.1	9.8
18	I have drunk alcoholic drinks in a pub under 16.	79.1		71.2		
19	I have been in a pub when I was under 16.	74.6	.01	86.4	58.6	66.9
20	I have taken things from big stores or supermarkets when the shop was open.	28.2		12.1 ⎫		
21	I have taken things from little shops when the shop was open.	39.8	.01	19.7 ⎭	47.0	21.6
22	I have dropped things in the street like litter or broken bottles	27.0	.001	83.3	81.0	80.0

TABLE 1.2 (*continued*)

Acts of delinquency	West and Farrington (1973) Boys (N = 397) per cent admit	Significance level of 2-tailed comparison between boys and girls	Campbell (1976) (N = 66) per cent admit	Jamison (1977) Boys (N = 781) per cent admit	Jamison (1977) Girls (N = 501) per cent admit
23 I have bought something cheap or accepted as a present something I knew was stolen.	57.4	.001	16.7	45.5	18.0
24 I have planned well in advance to get into a house to take things.	5.5		1.5	3.8	0.2
25 I have got into a house and taken things even though I didn't plan it in advance.	7.3		3.0	12.3	0.8
26 I have taken a bicycle belonging to someone else and kept it.	10.6	.06	1.5	7.4	0.4
27 I have struggled or fought to get away from a policeman.	12.9		12.1		
28 I have struggled or fought with a policeman who was trying to arrest someone.	5.0		1.5		
29 I have stolen school property worth more than about 5p.	53.2	.001	29.2	52.9	46.5
30 I have stolen goods from someone I worked for worth more than about 5p.	12.6		7.6		
31 I have had sex with a boy when I was under 16.			15.2		

No.	Statement					
32	I have trespassed somewhere I was not supposed to go, like empty houses, railway lines or private gardens.	66.8		54.5	81.4	58.1
33	I have been to an 'X' film under age.	89.7	.001	68.2	38.1	44.5
34	I have spent money on gambling under 16.	19.7	.05	31.8	51.0	8.2
35	I have smoked cigarettes under 15.	41.8	.01	59.1	44.2	41.7
36	I have had sex with someone for money.			0.0		7.7
37	I have taken money from slot machines or telephones.	17.9	.05	7.6	20.2	9.0
38	I have taken money from someone's clothes hanging up somewhere.	5.8		4.5	33.8	14.4
39	I have got money from someone by pretending to be someone else or lying about why I needed it.	9.8		10.6		
40	I have taken someone's clothes hanging up somewhere.			1.5		
41	I have smoked dope or taken pills (LSD, mandies, sleepers).	6.3		4.5	2.7	4.8
42	I have got money/drink/cigarettes by saying I would have sex with someone even though I didn't.			9.1		
43	I have run away from home.			10.6		

varied, and involves acts ranking much higher in their socially dangerous nature. (p. 43; present author's emphasis)

In contrast to that statement, Hindelang himself concludes:

> The rank order correlation ... indicates that the most and least frequent activities among the males and females are nearly identical. This finding is at odds with the conception of female delinquents as engaging primarily in 'sex' delinquencies. (p. 533)

In short, fewer girls than boys break the law (2.5 male offences to every 1 female), but when they do, they follow the same sort of pattern as boys in terms of which acts they commit. One other theoretically important point emerges from Hindelang's paper. It is possible to compute the degree of correlation between each delinquent item and every other. This intercorrelation figure answers the question: 'If an individual admits to any given act, how likely is he or she to admit to every other act in the inventory?' The answer for girls is that there is a 0.31 association and for boys a 0.19 association between act admissions. So for girls delinquent behaviour is a more general phenomenon than among boys. Contrary to Cowie et al.'s belief, girls are not 'specialists' in a particular sort of offence. Even more than boys, once they turn to crime they become involved in many different sorts of delinquent behaviour.

Similar work has been performed in England (see table 1.2). In 1976 I compared self-reported delinquency data taken from urban, working-class schoolgirls with similar data from boys (West and Farrington, 1973). Both groups were aged 16 and were given the same delinquent inventory, except that the girls were asked about five additional acts related particularly to the stereotypical view of female delinquency. The inventory consisted of 38 items and so gives a more extensive and more clearly differentiated idea of hidden crime than Hindelang's shorter 24-item checklist. The official figures for 1976 concerning the ratio of males to females with respect to findings of guilt give a figure of 8.95 to 1. Results from the self-report study show a ratio of 1.33 to 1. Girls admitted to 6 of the 38 items more frequently than boys. Statistical tests can be performed to establish the significance of the difference between two figures – they show which are the results of chance fluctuations and which should be considered real and reliable differences. Among the aggression items there were no significant differences except with respect to carrying and using offensive weapons. Of the 15 theft items, 7 showed no significant differences; boys did admit more often to shopbreaking, store- and shoplifting, accepting stolen goods, stealing school property and bicycle theft. Items relating to under-age offences actually showed that girls, significantly more often than boys, enter pubs, smoke and gamble. The correlation between admissions among the two sexes gave a value of +0.84, once again showing a striking similarity of patterning. The inter-correlation mean value for girls was 0.48, showing an even more general patterning of delinquency than in the United States study.

One way of investigating the validity of a study is to test it against other similar research. Jamison (1977) investigated the reported delinquency of 781 boys and 501 girls from three different areas in southern England, using a very similar inventory. His results show a similar patterning. The correlation between boys and girls on the 27 offences that were common to both studies was +0.61. In his sample of girls there was a higher rate of admission to carrying and using weapons, petty theft offences and drugs than in Campbell's, but there is no systematic difference in the quality of acts admitted by the different sets of girls. Some fluctuation is to be expected and may be attributable to different geographical areas providing differential opportunities for certain kinds of crime, as well as to the inclusion of younger subjects in his sample.

Both inventories include some items that might be regarded as minor forms of misbehaviour engaged in by many children in the normal course of growing up. If such items are included in the calculations, and if they are admitted by a large number of both boys and girls, they may artificially inflate the degree of similarity between the sexes expressed in the correlation. To check for this, it is possible to rework the correlation for *indictable* offences only. An indictable offence is a more serious act that may be judged by a higher court and is more likely, in the case of an adult, to result in imprisonment. For the

Campbell/West and Farrington comparison it provides a cross-sex correlation figure of +0.72, and for Jamison's data, +0.80. These figures assure us that girls are not simply admitting to petty items. Even when we restrict the analysis to serious crimes, the degree of similarity between the sexes remains very high indeed.

Hindelang (1971) and Short and Nye (1958) took measures of the reported frequency with which each individual admitted to having performed any delinquent act. On these frequency scores boys did score higher than girls. However, in and of itself this cannot adequately explain boys' greater representation in official crime figures. Farrington (1973) in Britain has noted that an index of frequency of involvement did not predict future official delinquency significantly better than the simple admission score. Gold (1966) found a +0.87 correlation between simple admission score and an index of frequency. Williams and Gold (1972) found that neither the seriousness of acts admitted nor the frequency with which they were performed was helpful in explaining which individuals would be picked up by the police. They conclude:

> having a police record is only slightly related to the seriousness of teenagers' delinquent activity, not at all related to its frequency, and is less indicative of both frequency and seriousness of delinquent behaviour than having a number of contacts with the police. (pp. 222–3)

This evidence from both sides of the Atlantic suggests that girls appear disproportionately less often in official crime figures than do boys. In view of this, the increase in the female crime rate over the last two decades is even more startling. The incidence of violence in girls in Britain today is 36 times as high as it was in 1955; for criminal damage, 108 times as high; and for burglary, 13 times as high. The respective figures for boys are 12, 61 and 7 times as high as 21 years ago. Of course, to demonstrate a bias in booking, trying and sentencing for girls in the 1970s does not necessarily mean that such bias has always existed. However, in common-sense terms, we would expect a reduction rather than an increase in differential procedures because of the greater public awareness of sex discriminatory practices publicized by the women's liberation movement.

In summary, it is clear that both institutionalization and official statistics must be rejected as a working guide to the nature of female delinquency. Self-report studies can give us a more accurate picture, but, like that provided by the two other approaches to female delinquency, it is a behavioural one. It assumes that delinquency is inherent in the act of law-breaking. We must move on now to consider the further notions of what delinquency might be: delinquency as statistical deviance and delinquency as a societal label. Neither of these definitions has yet been applied to females, but before they are we should ask where they would lead us.

Delinquency as deviance

Lemert (1951) borrowed the term 'deviance' from the notion of deviation used in statistics. His conception of deviants as those ranged at either extreme of any frequency axis representing an array of human behaviour has a marvellous versatility and universality. It can account for morons and geniuses, for our notions of insanity, for sexual 'perversions' and for criminality. Perhaps its greatest single contribution to learning is that it rejects a categorical notion of people. Instead of discrete types, it draws attention to the fact that all of us share the same traits to different degrees. Even something as fundamental and binary as gender can be re-evaluated with reference to the relative sensitivity of portions of the brain to male and female hormones. Similarly, it implies that everyone has the potential for criminality and indeed almost everyone breaks the law, wittingly or unwittingly, at some time in his life. Those who are considered criminals or delinquents are simply those who do it more frequently or more seriously than the rest of the population.

In connection with Lemert's definition, and with the criteria of Becker, who will be considered shortly, two fundamental questions have to be raised. First, there is the issue of the social relativism of the criteria. Second, if we accept this definition, towards what sorts of research will we be directed?

The relativism question effectively asks, 'Who will decide

what the axis should be?' The selection of variables profoundly effects what conclusions will be reached. Perhaps the most obvious choice would be the number of law-breaking acts in which the individual has engaged. Immediately we are plunged into difficulties. The axis must be bi-polar; that is, the two end points must represent true opposites of one another. But what is the opposite of law-breaking? It cannot simply be not law-breaking, for that would imply, for example, that the opposite of masculinity is sexlessness. We might argue, then, that law-breaking is anti-social, and that its opposite must be pro-social behaviour. But many illegal acts are not directly anti-social. For example, suicide, under-age drinking and offences relating to prostitution do not directly harm people other than those who willingly become involved. Similarly, many researchers in the area of altruism believe that there is no such thing as a 'selfless' act. Certainly, many forms of pro-social behaviour have distinct advantages, both genetically and socially. Apart from these conceptual problems, the task still remains of devising some form of measurement for the pro-/antisocial dimension. If a simple counting procedure were used, whereby the number of pro- and antisocial acts were traded off to establish a final figure for each individual, we might generate some strange anomalies. For example, a cold-blooded murderer who had never committed any other illegal act, and indeed had been responsible for many acts of generosity and kindness, would appear saintly. We could weight acts according to their seriousness, but this has already proved to be extremely difficult to do. Different sectors of society have quite different ideas about the seriousness of many acts. If agreement were reached that the taking of life is a particularly serious affair and if it were weighted accordingly, we might well end up with another anomaly. The selfless wife who, in an act of mercy, kills her husband who is dying slowly and painfully of cancer would then appear as a desperate criminal.

The problem is clearly that in attempting to hold on to a strictly behavioural criterion, it is necessary to ignore important issues such as extenuating circumstances, motives and justifications. Because these factors exist inside the mind of the actor, they are inaccessible to us. We may conjecture about them, but they are ultimately unknowable except by the actor himself and sometimes not even by him. There also remains the problem of where on the continuum to place the demarcating line that separates deviants from 'normals'. While some may dress it up in impressive statistical terminology, the question of how big a section of the public is going to be called deviant finally rests on the judgement of the individual.

The second question relates to the kind of work that would be implied by assuming such a criterion. Lemert's original formulation focuses the attention very heavily on the individual and his position relative to the population at large. Clearly, this leads to a view of the delinquent based on individual pathology. Regarding him as an isolated figure on a distribution, one is tempted to forget the social influences on him and to search for causation in some peculiarity of his physical or psychological make-up. This stance has been adopted *par excellence* with the female delinquent. Measurements have been sought of her IQ, physique, hormonal balance, early relationship with her mother, field dependency, subconscious motivations, psychoticism, neuroticism and extraversion. The search for some variable in which she shows abnormal scores has been tireless. At best, all that this work could produce would be a correlational relationship. It could reveal nothing that would explain which variable might have caused the other, or indeed whether both variables might not be the result of some third factor. This search for a pathological explanation also fails to take into account the transient nature of most delinquency. When a girl grows out of delinquent behaviour, what has happened to the internal and enduring personality disturbance that 'caused' it? It makes more sense to look at changes in a girl's social world over time than to pursue a fruitless search for some inherent difference.

Delinquency as a label

Lemert was also concerned with what he termed 'secondary deviance'; that is, the effect on the individual of being treated as deviant. This idea was taken up and popularized by Becker (1973). He moved away from a purely behavioural notion of deviance and stressed a more judgemental one. According to him, deviance should be defined as a consequence of the application of rules (and sanctions for rule infringements) by those who witness a particular act. Deviance, then, no longer inheres in the act itself but in the judgement of society about people who are found to engage in it. Several cogent criticisms have been put forward of Becker's ideas (see Walker, 1977). Again, they relate to the two central issues of social relativism and the appropriate foci of research.

First, Becker has not extricated us from the problem of who is to define deviancy. In the area of norms and norm violation this has long been a problem. An action that might be quite acceptable to one group of people may be severely sanctioned by another. A girl who shoplifts may be seen as deviant by her middle-class teacher but not by her peer group. How are we to decide whether her continued shoplifting implies the stronger influence of her peer group's values upon her or her failure to realize the negative view taken of it by her teacher? It might be argued that normality consists of adhering to the proscriptions of a certain group while they are present and not at other times – in other words, being aware of social context and its implications for behaviour. But an individual who fails to adjust his behaviour would be more likely to be judged stupid than criminal.

Another problem relates to what is seen as constituting an adverse reaction from, or a sanction by, others in the group. Such a reaction does not generally take the form of expulsion from the group, for social psychological research has shown that deviant members are often a valuable part of group dynamics. Marsh et al.'s (1978) work on soccer fans shows that the 'nutter' of the group fulfills an important function in underlining normative conduct; his behaviour is not only tolerated but even encouraged by other members. The breaking of a social rule may provoke a number of immediate reactions. It has been suggested that anger, embarrassment and humour are three typical reactions to rule violation. However, they are also reactions to behaviour other than rule breakage. Humour may be a reaction to joke telling and anger to failing a driving test – neither of these is a breach of any rule. Another problem exists with respect to discovering what the social rules are. Rule-following for the most part involves what has been called a 'tacit' knowledge. In other words, it is virtually impossible for someone to sit down and enumerate the rules of behaviour for, say, a dinner party. It is only when a breach occurs that we feel something has gone wrong – for example, when there is a long and embarrassing silence in the conversation, or when someone gets so drunk that he loses control over his behaviour. The *post facto* nature of many rules makes them conceptually problematic. Do the rules exist before they are broken? If not, then to enumerate them would be an infinite task as more and more rules are invented (or discovered).

Even if it were possible to solve these questions, we would be left with what has been acknowledged as the central problem of Becker's formulation. The act that is subsequently labelled as deviant precedes reaction to it. Labelling theory, in and of itself, cannot help us to explain why the act has occurred. Becker (1973) himself is clearly aware of this:

> We can construct workable definitions either of particular actions people might commit or of particular categories of deviance as the world (especially but not only the authorities) defines them. But we cannot make the two coincide completely, because they do not coincide empirically. They do not coincide empirically because they belong to two distinct, though overlapping, systems of collective action. One consists of people who co-operate to produce the act in question. The other consists of people who co-operate in the drama of morality by which 'wrongdoing' is discovered and dealt with, whether the procedure is formal and legal or quite informal. (p. 185)

If our focus of interest is the 'wrongdoers' themselves, we cannot invoke the labellers as the reason for their actions (unless we were to argue, improbably, that a girl steals in order to be detected and labelled as delinquent). So from the point of view of our delinquency criterion, we are still in some difficulty. It would be possible to use the labelling of deviance by officialdom, such as a finding of guilt or placement in an institution, but we have already seen the dangers associated with this. Equally, we could take the labelling of the newspapers and television. Let us consider these, with respect to female delinquency especially.

The media have two primary functions. The first is to make money, and the second is to put forward a particular, coherent world view or ideology. Sex and violence, as the old cliché goes, sell. These two in combination with females do even better. Not only is the combination titillating, but it is less common than among men – in other words, it does not accord with the stereotypical view of females. A woman recently tried in London for abducting a male and forcing him to have sex with her held the front pages for weeks. Similarly, female murderers and muggers get a disproportionate amount of attention. On the other hand, most newspapers are far from dedicated to the promotion of the feminist movement, so that such reports are usually censorious. They lead to a particular combination of fascination and moral outrage. In his book *Folk Devils and Moral Panic* S. Cohen (1972) has drawn attention to the way in which certain sectors of society, such as Hell's Angels or soccer hooligans, are singled out for condemnation and censure. Recently, this same process has begun to work against women in crime. The rise in crime figures among females receives more newspaper space than that among men and provokes a much more extreme reaction. If we were to take the labelling of newspapers as our criterion of female delinquency, we would devote rather little attention to the more mundane and frequent problems of shoplifting and petty theft and would focus instead on precocious sex, prostitution, violence, murder and child-beating. While the role of the media in shaping popular conceptions of morality is an interesting issue, taken as a criterion it may lead to a very unrepresentative view of female delinquency.

Negotiated delinquency

It seems, then, that the search for an absolute and universal definition of delinquency has to be abandoned. Laws change; labels change; and the same action may have a multitude of descriptions applied to it, depending on whether we look at behaviour or meaning, the actor or the observer. Indeed, Becker goes as far as saying, 'deviance is nothing special. Just another kind of human activity to be studied and understood.' But deviant behaviour is rare, newsworthy; it evokes extreme reactions, and mammoth institutions are set up to prevent it, contain it, punish it and research it. The general public, the Government and social scientists all want to understand it with an enthusiasm they do not channel into understanding the structure of more everyday activity. Delinquency has two particular properties – its salience with respect to the lives of the general public, and its relative infrequency in the population. If research is to be done, how are we to arrive at an acceptable definition of delinquency?

The answer depends on what it is we want to understand. If we want to investigate sentencing policy among magistrates, then it is their definition of what constitutes delinquency that is of interest. An investigation of social services with respect to juvenile delinquency would necessitate an understanding of what a social worker means by the term. A micro-social study of family dynamics during adolescence would lead to another definition of what constitutes delinquency. It is doubtful if any of these three definitions would fully accord with another, and this very disjunction of meaning would be yet another interesting area of study.

Most social behaviour involves joint action. This does not simply mean that people try consciously to fit in with one another. It means that individuals are usually aware of the implications of their actions for others and vice versa. This sensitivity is absolutely necessary for any kind of sensible and smooth-running interaction. When people go into a cinema or attend a dinner party, they have a common understanding about the sort of behaviour that is appropriate. They agree on the definition of what is going on. Imagine the chaos if half the people present treated a funeral ceremony as if it were a soccer game. Sometimes, however, a degree of ambiguity may enter the situation – for example, when an attractive female student is invited out to dinner with her middle-aged supervisor, ostensibly to discuss her work. The transition from one definition of the situation to another (or not, as the case may be) rests on a kind of tacit negotiation between the two parties as they conspire subtly to alter their behaviour towards one another, at every turn anticipating possible negative reactions from the other. Only when the whole episode is long finished and the couple have arrived unambiguously at a new role relationship can they safely look back and laugh at the stressful ambiguities of the transition.

However in head-on social collisions this tacit negotiation of definitions among the actors can become quite overt. Disputes among actors can arise over the labels used for one another and over their exact meaning and implication. A parent may call a teenage daughter a 'hooligan' because of her rowdy friends, a description which the daughter may strongly dispute. Similarly, a 'sexually liberated' young woman will hotly contest the use of a term like 'slut' to describe her. Different parties will almost certainly disagree over whether persistent truanting from school means they are 'delinquents'. These kinds of terms, their meaning and who qualifies for them are a constant source of discussion between teachers, parents, social workers, magistrates and young people themselves.

However, as Becker has noted, it is those with power who can usually make their definitions stick. In a juvenile court the tussle over the correct disposal of a young defendant takes place far above her head – between magistrates, social workers, lawyers and psychiatrists. Usually the girl is too overawed by the situation to express a very coherent view. Often her opinion is not solicited or not taken seriously. Her future is decided, and she is either excused, rehabilitated or punished, according to the definitions of those with power. This is not to argue that she is always attacked or persecuted. Sometimes things operate the other way round. The girl herself may admit full responsibility for what she knows to be a naughty or illegal act, only to hear her liberal social worker argue that she was not fully responsible or that the act was a legitimate expression of her anger at society's treatment of her. Indeed, it is romantically naive to assume that juveniles who break the law do so without being aware of the gravity of what they have done. Sykes and Matza (1957) have outlined the various ways in which juvenile offenders justify and excuse their actions to the police when they are picked up. Most of them also have the wit to ensure that they are not detected. They have a necessary and clear awareness of the view of society towards their behaviour. They understand this perspective as well as their own, which puts them in an interesting position, for very few members of the 'broader society' would claim to be able to understand and express the delinquents' point of view.

It is possible to conceptualize this set of relationships as a series of concentric circles (see figure 1.1). The individual is located within her immediate peer group, which in turn lies within the boundaries of outside agencies such as the school, the family, the police, her contemporaries and so on. Beyond this lies the unseen and abstract circle of the wider society. Each one of these groups will offer a particular view of deviancy, and an infraction of normality will require some kind of account or justification from the offender. But what requires accounting for will change depending on who the interrogator is, and so will the reply made by the offender. Let us take violence as an example. The peer group may question the individual within it, and the question may take the form, 'Why did you pick a fight with her when you knew you'd get pasted?' When the outside agencies interrogate the peer group, the question moves on to a different level: 'Why do girls in your group still fight when you know you'll all end up on care orders?' When wider society questions the agencies, they ask, 'Why is there such an alarming increase in violence among girls?' As one moves up through the

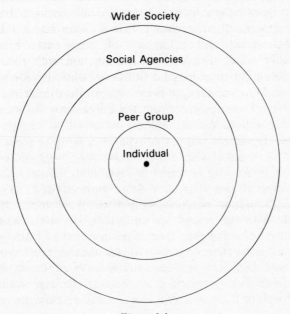

Wider Society

Social Agencies

Peer Group

Individual

Figure 1.1

hierarchical levels, the norm that has been violated alters. For the peer group it is normal to fight but abnormal to be 'nutty' enough to enter a kamikaze contest. For the agencies it is normal to be naughty but not to the extent of jeopardizing one's future by an illegal act. For wider society it is normal for females to be submissive and nurturant, and the question of why they should want to reject these positive virtues is problematic.

The issue, then, is to decide which of these interfaces interests us most. It is simply a matter of preference. The psychiatrist chooses the individual; the social psychologist, the peer group; the sociologist, social agencies; and the politician, broader society. To begin research from the centre outwards has advantages. Having acquired a detailed understanding of single units, we can put these units together into an ever more complex scenario as we introduce more actors and more viewpoints. If we begin with a macro-study of politics, we cannot reduce that to the psychology of the individual or small groups. Logically, then, the individual should be the beginning. But, as we shall see in later chapters, with respect to girls particularly this task has been tackled *ad nauseam*, with ambiguous results. It also, by its nature, asserts a pathological view of delinquency. The one thing criminologists have shown with unusual consensus is that delinquency is a *social phenomenon*. It is a group activity. It is the attitudes, values and behaviour of their peers that most profoundly affect teenagers. In conjunction with their peers, individuals come to a shared definition of what they do and how they do it. When challenged from without, they unite in a shared account of their lifestyle. From these accounts we should not expect too much. We are looking, after all, at one particular interface. Teenagers will not conveniently jump to a politician's account in terms of alienation or false consciousness, nor to a sociologist's account in terms of illegitimate opportunities and effects of high-rise flats, nor to a psychiatrist's account of Oedipal failure or reaction formation. With luck, they will negotiate with the researcher an agreement about what both outside agencies and they themselves consider to be delinquent. They may not bother to justify to one another their shoplifting or fighting, but they will certainly acknowledge that schools, parents and police demand explanations. The explanation they give is hard for them. If I were to ask a middle-class student why he persistently attends Bergman films, he would give a personal account rather than one in terms of cultural fashions for existential truths and their popularity among university students. Similarly, girls will give a personal response, and it is up to academics, if they wish, to place this in a broader social, historical or political perspective.

Such an approach may go some way towards answering a worthwhile plea made two decades ago by criminologists Cohen and Short (1958, p. 34):

It is our position that the meaning and function of any form of delinquent behaviour can only be inferred from rich and detailed descriptive data about the behaviour itself, about its position in a larger context of interaction and about how it is perceived and reacted to by the actor himself and by other participants in their interactive context. These data are largely lacking for female delinquency.

CHAPTER 2

Second-Rate Theories for the Second Sex

Before turning to a consideration of the theories that have been proposed to account for female crime, it is important to bear in mind three major points that affect the confidence that should be placed in many of the explanations.

First, chapter 1 has shown that many writers have had a faulty conception of the phenomena that they were trying to explain. Practically all took it as axiomatic that, as a sex, women were less criminal than men, and that when they did commit crimes, the offences were of a different kind from those of males. This was perhaps one reason why such a very different theoretical position was adopted in relation to females. It is also true that until relatively recently the differences between the behaviour of the sexes was ascribed largely to genetic or biological causes. These were held to determine the types of differential socialization that boys and girls received. Because by nature certain differences existed between the capabilities and interests of boys and girls, it was thought, these should be channelled and developed by different education and training. This assumption of fundamental, 'inherent' differences was reflected in the separate theoretical positions adopted for men and women.

Second, explanations of female criminality have been based on the view that criminal women are merely reacting like automata to forces beyond their control. The conception of mankind as a subject shifting like a billiard ball in response to different forces that strike him has been the foundation of all positivistic psychology. However, when sociologists finally broke away from this view by suggesting that internal, psychological representations might be as important as their external *reality*, and even that man was an active agent with plans and goals, this revision did not extend to females. They continued to be characterized as passive, vacuous, waiting for their parents or their sexuality to push them into delinquency. This assumption was made explicit by psychoanalysts, who spoke directly of the catabolic or inert nature of the female sex, and by post-Darwinians, who argued for the genetic basis of female passivity.

Third, it is important to remember that the validity of any theoretical formulation rests on its empirical failure to be falsified. But empirical data is only as good as the methodology used to obtain it. For many years the social sciences have restricted themselves to using fairly naive methodologies in their attempt to emulate what is thought to be 'real' science. This has meant an obsession with quantification at the expense of detailed descriptive data. It has also led to some conceptually naive treatment of data in order to comply with the tenets of acceptable statistical procedure. Frequently, comparisons have been made between the rate of occurrence of literally hundreds of variables in 'normal' and in 'deviant' populations. When a significant difference has been found, it has been assumed that the variable must be of etiological significance, an unwarranted assumption because we do not know the temporal relationship between the deviant behaviour and the variable – for example, delinquency may lead to bad family relationships rather than vice versa. Nor can we assume that one causes the other in any direct way, since not only delinquents but also schizophrenics, depressives, subnormals and divorcees have poor home lives. There must be some mediating variable that determines the home's effect on the child. In short, a lack of criticism of poor methodology has led people to assume that many inadequate theories have been proved (or at least have not been falsified) by empirical work.

Explanations of female crime can be categorized into three major types, which will be discussed in turn: first, biological and hormonal accounts; second, genetic explanations of the 'inherent' nature of women and female criminals in particular; and third, explanations in terms of the upbringing and socialization of females.

Biological explanations

Freud proceeded from the assumption that women are less prone to criminality than men. This results from his view that women are, by nature, passive. In 'Femininity' Freud (1973) argues:

> It is perhaps the case that in a woman, on the basis of her share in the sexual function, a preference for passive behaviour, and passive aims is carried over into her life to a greater or lesser extent. . . . (p. 149)

This difference in sexual function is attributed clearly to genetic differences between the sexes:

> The difference in the structure of the genitals is accompanied by other bodily differences which are too well known to call for mention. Differences emerge too in the instinctual dispositions which give a glimpse of the later nature of women. A little girl is as a rule less aggressive, defiant and self-sufficient; she seems to have a greater need for being shown affection and on that account to be more dependent and pliant. (p. 150)

This dependency is capitalized upon and employed in later development, when the girl makes the transference of affection from her mother to her father. Needing male approval and being by nature pliant, she is emotionally at the mercy of men and of their norms relating to appropriate female behaviour. She conforms to her sex-role stereotype faithfully in order to gain and maintain male approval. However, Freud himself notes that it is vain to expect women ever to achieve the higher moral precepts that men internalize and to which they adhere. Conscience, according to the Freudian explanation, results from the boy's resolution of the Oedipal situation. The boy's incestuous love for his mother is repressed by fear of his father's retaliation in the form of castration, and in its place he develops a severe superego. Girls, however, are at a disadvantage in developing conscience:

> In the absence of fear of castration the chief motive is lacking

which leads boys to surmount the Oedipal complex. Girls remain in it for an indeterminate length of time; they demolish it late and, even so, incompletely. In these circumstances the formation of the superego must suffer; it cannot attain the strength and independence which give it its cultural significance. . . . (p. 163)

This might reasonably be expected to predict a higher rate of delinquency and crime among women than men, were it not for the fact of female passivity and the need for male approval. What it does imply is a degree of expediency on the part of women in their search for a man. Lacking conscience, they will resort to almost any means in order to secure the love that they, by nature, need so badly. This argument is one that has been used to account for prostitution among females. An over-dependence on men, when its expression is not properly socially controlled by the family, may lead to a girl's exchanging sex for attention, affection or money. As Klein (1973) noted, this view fails to account for the fact that normal women, within the legitimate institution of marriage, have done exactly this for centuries. It also ignores the socio-economic pressures on women to turn to prostitution, and the fact that such a profession could not exist but for the fact that males show a demand for it. The study of pathology (if there has to be one) should focus on the male customer, as well as on the female who provides the service.

Freud's explanation of mental illness is based on the idea of deviation from normal development and so, for present purposes, can be seen as an explanation in terms of faulty socialization. However, he locates one form of pathology firmly in the genetic field. This is the girl who fails to achieve the 'normal' feminine state of passivity and dependency. Such a woman is destined to homosexuality and pseudo-male behaviour such as crime.

What can it be that decides in favour of this outcome? We can only suppose that it is a constitutional factor, a greater amount of activity, such as is ordinarily characteristic of a male. (p. 164)

Even Freud, who led the way to a study of the family as a major factor in pathology, was driven to genetic explanations of the 'masculine' woman.

Lombroso and Ferrero (1959; originally 1895) took a more explicitly genetic line but, together with Freud, assumed a lower incidence of crime among women. In accounting for this, they suggested:

> in the women of our time, the cerebral cortex, particularly in the psychical centres, is less active than in the male. The irritation consequent on a degenerative process ... leads more easily to motor and hysterical epilepsy, or to sexual anomalies, than to crime. (p. 111)

In short, women are less intelligent, and since they have less abstract reasoning capacity, they are more likely to show difficulties in motor areas. They also suggested that women are *by nature* passive and therefore less inclined to crime than are men, having clearly failed to take account of the fact that by no means all crime involves violence.

Lombroso and Ferrero attempted to show that male and female criminals were atavistic throw-backs to an earlier stage of evolution. In dealing with female criminals, their certainty of male evolutionary superiority involved them in some logical difficulties with their theory. Since women are less developed than men, they might be expected to produce more 'anomalies' and criminals. However, in their studies they were unable to find among imprisoned women such evidence of the stigmata of the born criminal. These signs took the form of misshapen skulls, peculiarities of height, weight, arm span and hand size, facial proportions, moles, prehensile feet, hairiness and voice pitch. They were disappointed to find the incidence of such defects among female criminals to be around 14 per cent, whereas among males atavism was found in 31 per cent of their samples.

However, Lombroso and Ferrero believed that some female criminals could be accounted for in biological terms. Their problem could be located quite simply in the fact that they were 'pseudo-males'. This fact was evidenced by their physical similarity to men, most particularly by their stature, cranium, brain and muscular strength. They were thought to be genetic relics of a time when females had not fully differentiated themselves from males. This is strange, because given the glowing terms in which males are portrayed, we might expect that only advantage could be conferred on the females who approximated to them. Apparently these 'pseudo-male' women had unfortunately chosen to resemble men only in their more unattractive facets. Lombroso and Ferrero also assumed, from biblical rather than Darwinian evidence, that the male was the prototype from which the female evolved.

It is easy to look back on Lombroso and Ferrero's writing with amusement and see it merely as testimony to the historical chauvinism of males. But this would be to ignore two important ideas to which they drew attention and from which the study of female criminality has never fully recovered. First, the idea that the cause of a socially generated phenomenon might be reduced to a genetically transmitted biological unit. This quest for a visible, physical manifestation of the cause of delinquency has been maintained even up to the last decade. Second, both they and Freud embraced the idea of pathology or clinical abnormality as the cause of law-breaking. Among female criminals particularly, this idea of individual maladjustment has never been fully abandoned. Although we are now prepared to accept that delinquency among males may be a subculturally normal response to societal frustrations, it is remarkable that even among female urban guerrillas, who offer highly articulate accounts of their social grievances, we still ascribe their behaviour to clinical disorder.

More recently, Cowie et al. (1968) have presented data from a female approved school sample on age, IQ, family relationships, siblings and many other social variables, but in their concluding chapter they come down heavily on *genetic* factors as the major cause of delinquency. They account for the lower rate of delinquency among girls by suggesting that they are less genetically liable to anti-social acts. Girls require a more extreme push from the environment (in the form of poor home lives) to overcome their relative immunity to delinquency. It is for this reason, they argue, that there is a much higher rate of psychiatric disorder among delinquent females. It should be remembered that the girls to whom they refer are all 'officially delinquent', in the sense that they have arrived through the courts at an approved school. This is important, since we know that girls are more likely to be placed on care orders if they come from broken or disrupted homes (Smith, 1978). Similarly, studies of diagnostic practices among psychiatrists have shown that they operate on a perceptual 'set'. Their diagnosis of mental illness rests heavily on the social context in which they find their patients. Rosenhan (1973) has shown that 'normals' will be judged to be schizophrenic by doctors and nurses in a psychiatric hospital if they are so labelled when they are first encountered. A psychiatrist who encounters a girl in an approved school is likely to be predisposed to find signs of psychological disturbance, since, like many other people, he views deviation from traditional female stereotypes as a sign of abnormality.

Cowie et al. go as far as to suggest that these genetic factors may be specific enough to determine what sorts of crimes the sexes will commit:

> It is more natural to suppose that the male–female difference, both in delinquency rates and in *the forms that delinquency takes*, would be closely connected with the masculine and feminine pattern of development of personality. This again *would be related to biological and somatic differences*, including differences in hormonal balance; and these would at the ultimate remove be derived from chromosomal differences between the sexes. (p. 17, present author's emphasis)

In favour of this contention, Cowie et al. present no data of their own but cite a twin study undertaken in 1941 by Rosanoff et al. (see table 2.1). The genetic inheritance of monozygotic twins is believed to be identical. If delinquency were genetically determined, a high concordance rate in the delinquent behaviour of each identical pair would be expected. If environmental influences were paramount, the dizygotic twins (non-identical pairs) should show as much concordance as identical twins. As Cowie et al. admit, the results show no persuasive evidence of any genetic component at all. Undeterred however, they continue with their argument.

In studies of male criminality, researchers claim to have found evidence of an extra Y chromosome in the genetic make-up of highly aggressive prisoners. This accounts for very few of the

TABLE 2.1   *Concordance rates in delinquent behaviour of monozygotic and dizygotic twins*

	Monozygotic twins		Dizygotic twins	
	Both delinquent	One delinquent	Both delinquent	One delinquent
Boys	29	0	12	5
Girls	11	1	9	0

SOURCE: Rosanoff et al., 1941, quoted in Cowie et al., 1968, p. 173.

total population of criminals, and its rate of occurrence in the normal, non-criminal population is still in some doubt. Cowie et al. conclude that the greater the degree of masculinity, the greater the delinquent predisposition and, by extrapolation, the more likely delinquent girls are to have a Y chromosome. As evidence of this, they point to the fact that delinquent girls are large for their age (Healy and Bronner, 1936); that psychoanalysts have commented on the presence of masculine traits; and that girls in care for prostitution show high rates of 'homosexual tendencies'. It has not been shown that height in males or females is linked to genetic abnormality, and the presence of masculine traits in no way implies elements of masculine gender in women. This confusion of sex role with biological gender has lingered on from Lombroso and Ferrero. The evidence that was used to infer homosexual tendencies is unclear, but again homosexuality is neither linked to genetic abnormality nor is it noticeably more prevalent among female prisoners than among males. Homosexuality among males in single-sex, long-term institutions such as the forces or prison is regarded as an understandable, although undesirable adaptation to their circumstances. In women it seems to be enough to call their genetic composition into question.

Gibbens (1971) has reported a high rate of autosomal and sex chromosomal abnormalities in delinquent girls. Kaplan (1971) investigated the incidence of chromosomal abnormality in female convicts and juvenile delinquents. Not one instance of a female with a Y chromosome was found. Two syndromes were noted. Hyper-femininity (an extra X chromosome) was found in 1 per cent of the population, as compared with a rate of 0.12 per cent in a 'normal' group. An X0 constitution (phenotypically female, although sterile) was found also in 1 per cent of the sample, compared with 0.48 per cent for non-criminal women. If genetic factors such as these are relevant at all, they play a very small part in any final explanation.

Some writers have noted the incidence of syphilis in incarcerated women, although to what purpose is not always clear. Given that syphilis has a genetic form and may be passed from parent to child, the implication is clearly that it may be a predisposing factor to delinquency. Early reports by Spaulding (1914) and Anderson (1917) put the incidence of syphilis among criminal females at 46 per cent and 39 per cent respectively. However, later studies by Cowie et al. and Richardson (1969) give figures of 0.3 per cent and 1 per cent respectively. Either preventative and curative measures have increased dramatically in efficiency, or diagnostic practices have changed. However, since the crime rate among women has actually increased with time, while the incidence of syphilis has decreased, it may be concluded that its etiological importance is not very great.

Many writers, perhaps influenced by Guibord (1917), have investigated poor physical health in relation to criminality. Guibord argued that persons of low intelligence living in a state of poverty are more prone to physical defects and ill-health, which may in turn predispose them to delinquency. His aim as a doctor was to prevent such diseases and so reduce delinquency. His assumption of the homogeneity of criminal behaviour was a necessary rationalization for the medical explanation and model that he wished to use. Delinquency was seen as a symptom of an underlying malfunction, which was thought to be common to all criminals. This simplification made a neat, universal answer possible. However, the implications of this idea – that a predisposition to ill-health and criminality was genetic – were horrific. He suggested that operations to render criminal women sterile might be made with the 'highest ethical propriety'.

Spaulding (1914) and Anderson (1917) divided their samples into those with good, fair or poor health. Both authors considered 46 per cent of their sample to be in poor or bad physical condition. Spaulding, more optimistically, rated 21.5 per cent as in good health, compared with Anderson's figure of 14 per cent.

In recent years less poor health has been noted. Cowie et al. consider 10 per cent of girls to be unhealthy, and Richardson 6 per cent. Once again, improvements in the area of community health have not brought concomitant decreases in the rate of delinquency.

Many writers have noted in this connection the high incidence of sexually transmitted venereal disease among institutionalized girls. Spaulding reports only 11.2 per cent of her sample to be free from disease, and Anderson found that 61 per cent of his sample were infected. By the late 1960s the incidence had dropped to 23 per cent (Richardson, 1969) and 14 per cent (Cowie et al., 1968). It is interesting that there is a lack of data on venereal infections among males, clearly reflecting the differential attitude of researchers (and of the general public) to females' assumed sexual promiscuity. It is worth remembering too that by 1970 venereal disease was the second most common infection in Britain, and that even the above writers would not claim VD to be of *etiological* significance. They are more likely to be the result of the girls' sexual 'delinquencies'.

Following the work of Kretschmer (1925) and Sheldon et al. (1949) on body types as a factor in the predisposition to delinquency, recent literature has paid attention to this factor among girls. Sheldon argued that body build was related to the differential development of the viscera, the connective tissue and the nervous system. Mesomorphs (muscular, of heavy build) were thought to possess certain characteristic temperaments (they were regarded as boisterous, aggressive and undisciplined) and to account for the majority of delinquent boys. Such males were thought to descend directly from the predators of man's hunting history, an explanation reminiscent of Lombroso. Controlled breeding among such individuals was suggested to be the long-term solution to criminal behaviour.

Lombroso was the first to comment on the sturdy physique and physical and facial unattractiveness of criminal women. Cowie et al. note the above-average weight of their institutionalized sample and attribute etiological significance to this finding. They suggest that physical over-development tends to draw a girl's attention to sex earlier in life, resulting in moral 'degeneration'. Richardson (1969) categorizes 43.2 per cent of her 500 sample as mesomorphs, while a further 10 per cent were considered to be plump or 'tubby'. Epps and Parnell (1952), in a study of Borstal girls, also noted a preponderance of mesomorphs, and Healy (1925) found 70 per cent of female delinquents to be overweight. Morris (1964) has also commented on the plumpness of institutionalized girls, as well as on their unattractive appearance. Like Cowie et al., she takes this to be a causative factor in their delinquency, related particularly to the parents' emotional rejection of these unattractive children.

Since estimates of body build are largely based on a weight/height ratio, what is being considered is, in fact, plumpness. As all the samples were in approved schools and Borstals at the time that these measurements were taken, a fairly obvious explanation presents itself. Within such institutions exercise is relatively rare because of the low staff numbers and need for constant supervision. The diet is designed chiefly to fill the girls up at modest expense and is composed mainly of bread, potatoes and suet. With no incentive to work actively at weight loss, and with the prevailing level of depression and boredom, substantial weight gain is almost inevitable.

Another biological factor that has received attention is what Pollak (1961) calls the 'generative phases' of women. According to psychoanalytic theory, menstruation is a constant and distressing reminder to women that they can never become men. At times of such distress, it is argued, they become increasingly prone to delinquent acts. Evidence to support this contention is scarce. Neither Healy (1925) nor Epps (in Gibbens and Prince, 1962) was able to find a significant relationship between the menstrual period and crime. However, later medical evidence suggested that hormonal changes immediately before and after menstruation may lead to emotional lability and predispose to crime. Dalton (1961) believed that she had found a significant relationship between the menstrual cycle and crime. She demonstrated that in the 16-day period covering pre- and post-menstrual hormonal disturbance, as well as during the menstrual period itself, 59.8 per cent of a sample of imprisoned women had committed their offences. It takes little mathematical competence to work out that the reciprocal statement must also be true; 40.2 per cent of women committed detected crimes when they were hormonally undisturbed. This is scant proof indeed of such a biological argument. It is always dangerous to deal with detected offences, since any difference that might be found could be attributed to slower reactions in the detected criminal and increased likelihood of detection, rather than to criminality itself.

Ellis and Austin (1971) conducted a study of patterns of aggression in relation to phases of the menstrual cycle. The study was performed in an American prison, using 45 subjects, the regularity of whose cycle had been checked over a three-month time span. Although information on aggression was taken both from the prisoner subjects and their wardens, the subjects' own self-reports were discarded from analysis, since it was felt they were not honest accounts. Physical and verbal aggression were noted, the latter comprising 64 per cent of the total number of instances. Significance tests were not performed, but 41 per cent of aggressive acts occurred in two-sevenths of the time base (that is, on 8 out of the 28 days). However, since all figures are given for the total number of acts across all women, doubts remain about the extent to which a few women may be contributing disproportionately to the overall levels. Results may also have been affected by the all-female environment and the high levels of aggression provoked in artificial social situations such as institutions.

Pollak also suggested that pregnancy and the menopause were likely to increase female criminality. If we total up the entire 'danger time' for women from a hormonal point of view, we might expect any given female to be predisposed to crime for 75 per cent of her life. Clearly, this type of account postulates a great deal more delinquency than actually occurs. Nor is it theoretically clear what the nature of the relationship between hormonal imbalance and crime is supposed to be. Should we not also expect, during these times, a higher incidence of nervous breakdowns, suicides and depression? Unless some mediating link can be specified to predict in advance the behavioural form that the hormonal imbalance will take, such a statement, even if empirically true, is useless.

Explanations of human behaviour in terms of genetics or biology are always dubious. Genetic factors are extremely hard to demonstrate empirically although they are often inferred from analogy with the behaviour of subhuman primates such as baboons or gibbons. When we come to consider crime any biological explanation faces severe difficulties (see Taylor et al., 1973). Since what is criminal is a relatively arbitrary matter, changing across time and place, how could a gene (developed over millions of years of evolution) account for criminality? It might be argued that there is a non-specific gene determining adherence to group norms, but if there were, it would account not only for criminals but for all deviants – saints, innovators, revolutionaries and so on.

Biological variables have been particularly popular in explanations of female delinquency. Deviation from the female stereotype is frequently confused with physical disorder, since no 'normal' woman, it is claimed, could be unhappy with her lot in life. The equation of female assertiveness (and its implied questioning of the *status quo*) with abnormality has been a recurring theme. It is hardly surprising that many female prisoners in Holloway refused to answer Dalton's questions about their menstrual cycles. To be reduced to the status of a faulty biochemical machine is insulting to anyone.

The nature of women

The basis of much writing in the area of female criminality relates to the assumed 'innate' nature of women. While biological explanations focus on somatic and hormonal aspects, this latter kind makes reference to the inherited psychological make-up of females. Some claim an empirical foundation for these sex differences; others are based only on 'common-sense' ideas about femininity. Some have no *a priori* foundation at all and are simply summaries of studies in which various psychological tests have been given to female prisoners, showing them to be 'abnormal' in some respect.

One of the most popularly held ideas relates to the lack of *aggression* in normal women compared with men and the consequent double deviance of the female criminal. Now, it is important to bear in mind that by no means all criminal acts involve aggression. Blackmail, fraud, burglary and prostitution may have no aggressive component at all, and even ostensibly violent acts may be performed without any experienced emotion. Nevertheless, the semantic confusion between aggression, assertiveness and ambition has clouded the issue. Theories related to the very low incidence of violent crime among women have certainly employed this kind of genetic argument. They rest on two major factors; the early differentiation of the brain in the two sexes, and the levels of circulating hormones.

All the experimental work has been performed, for obvious reasons, on rats. Shortly after birth the rat brain becomes irreversibly male or female, depending on the differential levels of androgens (male hormones) and oestrogens (female hormones). The earlier the castration of a male neonate, the less 'male' the brain will be and the less overt aggression will subsequently be demonstrated. Conversely, if female rats are exposed to artificial levels of androgens early in life, their later level of aggression will be indistinguishable from that of males. It has now been suggested that human females exposed to androgens prior to birth became more tomboyish and assertive than normal females (Money and Erhardt, 1972).

Rose et al. (1971) have shown that the most aggressive male monkeys in a group had higher levels of plasma testosterone than more submissive males, and Persky et al. (1971) claim to have shown a relationship in human males between testosterone levels and some rather dubious measures of aggression and hostility.

The issue of early brain differentiation is the most central, since levels of circulating hormones in later life can have their effect only on an already differentiated brain. Such studies have, by necessity, to rely on animal work. Extrapolation from rats to humans is extremely hazardous, and even animal behaviourists are loath to assume correspondence between primates and humans. What seems to be at issue here is the *degree* of influence that such genetic factors exert. Clearly, females as well as males have and exercise the potential for aggression. The expression of any genetic endowment depends on environmental factors, which modify and direct it. Extreme environmentalists deny any genetic predisposition, claiming that any visible differences in aggression between the sexes are exclusively the result of differential socialization of males and females. Since we know that hormones and behaviour have a two-way causal connection, it might even be argued, from an evolutionary perspective, that early social conventions actually accentuated what were originally negligible sex differences in temperament.

Such an argument is put forward by Marsh (1978). He argues that differences in the overt expression of aggression between the sexes came about because of the different roles of males and females. Aggressive males were an asset to the primitive social group, as they defended territory, drove out invading males and ensured the availability of food. Women, who bore the children and fed them, found it in their interests to produce strong male offspring to ensure the continued safety of the group. In order to contain what might easily have become highly destructive intra-group aggression among the males, cultures developed aggres-sive rituals or displays so that dominance could be established without unnecessary harm. This ritualization can still be seen today, Marsh claims, on the football terraces and in bar 'brawls', in which there is much threat and bravado but considerably less physical damage than one might anticipate in such an explosive situation. Males come to 'know the rules' of fighting, whereas women have never had reason or opportunity to learn them. Historically, women have fought only to protect their offspring, and this kind of 'basic survival' aggression is not bound by any such social conventions. Women then, by nature, are not atuned to the same kind of fighting as men; consequently, now that social and economic factors conspire to encourage female aggression, they mishandle it by going at their opponents 'tooth and nail' instead of by 'ritually' subduing their rival.

Marsh's argument is by no means an extreme genetic viewpoint. In fact, he stresses heavily the different ways in which various cultures have developed their own means of defusing aggression. For our purposes, the important point is that women are not predisposed to react to provocation in the same way as males. However, given that this is true, there seems to be no reason why contemporary females should not learn from their male counterparts. It is also important not to discount the more obvious and immediate impact of social structures on women. If it is arguable that women today overreact in agonistic situations, we must remember that for hundreds of years they have been scorned and rejected for any display of assertiveness or aggres-sion. Like any oppressed group, they feel hypersensitive about their attributed weakness, and in order to force any social change at all, they must overstate their case in order to draw attention to it. Many middle-class women feel that they must be not merely competent but outstanding professionals to show society that they can both compete and excel. Similarly, if delinquent girls wish to be taken seriously by their male friends, they must fight not just adequately but outstandingly to gain their respect. This is evidenced by a new phenomenon: girls who pick fights with men rather than with other girls. Intra-sex fighting between girls is viewed with indulgence and a patronizing smile by boys. They cannot be so superior when they themselves are challenged. Since there is such a clear disadvantage in terms of size and weight for females, they may resort to the use of weapons to equalize the fight (see chapter 5). Because of this, they are accused of fighting 'dirty' and failing to know the 'rules' of a real fight.

Ambition has similarly been an issue of contention. Hutt (1972) has argued that ambition in both males and females is related to adrenal androgens. Male hormones, artificially administered, not only increase the sex drive but also alleviate fatigue and facilitate sustained concentration and performance by their affect on the neuro-humoral control of attention. Some workers claim to have found raised levels of androgens in highly competitive women such as graduate students and women's liberation workers. (It should be stressed that both sexes have present in their body both types of hormone, male and female. It is the predominance of one or the other that determines gender and secondary sexual characteristics.)

Thomas (1967) considered the ambitions of females as opposed to males in his book *The Unadjusted Girl*, although from a less scientific stance. He argued that the human species is driven by four wishes (or ambitions): the desire for new experience, for security, for response and for recognition.

> We may therefore define character as an expression of the organization of the wishes resulting from temperament and experience, understanding by 'organization', the general pattern which the wishes as a whole tend to assume among themselves. (p. 39)

These wishes correspond to drives necessary for evolutionary survival and are manifested in the somatic reactions of the nervous system: hunting (new experience), fear of death (security), maternal and sexual love (response) and dominance within the group (recognition). In women, Thomas argues, the wish for response is greater than in men. This desire originates in their 'natural' maternal instinct, and the need to give and receive love carries over into male–female relationships. Thomas's romanticism seems to get the better of him, and he relies more on literary conceptions of the archetypal Mother Earth figure than on reality. He assumes that the delinquent girl's problem is not criminality but immorality and confines himself almost exclusively to consideration of the phenomenon of prostitution. The major cause of this, he argues, lies in the girl's need for love, which is glorified into an almost altruistic act, with her own sexual feelings taking a minor role.

> I have seen ... the life history of a woman who has had sexual relations with numbers of men. ... She has kept a restaurant, partly I think to feed men. ... While she was sexually passionate her concern was mainly to satisfy the sexual hunger of others, as she satisfied their food hunger. When two of her lovers were jealous, unhappy and desperate, she ran from one to the other like a mother visiting two sick children in different hospitals. (p. 21)

A secondary factor in the predisposition to prostitution is the wish for recognition – in other words, ambition. However, this drive takes a peculiarly trivial form in women and expresses itself in their desire for material possessions, particularly clothes. This forces the impoverished woman into criminal activity.

Women's deceit is a strong theme in Pollak's work. He proceeds from the assumption that criminal statistics underestimate the true amount of female crime, an assumption that subsequent empirical work has endorsed. However, his speculations concerning the true nature and extent of women's crime suggests a degree of male paranoia. Women commit crimes of violence and sexuality; they are not seen as property offenders or as white-collar criminals. In other words, he endorses the view that while men respond to societal injustices, women react to interpersonal ones. Their failure to feature in official statistics he attributes partly to chivalry on the part of police and magistrates but largely to the devious and cunning nature of women, which is reflected in their *modus operandi* in crime. Women are deceitful as a direct result of two biological facts. First, menstruation is held in many cultures to be repellent and dirty. Women learn to tolerate the physical and practical discomforts associated with it in silence. Pollak points to the fact that women on trial for murder would rather have their guilt assumed than admit that a blood stain on their clothing results from menstruation rather than the victim's wounds. Second, interest in the sexual act cannot be feigned by a man; without sexual arousal on his part, intercourse is impossible. Women, on the other hand, can go through with sex without any physical passion and can feign both interest and enjoyment (once again, women are seen as sexually frigid). From these two facts, women come to practise, and even to take pride in, their ability to deceive men. Pollak himself acknowledges the sexual suspicion that exists in men:

> Suppressing them [women] and needing them at the same time, men have never been completely comfortable in their apparent state of social superiority and have always been apprehensive of the possibility of rebellion or revenge on the part of women. (p. 149)

It is unfortunate that, given this insight, he did not see its social and political implications for the alleged deviousness of women, but instead stressed its sexual root. In view of the fact that women had no power (social, economic or political), it is hardly surprising that they had to resort to manipulative strategies to effect change. The nature of female crime (as speculated upon by Pollak) involves the cunning abuse of the female role. By virtue of motherhood, woman gains access to children and the possibility of abortion and infanticide; by virtue of her role as caretaker of the sick, to poisoning and torture; by virtue of her sexual desirability, to prostitution and to baiting victims for blackmail and robbery. In explaining why some women become criminal while others do not, Pollak falls back on largely biological explanations:

> Thus alerted by the comparatively high criminal liabilities of women in the brackets of childbearing age and of married

women independent of age, we turned to an investigation of the biological and social factors. (p. 157)

This age range includes almost all females who are not actually children and seems unhelpful in directing us to any particular sort of explanation. Nevertheless, Pollak points to the effects of the menstrual cycle and, less strongly, to the irritant effects of the double standard of sexual morality, methods of sales promotion in modern stores and the burden of housework. Since all women of 'childbearing age' are subject to all these pressures, Pollak's argument does nothing to help us understand why some women and not others become criminal.

Konopka's (1966) conception of delinquency relies heavily on the notion of individual pathology; only a girl who is 'sick' can become delinquent. Once again, in females delinquency is clearly equated with sexual promiscuity. The root of girls' problems lies in their *need for love* and their wayward rejection of the normal female means of attaining it.

While these girls also strive for independence, their need for dependence is usually great – and almost completely overlooked and unfulfilled. This need for support seems to exist in all adolescent girls. (pp. 40–1)

Konopka implicitly rejects this search for independence and decides that women's salvation lies in the time-honoured tradition of making themselves lovable to men – without, of course, using sex to do this. Delinquent girls' difficulties are seen in a neo-Freudian framework, arising largely from unloving parents. But the real problem can be traced back further, to the supposed greater need to love among women than among men. As Smart (1977) pointed out, Konopka makes no attempt to question or analyse the social forces that conspire to generate this exaggerated need for dependency by denying women the physical and psychological resources to overcome it.

After the Second World War there was tremendous interest in the application and development of paper-and-pencil psychological tests. Constructed for purposes of screening in forces selection, they then grew in popularity and were applied ad lib to any and every section of society that might fall into the category of 'deviant'. In most cases there was a complete absence of any theoretical framework or *a priori* hypothesis. It was assumed that the continued application of a vast battery of tests would reveal the ways in which deviant populations differed from normals. Such work rests on the assumption that there are structural differences in the personalities of delinquents and normals. These differences, in the absence of any other explanation, are assumed to be innate (Eysenck, 1964). It would be a lengthy undertaking to review all such work, but since the bulk of it has revealed no signficant or replicable differences between delinquent girls and normals, perhaps such an omission is not too grave.

Felice and Offord (1971) and Widom (1978) provide a review of such work. There are three major areas of interest: intelligence, clinical abnormality and personal idiosyncracies. No differences could be found for IQ when delinquent girls were compared with controls suitably matched for socio-economic status and education (Woodside, 1962; United States Department of Labor, 1972). Clinical tests succeeded in producing some results, but these were hardly ever replicated by other workers and almost certainly resulted from the selection bias in girls' institutions. Almost all such studies used institutionalized girls, and, as we have shown, it is the most disturbed girls in the community who are likely to receive residential treatment. Even using the same inventory, workers could not agree about the particular way in which female delinquents' personalities differed from normals (Price 1968; Cochrane, 1971), and American female prisoners showed a personality pattern different from that of a British sample (Barack and Widom, 1977).

Among females the most stable results have come from administration of the Minnesota Multiphasic Personality Inventory (MMPI). Hannum and Warman (1964), Beall and Panton (1956) and Panton (1974) have all reported raised scores on the psychopathic deviate scales for female prisoners. However, Panton notes that female prison inmates appeared significantly less deviant than males on many of the scales. Blackburn (1974a), using a different questionnaire (SHAPS), also reported peaks for incarcerated women awaiting trial on hostility, tension and psychopathic deviate scales. Other tests concerned with specific idiosyncracies (such as time perception, sensation-seeking, awareness of impulsivity) produced quite inconclusive results. Some writers, when they failed to find differences between delinquent girls and normals, even questioned the validity of the scale itself rather than assuming that delinquent girls were not suffering from any personality disturbance.

There are numerous problems associated with the use of formal personality tests. These are considered in detail by Mischel (1968), but a few should be noted here. First, the repeated use of multi-factor personality inventories on a wide enough scale will eventually produce significant results in group comparisons *by chance alone*. Such inventories are of interest only if such differences appear reliably and take a stable form, which they have not done in studies of female delinquents. Second, there are enormous difficulties associated with any superficial, multiple-choice test because subjects are at liberty consciously or unconsciously to distort their replies. Such factors are called 'response bias' and cover well-recognized syndromes of yea-saying, acquiescence and positive self-presentation. One questionnaire asks, 'Do you enjoy watching people in pain?' Clearly, the cultural pressures against agreeing with this statement are enormous, and only highly disturbed individuals (or those with a sense of humour) would endorse it.

More important than the methodological and procedural objections are the theoretical ones. These have been documented and empirically demonstrated by Argyle and Little (1972). Psychometric testing assumes the stability of certain enduring modes of response – this is the definition of personality. However, it has been shown that a person's reactions are more clearly related to situational constraints than to internal personality factors. In particular situations we are highly affected by the specific norms of appropriate social behaviour. Behaviour always exists in a social context, a fact that personality tests and testers tend to ignore. Also, people change with age and experience. A test used on the same individual at different times in his life shows an average correlation of about +0.30; in other words, he gives the same response to only 9 per cent of the questions. In terms of predictive ability, such tests are not useful. The thing that they attempt to measure, if it exists at all, fluctuates wildly with age, time and situation.

Sex roles and socialization

A third type of explanatory schema for female criminality has addressed itself to socialization differences in the two sexes. Sociologists and psychologists have employed this rhetoric, but the focus of concern has been different in the two cases. It is sociologists whom we shall consider first.

Basically, their argument states that the paucity of female crime is attributable to the constraints that are placed on women's lifestyle by society. The rise in female crime figures reflects, directly or indirectly, the change brought about by the liberation of women. Adler (1975) takes the 'direct' causal argument and states:

> In both hidden delinquency and overt deviancy, girls of all classes have departed from previously prescribed sex role behaviour for the same reason that their sisters are choosing careers over domesticity or sexual experience over chastity. (p. 90)

She implies that the new ideology of female assertiveness and equality, when accepted by girls in certain sectors of the community, leads directly to criminality. However, the liberation movement has always been a notably middle-class phenomenon, and a visit to any local community school will confirm that the bulk of girls still voice a desire for marriage, children and settling down; moreover, girls who have become delinquent (and who often have very little opportunity for a rewarding career) reject the idea of the self-supporting and independent woman. Widom (1977) has shown that young female offenders in the United States endorse very traditional values about the role of women. To imply that their delinquency is an inarticulate plea for female equality is unrealistic, and even the idea that they are responding to women's new-found position in society is simply not borne out by the facts. Smart (1977), on the other hand, subscribes to the mediationalist view that the day-to-day changes in girls' lives (brought about by ideological changes related to women) have opened up the same kind of freedoms and challenges to which boys are subjected, resulting in a heightened incidence of delinquency. Higher rates of female employment, the increased divorce rate, the stress on self-fulfilment and the earlier rejection of the family have all opened up to women a greater part in society as a whole, rather than simply in the nuclear family. We are still left with the question of why some females, brought up before such changes took place, became delinquent, as well as why the majority of girls today do not. But perhaps such a question should be left to the psychologists.

Hoffman-Bustamante (1973) has written perhaps the clearest and most comprehensive sociological account of the lower incidence of crime among women, although many of her points are contained within the work of various other writers also. First, she claims that differential role expectations for men and women lead to different socialization practices. Such practices equip men, but not women, with the necessary skills for certain kinds of criminal activity. Boys learn how to handle guns and how to use their fists in a fight, and they have the strength required to break into houses. The nature of female crime is dictated by the kinds of crime that women are capable of committing. Female murderers, more often than males, tend to choose victims from within their families, to use weapons that are convenient household implements and to choose occasions on which the victim is unable to defend himself, being asleep, drunk or off-guard. Previous writers had restricted this kind of argument to the fact that women lacked the physical strength to perform violent crimes. However, it requires little strength to aim and shoot a shotgun, although it does require some familiarity with the weapon – a familiarity that females are unlikely to have. Closely linked to this factor is the question of differential opportunity to commit certain crimes. Pollak points to the high incidence of shoplifting and infanticide among women, reflecting the day-to-day activities in which their criminality is likely to be expressed. Oakley (1972) also subscribes to this view, pointing out that

as some of the differences between the sex roles are reduced by the conditions of modern life, the deviance of male and female becomes more alike. For both male and female, the most common offence is against property. (p. 70)

Hoffman-Bustamante performs a more detailed analysis of crime types in terms of mode of commission and differential opportunities for males and females. She also points out that the vast bulk of female larcenies are for shoplifting of low-value household items rather than personal luxuries. Burglary is an untypical female offence, since it requires the perpetrator to be out alone on the streets at night and to possess certain 'masculine' skills such as the ability to force entry or pick locks. Forgery is primarily a white-collar, low-visibility crime, and middle-class women have a relatively high rate of passing bad cheques. Female embezzlers usually steal from charities, which are rarely audited, so that the detection rate is low, and a woman who works voluntarily for a good cause is rarely a prime suspect.

Hoffman-Bustamente also stresses the importance of the stronger social controls employed in the socialization of girls and maintained in marriage by the husband. This theme has been echoed by many writers, including Adler (1975), Heidensohn (1968), Oakley (1972) and Pollak (1961). Smart (1977) writes:

> Where it is more heavily impressed on girls [than boys] that certain types of behaviour are morally wrong or inappropriate it seems likely that a greater level of conformity will result or, failing that, a stronger feeling of guilt will accompany deviant action. (p. 67)

In support of this contention, she cites a study by Morris (1966), who shows that girls are more censorious of delinquency in their own sex than boys are, and that delinquent girls are more likely than boys to lie about their misbehaviour. Social workers engaged in full-time treatment of young offenders often express the view that girls feel guilty about their delinquency, and that this accounts for the higher rate of self-mutilation, tattooing and suicide attempts by girls in care (Hoghughi and Nethercott, 1977). Their higher rate of conformity to norms and laws has even been attributed to greater levels of field dependency in women. Certainly, girls are taught from an early age to suppress aggressive and anti-social behaviour and are rewarded for obedience and plasticity (see Hutt, 1972; Oakley, 1972), and they come to rely heavily on the approval of significant people in their lives; but such a statement might equally well be offered to account for the levels of delinquency among girls who enter delinquent subcultures. Trained to need approval through conformity, this must equally apply to their behaviour within delinquent peer groups who, at adolescence, become very important sources of self-esteem. While on face value such an argument has a ring of truth, we must go on to ask why some girls become *instigators* of delinquent behaviour. In the framework of sex-linked social control arguments, we find ourselves invoking the notion of pathology to explain individual deviation – a false step that has been taken by many 'common-sense' writers such as Cowie et al. (1968).

One of the direct forms of social control that intimately affect a girl's chance of delinquent behaviour is the fact that girls are kept at home under supervision while their older brothers are allowed to roam the streets. McRobbie and Garber (1975) describe the female teenage subculture as taking place inside girls' homes. They listen to records, exchange pictures and records of their favourite stars and spend a good deal of time in a fantasy world, insulated from the reality of the streets. Hoffman-Bustamante maintains that even when they do become involved in heterosexual delinquent cliques, their role is secondary and marginal. Patrick's (1973) analysis of Glasgow gangs shows the girls as hangers-on, whose main functions are to conceal the boys' weapons, buy drinks and provide sex. Work by Hanson (1964) and Smith (1978) suggests that this role is changing and girls now engage as fully as boys in criminal activities, instigating them and even rejecting boys in favour of all-female gangs. Certainly, the freedom now accorded to girls by their parents (relieved by the pill of any visible proof of misbehaviour) has opened up to them more 'street-corner' life than ever before.

Rather than the broader concern of sociologists with sex stereotypical behaviour and training, psychologists have shown interest in socialization practices within the family. Their orientation is generally clinical and constitutes an attempt to

understand the types of parental behaviour that may predispose
the child to a delinquent future. Blos (1957) has analysed female
delinquency from a Freudian perspective and makes it clear that
his interpretation is psychiatric: 'anti-social behaviour has been
on the rise for some time; this goes hand in hand with a general
rise in adaptive breakdowns in the population as a whole'
(p. 230). He confounds an increase in psychiatric diagnosis of
symptoms with a true increase in the phenomenon of
breakdowns, and the immediate equation of anti-social
behaviour with clinical disorder leaves one almost breathless.
Once again, he makes some 'common-sense' assumptions about
the nature of female crime:

> The girls' wayward behaviour is restricted to stealing of the
> kleptomanic type; to vagrancy; to provocative, impudent
> behaviour in public; and to frank sexual waywardness. In the
> girl it seems delinquency is an overt sexual act, or to be more
> correct, a sexual acting out. (p. 232)

In this way, he reduces all female crime to a fundamentally
sexual level, seeing even shoplifting as an expression of
sexuality.

Female delinquents, he claims, are of two types: one that has
regressed to the pre-Oedipal mother, and the other that clings
desperately to a foothold on the Oedipal stage. Both types result
from the same difficulty: a distant or unsympathetic father to
whom the girl feels unable to transfer her original mother love.
To make matters even more complicated, both types of delinquent show exactly the same symptoms: 'wild displays of
pseudo-heterosexuality'. In the first case the girl has never
succeeded in leaving her mother emotionally and sexually and,
to protect herself against the natural consequence of this
(homosexuality), engages in joyless sexual adventures to
demonstrate her heterosexuality. In the second case, the girl
perceives her father's faults but blames her mother, feeling that
she herself could be the 'good woman' who saves him. To
express this rivalry with her mother, she characteristically
chooses sexual partners with glaring personality defects, which
'she denies or tolerates with masochistic submissiveness.'

However, Freud has been vociferously attacked for the

unfalsifiability of his theory, the absence of corroborative evidence from the few empirical studies that have been undertaken and, more recently, from a feminist perspective. The real danger of psychoanalysis for the present discussion is that it inevitably turns a social and psychological issue into a psychiatric one, once again underlining the view that only a woman who is 'sick' engages in antisocial behaviour. It stresses exclusively sexual aspects of both symptoms and causes, thus failing to account for the massive increase in violence and property offences. Quite apart from the question of its validity as an explanatory scheme, psychoanalytic treatment has been shown to offer no speedier 'recovery' than if no intervention had taken place at all. However, the impact of such explanations should not be underestimated; they are learned by social workers, doctors and psychiatrists and carry weight with magistrates and others who decide on the treatment of juvenile offenders. Such theories, until they are rejected, will continue to hamper any attempt to understand and treat young people with problems.

After Freud the writings of Bowlby (1953) took first place in connection with delinquency. He stressed that the relationship between the child and the mother in the first five years of life was crucial to healthy psychological development. Children deprived of mother love were thought to develop a host of psychological disorders, ranging from subnormality, through schizophrenia and neurosis to delinquency. Criticisms have been offered of Bowlby's work largely in terms of its failure to specify in detail either the independent or dependent variables (see, for example, Rutter, 1972). What is it about the presence of the mother that is so critical? Critical to what aspects of development? Which deprivations lead to which particular disorders? The vagueness of Bowlby's hypotheses has doubtless added to their popularity since, like Freud's, they could always be invoked after the fact to explain almost anything. They also followed the liberal fashion of the times by laying the blame squarely at the feet of the parents and by denying the ability of the child to control its own destiny. The appeal of Bowlby's work in connection with girls was strong, since it viewed the delinquent as a helpless victim of circumstances rather than as an individual with free will or a 'bad streak'. Glueck and Glueck (1934) claimed that 90 per cent of women from a Massachusetts reformatory had broken or poorly supervised home lives, and many post-war studies measured the prevalence of maternal deprivation in incarcerated girls, giving figures that ranged from 27 per cent (Richardson, 1969), through 33 per cent (O'Kelly, 1955), to 43 per cent (Cowie et al., 1968). Yet none of these studies used a control group against which to compare its figures, and the only study to do so (Riege, 1972) found no significant differences between delinquent and non-delinquent girls. However, an Australian study by Koller (1971) reported that 62 per cent of training-school girls had experienced parental loss or deprivation, compared with 13 per cent of the control group.

It became obvious that such a theory notably failed to explain the peculiarly adolescent nature of delinquency. If it results from such an early disturbance, why is it not manifest until puberty? And if it has an enduring effect on personality, why does delinquency usually end in the later teens? Attention turned instead towards the current child-rearing practices of delinquents' parents. Studies by Nye (1958), Riege (1972) and Morris (1964) found that the factors held to be important in male delinquents' homes were equally true of the homes of delinquent females. The frequency of separation and divorce among parents varied widely depending on the definition of delinquency and of the intact family. In general, the incidence of marital break-up was higher in delinquent than non-delinquent populations, and this was particularly true of girls. For both sexes quarrelling and discordance were found in the home (with the exception of Riege's startling finding that the parents of non-delinquents quarrelled more frequently in front of their children than did the parents of delinquents). Often the child reported a feeling of being rejected by either or both parents. Supervision over the child's activities and discipline was lax and erratic, and parent and child spent little time in recreational activities with one another. It would appear that the precipitating factors within the family for delinquency in females are not substantially different from those for males.

The question of parental supervision and discipline is particularly interesting, as it is an area in which attitudes to girls have changed in the last few years. Campbell (1976) reports significant correlations between self-reported delinquency and laxness of parental supervision. Such a linear relationship would imply (though would not prove) that an increase in parental laxness should predict an increase in delinquency over time, and with respect to girls this seems to be true. As girls spend more time out of the home and on the streets, the possibility of their becoming involved in delinquent subcultures increases, particularly in urban, working-class areas. This would seem to focus attention on the peer group rather than the family. While great attention has been paid to this factor in studies of boys, such analysis of girl delinquents is almost completely lacking. We know virtually nothing of their life beyond the family, and this reflects the prevailing belief that the behaviour of females can be explained exclusively by recourse to their biology, psyche and home life. In Chapter 3 we shall contrast these rhetorics with the types of explanations current in connection with male delinquency. We need to ask why females have been considered in such limited terms, and whether with changing sex roles, we might not usefully apply some of the male theories to the 'second sex' as well.

Borrowing from the Boys

In spite of the manifest similarity in the delinquent activities of boys and girls (Brown, 1977; Campbell, 1976; Hindelang, 1971), there have been few attempts to apply 'male' theories of delinquency to females. Yet although each sex has received its own characteristic type of explanation in the literature, there have been some areas of overlap in the foci of delinquency research for boys and girls.

For many years the family was the major target of study in the search for an explanation for delinquent behaviour in both sexes. By 1970 the number of such studies had dropped very dramatically. This shift of emphasis in research resulted from changes in prevailing political viewpoints and a dissatisfaction with the available methodologies, which particularly affected paradigms in psychology. Freud and others who followed him rooted the etiology of all behaviour disturbances firmly in the family. The notions of repressed sexuality and the dark recesses of the subconscious at first had enormous appeal, particularly to the middle classes, and in the 1950s hundreds of popular books on child-rearing practices predicated upon Freud's doctrine were sold. For the new aims of psychology, however, psychoanalysis was unsatisfactory. Psychology wanted to become a legitimate science. It required clearly articulated theories, logically related hypotheses and empirically testable statements of human behaviour. Psychoanalysis was in no position to supply any of these. In its wake, behaviourism grew in popularity largely because of its clear and conservative statements about human action. The initial work by pioneers of behaviourism (Hull, 1952; Skinner, 1953) was performed exclusively on lower 'organisms' – most often rats and pigeons. Slowly, however, the basic tenets of reward and punishment were translated to humans. Sears et al. (1957) amalgamated, rather uncertainly, the views of behaviourists with the old language of psychoanalysis. 'Identification' was still a much used word but was by now being taken over and operationalized more stringently by Bandura and Walters (1959). Instead of the intra-psychic struggles of the first half of the century, childhood development was now discussed in terms of reinforcement schedules and appropriate 'role models'. Delinquency research became obsessed with the frequency and severity of punishment and with the number of hours that parents spent with their children (see, for example, Andry, 1960; Nye, 1958). Nevertheless, the prevailing view remained that delinquency was a direct result of the parents' behaviour and that delinquency was a pathological condition.

The stress that was placed on the family was certainly related to the prevailing political climate. With increased industrialization and the creation of an ever-enlarging middle-management stratum, the old extended family and neighborhood roots began to break down. Workers moved to wherever jobs were, and the geographical dispersions caused by the Depression and the Second World War and its aftermath almost completely succeeded in breaking down practical kinship relations and replacing them with the nuclear family. In the 1960s this thrust continued in the building of high-rise blocks for small family units. All these changes resulted from the requirements of the economic system. Broken into domestic units, the race to keep up with the neighbours began in earnest. Each unit had at least to be self-supporting and at best upwardly mobile. The role of the state was to intervene minimally in the 'natural' equilibrium of capitalism. This meant, however, that indoctrination of proper social motivations was left to parents. As delinquency began to increase, the blame was directed not towards the social disorganization that the state had engineered, but towards the parents who had failed properly to inculcate pro-establishment values. Delinquents' parents, predominantly working-class, were made to feel guilty about their 'neglect' of their children. Parents working long over-time hours to achieve a reasonable standard of living were simultaneously berated for sacrificing their children. As usual, the law lagged behind the changing social climate, but by the 1950s in Britain and the United States legislation embodied the fact that it was parents who created delinquents. They became known as children 'in need of care and protection'. The state assumed the right to remove potentially delinquent children from their families and to provide them with institutional homes, designed to succeed where the natural parents had failed in teaching pro-society attitudes.

Psychologists were at the same time becoming disenchanted with the family as an area of study. Scientifically, it was a difficult subject with which to work. Adequate studies (of which there were few) had to be longitudinal, which cost enormous sums of money. Because it was impossible to predict which children would become delinquent in the future, huge samples had to be taken and data regularly obtained.

Most workers were content to take groups of adjudicated delinquents and controls and to compare them on indices of home climate. The use of different questionnaires, different definitions of delinquency, retrospective information and uncontrolled race and class effects made the resulting body of work inconclusive. Most studies found delinquents' home lives to be worse on at least some dimensions (see Peterson and Becker, 1965, for a review). In the lull that followed the 1950s psychology retained its pathological view of delinquency but moved towards personality-based views of human behaviour. Eysenck (1964) offered one of the most coherent theories of personality and delinquency, rooting the problem in an interaction between genetically based personality traits and parental disciplinary practices. Most workers, however, were prepared to employ trait tests in a theoretical vacuum. As the criticisms of such approaches multiplied (Mischel, 1968; Argyle and Little, 1972), attention turned instead to self-concept. Just as quantitative and *a priori* as the personality tests, it employed rating scales designed to show that delinquents devalued themselves, their masculinity or feminity, their families, their towns or their friends (see, for example, Reckless and Dinitz, 1967; Bhagat and Fraser, 1970). The methodology was simple, quick to administer, easy to score and almost guaranteed to show a significant effect on at least one of the scales.

The wave of liberalism (or radicalism) that swept the middle classes in the late 1960s and 1970s had been apparent in sociology for some time. The Vietnam War, equal rights movements, increases in unionism and women's rights were all part of the tide that turned popular opinion. In academia writers who for years had pointed to social class as an important factor in delinquency were recognized by policy-makers and pundits. In psychology, to match the new consciousness, there was a cry to take the views of the people who were studied more seriously. Deviancy was no exception. In the area of mental health writers suggested that psychiatric labels were meaningless, even that mental illness did not exist. In that of delinquency there was an increased awareness that the delinquents might have something sensible to say, and that their viewpoint should be taken into account. The fashion for introspection and openness, capitalized upon by encounter groups and consciousness-raising courses, even took on a respectable face in methodology (Cicourel, 1968; Harré and Secord, 1972). In wider capitalist society the family was breaking down. Marriage rates dropped, and divorce figures rose in Britain and the United States. The family, which had been such a convenient target for blame, began to collapse. Instead, the responsibility for delinquency was put in the hands of the subculture and the peer group in the context of social class. A new social conscience emerged, and guilt found its expression in listening at last to the words of delinquents without dismissing them as 'disturbed'.

Somewhere along this political and social progression studies of female delinquency halted. For girls, even in the 1980s, blame is still attributed to the parents. In this chapter two contemporary theoretical positions forwarded by studies of male delinquency will be considered: first, societal-level explanations that focus on the disjunction between predominant middle-class values and those of the delinquent; second, an approach that focuses on the particular norms and behaviours of subcultural delinquent groups and the manner in which the individual relates to his peers within them. The reasons why such approaches have so rarely been adopted in studies of females will be discussed.

Societal explanations

This is by no means a homogeneous category, and a number of sociologists have offered alternative accounts of the relationship between societal values and the delinquent individual. It will be helpful to take them in roughly historical order, which broadly corresponds to a movement along the political spectrum from right to left.

It was Durkheim (1951) who coined the term 'anomie' to refer to a state in which normlessness prevails and social mores no longer control the actions of individuals. Deviance and criminality were thought to represent anomic subcultures Durkheim drew a distinction between two types of human need: the physical, which is kept in check by physiological structures that automatically regulate the desire for food, drink, sex, exercise and so on, and social needs, which are controlled and satisfied by the social order. In industrial societies the need or motivation to acquire wealth and prestige is infinite, and this insatiable desire threatens the prevailing rules of society. This drive results in a societal structure that encourages all members to strive for success in order that the most able and talented can be selected in a competitive struggle for status. However, this process, which may be adaptive for society as a whole, has the unfortunate side-effect of producing a feeling of 'uninterrupted agitation' that for many will never lead to fulfilment in socially recognized terms and so can become a force for deviance. Merton (1957) extended this argument to the cultural structure that dictates both the goals that people are encouraged to pursue and the approved ways in which they are expected to do this. Merton directs attention to particular ambitions (rather than rampant, insatiable aspirations) and to the way in which certain sectors of society are more likely to fail to attain these goals. He takes both legitimate and illegitimate goals and means as social objects that people may accept or reject and from these derives a typology of social deviance. It was Cloward and Ohlin (1960) who further explored these ideas, most particularly in relation to delinquent gangs. All young people in a highly competitive and industrialized society such as that of the United States are encouraged to attain the visible manifestations of success and status. They are exposed to the influence of this aspiration by their schooling, the media and often their parents, who hope to see their children achieve higher levels of success than they themselves have attained. However, working-class youths are at a distinct disadvantage in achieving these aims. Education is seen as the passport to money and prestige, but working-class boys often come from families in which academic success is not valued, funds for a college education are not available, school lessons are seen as irrelevant to daily life and the social contacts required for business success are absent. In the face of these disadvantages, such youths must seek alternative avenues to the goals to which they aspire. In sport and show business, for example, the working-class kid can make good legitimately, although the competition is just as intense as in the less glamorous middle-class professions. Instead, boys may turn to a life of crime, which is likely to take one of three forms, corresponding to different subcultural solutions. The *criminal subculture* is devoted explicitly to the acquisition of money by illegitimate means. It involves a career structure whereby younger boys are apprenticed in the necessary arts of burglary, theft and 'fencing' and, through the subculture, make connections with older, more established criminals, into whose circles they will eventually graduate. The *conflict subculture* is more concerned with the acquisition of status or 'rep' (reputation), rather than with money. The boys form gangs that are territorial in nature and devote their efforts to fights with rival gangs to ensure their position as respected warriors. The *retreatist subculture* is devoted to the world of 'kicks' gained through drugs, drink, sex and other sensory experiences. Members opt out of the competition for both wealth and prestige, although they may engage in theft incidentally in order to support their main activities. The stress is on 'coolness', embodied in language, dress and music, and through these values they demonstrate their contempt for the world beyond.

A. K. Cohen (1955), another subcultural theorist, offers an alternative account of delinquent gangs. He argues that such youths no longer aspire to the goals set by middle-class society. They have been blocked in their effort to achieve them legitimately not only by their lack of education but also by their ignorance of the values and norms of the middle classes, which are the prerequisites of success − the virtues of ambition, individual responsibility, the acquisition of academic and sporting skills through competition, the ability to defer gratification, rationality, middle class manners, the rejection of physical aggression, constructive leisure and respect for property. This failure generates a sense of deep frustration, which demands a collective or group solution. Within the subculture the boys invert all the values of the middle-class and live by their antithesis. Through these values, they can at once indicate their disdain for the 'college boy' and gain status within their group:

> The delinquent subculture ... permits no ambiguity of the status of the delinquent relative to that of anybody else. In terms of the norms of the delinquent subculture, defined by its negative polarity to the respectable status system, the delinquent's very nonconformity to middle-class standards sets him above the most exemplary college boy. (A. K. Cohen, 1955, p. 131)

Miller's (1958) account of the delinquent subculture stands in striking contrast to the preceding accounts. While other writers see delinquent values as a reaction to, or a substitute for, middle-class norms and aspirations, Miller points instead to the 'focal concerns' of the working-class culture from which most delinquent gang members come. The working class has its own cultural history, he argues, and to see the delinquent's value system as simply an inversion or perversion of middle-class values is to ignore the unique adaptiveness of the 'focal concerns' of the boys' own cultural background. Working-class males in general are concerned with certain behaviours or traits that are perceived as integral to the male role: trouble (involvement with police or official authorities); toughness (physical prowess, skill, bravery, daring); smartness (ability to outsmart or 'con'; adroitness in repartee, gaining money by wits); excitement (thrill, risk, danger); fate (being favoured by fortune), and autonomy (freedom from superordinate authority, independence). These concerns are particularly salient at adolescence when the boy, who has been raised in a primarily female home, seeks to establish both his manhood and his adult status in the eyes of his peers. His peer group offers him the possibility of trying out these values in words and practice and, through his mastery of them, of achieving what Miller terms a sense of 'belonging' and status. Of course, such aims can be realized in a law-abiding way, and the question remains of why some boys and not others become delinquent. Miller contends that adherence to these male working-class values implicitly demands the violation of certain laws. Fighting is a necessary part of being tough but is also illegal. Similarly, smartness may easily involve illegal financial gain ('conning', receiving stolen goods, betting). Miller's first and most explicitly discussed 'focal concern' (trouble) involves, by definition, a willingness to break the law. He also argues that although law-abiding channels *may* be available in the neighbourhood, illegal activities provide a greater and more immediate return for a smaller outlay of energy. Miller hits out at the formulation offered by Cohen: 'Such characterizations are obviously the result of taking the middle-class community and its institutions as an implicit point of reference' (p. 19). Miller's work will be mentioned again when we turn to a consideration of the peer group and its influence on the individual.

Social control theorists such as Hirschi (1969) proceed from the assumption that man is, by nature, amoral. Actions labelled by society as deviant or delinquent represent the quickest and most effective means of releasing aggression or gaining material possessions. Through socialization we are taught to develop conscience and 'morality', but for some individuals this learning is discarded. It is rejected by those who have little stake in conformity because of weakened bonds with the family, the education system and peers or all three. This weakened relationship and the rejection of social norms frees these individuals to engage in delinquent acts. Such a theory is not aimed exclusively at explaining working-class delinquency, for anyone may become nonconformist for a variety of reasons, arising either internally or externally. It implicates the peer group as an important influence by suggesting that boys enter delinquent peer groups in a search for like-minded others after they have lost their stake in conformity. The hallmark of such a position is explained by Hirschi: 'The question "Why do they do it?" is simply not the question the theory is designed to answer. The question is "Why don't we do it?" There is much evidence that we would if we dared' (p. 34).

During the 1960s attention turned towards the role of society in perpetuating rather than causing delinquency. Wilkins (1964) offered a theory of deviancy amplification that rejected causal links and suggested instead a cyclical positive-feedback loop. In large and depersonalized society people lose sight of individuals and categorize them as types. Groups falling at extreme ends of the normal distribution with respect to, for example, law-violating behaviour are the objects of increasingly severe social judgements and action. Such treatment increases the target group's feeling of separateness and produces increments in the very behaviour that makes them different. This leads to even more forceful condemnation by society, and the cycle continues to repeat itself, resulting in greater and greater levels of criminality. Such a view was popularized by Becker (1973), who gave the message a more political tone by drawing attention to the moral entrepreneurs who dictate what shall constitute deviance and to those individuals who fall victim to such criminal labelling and are effectively prevented from re-entering normal society. S. Cohen (1972) further elaborated this view by studying the way in which the media single out certain youth groups for censure and create 'moral panics' about them among the general public.

The 1970s saw the emergence of radical criminology in Britain. Its orientation is Marxist, and this theory is used both to explain 'delinquency' among youth groups and to direct attention to appropriate research topics. Youth subcultures are discussed in relation to a basically two-dimensional explanatory schema of historical dialectic and social class. Fads and fashions in the values of youth groups are intimately connected with the social stratum from which they spring. The criminologist's role, the theorists argue, is to interpret the statements and actions of youth, police, media and Government in coherent political terms. They claim that any criminological theory or theorist is political, whether explicitly or not. Conservative writers, such as behaviourists and control theorists, attempt to define deviants as maladjusted and direct their attention towards the 'rehabilitation' of the individual. Liberal writers, such as Cloward and Ohlin or Cohen, point to inequalities in the system but are committed to the belief that increased opportunity or cultural change could solve the problem. They settle for piecemeal revision rather than a direct confrontation with the ideology that generates such inequality in the first place.

A socialist conception of man would insist on the unlimited nature of human potential in a human society, and specifically in a society in which man was freed from having to engage in the essentially animalistic pursuit of material production in order to feed, consume and exist. It is not that man behaves as an animal because of his 'nature' (under capitalism): it is that he is not fundamentally allowed by virtue of the social arrangements of production to do otherwise (Taylor et al., 1975, p. 23).

Much concrete work on youth subcultures, their form and social meaning to both actors and observers, came from the Birmingham group (see Jefferson, 1975).

Virtually all the writers who have been mentioned here have ignored the problem of female delinquent behaviour. In most cases they seem unaware of its existence, at least in any sizeable quantity. A. K. Cohen (1955) is one of the few writers who devotes at least a few pages to explaining why female delinquency lies outside the scope of his theory.

First, he argues, female delinquency is much less common than male delinquency (although why this should render his theory inapplicable is unclear). Second, he accepts unquestioningly the fact that female delinquency is sexual and therefore cannot be said to be a gang-based phenomenon. He quotes Kvaraceus and Miller (1959), who disparagingly explain away the fact that the incidence of group delinquency is virtually identical for males and females thus:

> Since the majority of delinquent girls, regardless of the 'reason for referral' are in some degree sexually delinquent, the 'number of companions' has a different connotation from what the same item has for boys, the episodes occurring with different boys at different times, except in the comparatively rare episodes of delinquent girls who have sex episodes with groups of boys in rapid sequence. (pp. 116–17)

This view of female crime as exclusively composed of promiscuous sexual adventures is not only inaccurate and value-laden but implicitly views the girl as being able to relate to others only from a horizontal position. It implies that she is a complete social isolate except when her body is being 'used' by boys. To bolster this asocial view of delinquent females, Cohen quotes five writers who have mentioned the relative infrequency of female gangs, the most recent reference being 1946, a decade before his book was published. In terms of facts, Cohen's dismissal of the comparability of male and female delinquency at an explanatory level is misguided. Later, however, he offers further argument at a theoretical level.

Delinquency represents a solution to an adjustment problem, and this solution must take a form that is consistent with the stereotypical sex role.

> In short, people do not simply want to excel, they want to excel as a man or as a woman, that is to say, in those respects which, in their culture, are symbolic of their respective sex roles. ... Even when they adopt behaviour which is considered disreputable by conventional standards, the tendency is to be disreputable in ways that are characteristically masculine and feminine. (p. 138)

The male's role is within society. His success is defined with respect to education, income, power and status. The female, Cohen argues, derives her self-respect exclusively from her relationships with men. The delinquent solution offered would, he argues, not only be irrelevant to a girl; it would also be positively damaging. By attacking society so provocatively, she would be actively damaging her status as a female. Cohen does, however, permit himself some observations on the sexual nature of girls' delinquency. The equivalent of the 'college boy' is the girl who learns to defer sexual gratification in order that she may offer her virginity as a bargaining device for marriage and therefore achieve a higher social status. As the male delinquent inverts the middle-class value system with respect to status, so the delinquent girl does with respect to sex. By openly 'sleeping around', she expresses contempt for a system in which she has no hope of success. It is unclear from Cohen's writing whether the girl lacks the self-discipline (a middle-class ethic) to refrain from sex or whether she actively elects to demonstrate her contempt by promiscuity. It would seem that the working-class girl has a relatively greater chance of upward social mobility than the male and experiences considerably less hostility and frustration than her male friends. Cohen's simplistic view also fails to explain the fact that 'loose' sexual behaviour is likely to generate just as much disapproval among working-class and 'delinquent' girls as it does in any other strata of society. Even in the liberated 1980s teenage girls in Borstals still express contempt for promiscuity and prostitution. Cohen argues that the delinquent boy is a rogue male whose *behaviour* may be condemned but never his masculine status, but the same is clearly not true for sexually 'delinquent' girls. The promiscuous girl, far from being applauded in the subculture for her femininity, is condemned by both males and females alike. This explanation certainly does not offer a delinquent a solution compatible with excelling in her female role.

Cloward and Ohlin (1960) make passing reference to the possible existence of female gangs but are happy to conclude, 'they are likely to be affiliated in some subordinate relationship with a group of delinquent boys'; for this reason they are discounted from further consideration. Morris (1964, 1966), however, took up Cloward's and Ohlin's ideas and implemented them in two studies, which, she claims, give support to their view. Her contention is that *relational* problems are the female equivalent of male status problems. The male is driven to delinquency by a perceived failure to achieve success and prestige, while girls are impelled by a sense of their own failure to deal effectively with personal relationships within the family. This they take presumably as evidence of their inability to cope with heterosexual relationships and with marriage in the future. Morris's first study compared male and female delinquents and non-delinquents. She predicted that delinquent girls would be most likely to come from broken homes and/or homes with many family tensions and to be physically less attractive than non-delinquent girls.

She found significant differences between the two sets of girls with respect to all three areas of inquiry. However, as has already been mentioned, evidence suggests that girls from disrupted homes are more likely to come to the attention of the police and so be defined as delinquent. The significance of Morris's hypothesis is not very obvious. First, she implies both that unattractive girls are less likely to be loved by their parents, which seems a rather harsh assumption, and that their chances of marriage are directly related to their looks. How an objective measure of physical attractiveness was established is unclear, but one cannot help but suspect a strong 'experimenter bias' in this evaluation. The fundamental objection to the whole inquiry lies in the very tenuous link between Cloward's and Ohlin's theory and Morris's operationalization of it. The fact that there is more conflict and more broken marriage in the homes of delinquents has been shown many times for both boys and girls, always at a correlational level. Second, Morris's claim that she has demonstrated 'the particular relevance of relational problems to female delinquency' is simply untrue. To demonstrate this, she would have had to test a number of other dimensions of possible importance to establish the superordinate salience of the family to girls. She would also have had to demonstrate that these family tensions exercised a greater impelling force on girls than boys. To show a difference is not necessarily to show an important, causal difference.

In her second paper Morris deals with the hypothesis that there is a relative absence of a deviant subculture among female delinquents and an absence of subcultural as well as cultural support for female delinquency. To do this, she compiles a list of eight delinquency items and asks subjects to estimate their friends' probable attitude towards the commission of such acts. Again, she employs male and female delinquents and non-delinquents. However, while four delinquent items are common to both sexes, the remaining four deal with sexual activities in the case of girls and violence, theft and vandalism for boys. The results over the total inventories do indeed support her prediction; non-delinquent girls and boys are more condemning of these forms of behaviour than are delinquents. This comes as no surprise, since girls are often even more censorious of promiscuity among their own sex than are boys. When she goes on to analyse the four items common to both sexes, she does not split her subjects by sex and so fails to answer her central question: do girls condemn their own sex particularly for the same offences that boys commit? She also claims to have shown that delinquent girls have fewer like-minded friends than delinquent boys, in spite of the fact that such a comparison showed no significant difference between the two groups.

A second study that attempted to investigate subcultural support and perceived opportunity theories among girls was performed by Datesman et al. (1975). A large sample of boys and girls was taken from public schools and compared with a group of teenagers who had appeared before a family court. As a measure of subcultural support for delinquency, subjects were asked to rate themselves on ten bipolar adjectives, the hypothesis being that subcultural support would have the effect of immunizing delinquents from lowered self-concepts. This seems a very oblique way of investigating subcultural support. Since no information is given on the subcultures to which they might have belonged, it seems more likely that the subjects responded in terms of general, stereotypical sex-role values congruent with their age, race and background. The results revealed no overall relationship for males but a weak association ($p < 10$) between delinquency and poor self-concept for girls. When the subjects were partitioned by race, only black girls and white boys showed the predicted relationship. This effect could not be explained by further analyses of offence history or offence type. The authors conclude:

> Perhaps the larger gap between the self-concept scores of black female delinquents and non-delinquents reflects a relative absence of subcultural support for female delinquency as compared to male delinquency. (p. 112)

In one sentence they have conveniently forgotten that the relationship held for black girls only. Since blacks constituted only 34 per cent of the total sample, there can be no justification for this generalization. In a footnote the authors point out that 90 per cent of the black sample came from the lower half of the income distribution, compared with 30 per cent of whites. Moynihan (1965) has pointed out that black girls are encouraged to integrate racially more than boys and to aspire to success in the mainstream of American culture (rather than exclusively within black ghettos). If this is indeed the case, the lowered self-concept of black female delinquents may be explained as much in terms of class as of race. However, if self-concept is in any sense related to subcultural support, the authors' most striking finding must be that for females as a whole there is more subcultural support than for males. This fact is not related to the degree of seriousness of delinquent behaviour nor to the length of involvement with labelling agencies such as police and courts.

The second half of the paper deals with the perception of

opportunity by delinquents and non-delinquents, as a test of Cloward's and Ohlin's theory. Opportunity was operationalized in terms of degree of agreement or disagreement with 14 questionnaire items. It is unfortunate that these items are not made available in the text. Nevertheless, the results show that among both male and female delinquents there is a significantly lower level of perceived opportunity. The degree of significance is identical for both sexes and remains constant when the sample is partitioned by race. When the delinquents are analysed in terms of offence type, there is a significant relationship for white girls only, with public policy offenders tending to perceive the lowest opportunity. The authors conclude:

> Sexual delinquency among girls may thus be an attempt to fulfil their marital goal by gaining male attention or, alternatively, it may represent retreatist behaviour in which the long term goal of marriage has been supplanted by the short-term goal of immediate popularity with males. (p. 119)

Once again, opportunity for girls is perceived as linked directly with matrimony, even though the 'opportunities' investigated in the questionnaire were identical for male and female. Sandhu and Allen (1969) showed that delinquent girls are less committed to marriage as a goal and perceive fewer difficulties in reaching that goal than do non-delinquent girls. Nevertheless, marriage is once again invoked by the authors as the only legitimate goal for a girl. Would it not be more sensible to view the causal link between perceived opportunity and public policy offences as operating precisely the other way around? Girls who are publicly stigmatized for their personal and sexual lives (which are probably no more promiscuous than any other teenagers') come to view their futures as much more circumscribed than those of other girls. The intrusion of police and courts into such private matters probably has a far more traumatizing effect than a straightforward accusation of petty theft. The stigma that accompanies it perhaps makes the girl feel that her future has been irreversibly altered.

In summary, empirical attempts to implement subcultural theories in girls have been hampered by a sexist translation and distortion of the original statements. It has been taken as axiomatic that the acquisition of a man is the only legitimate goal of females, and that subcultural support can come only from members of the same sex. There has been little work on the heterosexual adolescent group and on the position of girls in relation to societal achievement.

The notion of social control is one that has not been viewed explicitly in relation to girls. The notion has both an active and a passive application. The passive stance explores the rejection of an individual *by the system*. Needless to say, this passive view has been applied to girls by workers who have investigated maternal and parental rejection and scholastic performance. There is no empirical work investigating rejection by peers as a precursor of delinquency, although the view of the female delinquent as a social isolate is prevalent in the literature. The active stance credits the individual with asking the question, 'What incentives are there to commitment to conformity?' This position seems particularly relevant with respect to females since the advent of the women's movement. The hypothesis would be that an individual who perceives that little satisfaction is to be gained from adherence to conventional social norms about law-abiding and feminine behaviour becomes free to 'deviate' without risk. Such a theory would seem more relevant to girls than boys. The successful and conforming male certainly appears to have more to gain (in terms of status and wealth) than the equivalent female, who can hope at best for a 'good' marriage and a lifetime of poorly paid domestic or industrial labour. Work in this area might well prove fruitful now. Dissatisfaction with the female role as a cause of crime would imply that social change might alleviate it. On the other hand, dissatisfaction arising from the fact that females now see their new and equal role in society to be as meaningless as their old one within marriage would be an altogether more socially threatening matter. The lack of research into social control theory in its *active* sense seems to reflect the view that women could not or should not be frustrated by what conformity offers them. The stress on the female as a passive victim of rejection by others not only takes a pathological stance but, once again, views her as an object of sympathy, not censure – as a casualty rather than a critic of society.

Another fruitful area of inquiry might be interactionist or amplification theory. Figes (1975) has pointed to the way in which the female criminal in prison is treated as psychologically disturbed rather than just plain 'bad'. To suggest that criminality results from stress or anxiety is to imply that its cause is transitory and situational. It also implies that a 'cure' is possible, and that the prison can provide this. From a deviance amplification point of view, it might be hypothesized that fewer women than men are defined as 'criminal'. They are likely to generate less hostility and to provoke less punitive reaction because they are deemed to be under the control of their husbands or families, and their criminality presents less of a danger to society. This creates smaller positive feedback into the control system and might predict a lower rate of increase in female crime. Once society does begin to censure female crime as strongly as male crime, there may be a substantial increment in the rate of female delinquency and of recidivism. An investigation of media treatment of women and crime might well help to promote understanding of the degree of public censure directed towards them. Once again, the time is right for such an investigation. Newspapers are beginning to generate a strong sense of outrage against the 'gentler sex' who are now turning to violence. Female baby batterers, muggers and vandals provoke a storm of public reaction, and the media are predicting the downfall of society as women become as violent as men.

Even among the radical criminologists (Taylor et al., 1975) there has been an unusual silence on the topic of female crime. A search through the subject index of such books reveals only a few references to the women's liberation movement but no mention at all of women's position in the legal system. This seems an important omission on the part of those purporting to be on the side of the unheard voices of the oppressed. Other writers have begun to address the issue, notably members of the Birmingham group and Carol Smart (1977). McRobbie and Garber (1975) discuss the 'invisibility' of girls in many of the studies of youth subcultures. They consider that the cause may lie partially with male researchers, who impose on their work normative male views about the subordinate and sexually defined role of females and therefore assert that girls play a minor part in the activities of Hell's Angels, Mods, Rockers and so on. McRobbie and Garber point out that while girls *may* be marginal to the activities and views of such groups, teenage girls do develop their own culture – the culture of the bedroom. Here girls gather to swap pictures of pin-ups, listen to records, size up boys and experiment with clothes and make-up. They continue to pursue interests that constitute a training ground for their future position as decorations for, and supporters of males. The extent to which delinquent girls transcend this culture and move forcefully into more active positions within heterosexual groups is rarely discussed (see Smith, 1978). Powell and Clarke (1975) look at career and leisure possibilities for working-class girls. Their stress on the class structure and the way in which it both dictates and trains for only a limited number of female lifestyles is important. The work of Miller (1958) is relevant here: delinquent activity needs to be investigated with reference to the values upheld by highly delinquent girls and the lifestyles that they adopt. Part of the shock value of female crime (particularly acts of violence) arises from the stereotypical view of women as middle-class ladies. Comparisons between middle-class girls diligently studying for university entry and delinquent working-class school leavers are not meaningful ones. Girls who habitually become involved in violence, theft and so on have to be seen in terms of their own peers who do not, and evidence provided by a study of such girls may suggest that they are not 'deviants' but individuals who have taken certain values and norms one step further than their friends. It is astonishing that so little has been written about current values and lifestyles among working-class women. Young and Wilmott's (1957) study of East End family life is now outdated. Fewer families are left in urban slums, and economic changes have brought about an *embourgoisement* of values, which was perhaps best reflected in the consumer-oriented culture of the Mods.

From my own research (Campbell, 1978) it is clear that the working-class girl still aspires to be a 'coper' – an attractive wife and mother, certainly, but for all that a character to be reckoned with. She must be a woman who can provide materially and yet does not lose her sense of fun, her ability to 'have a laugh'. Other values that will become prominent in later chapters are those of loyalty and integrity. The quintessential woman is one who will defend the good name of her friends and family against all-comers and who is prepared openly to challenge anyone who, by his or her speech or behaviour, belittles her or her acquaintances. To take all these values one step further is to find that being attractive on very low pay may require shoplifting, that having a laugh may involve breaches of the peace and that loyalty may often end in a physical confrontation. As with Miller, such behaviour is not condemned or sanctioned by girls but taken as evidence of appropriate, if extreme, value systems. The capacity to 'bite one's tongue' and suffer in silence, so beloved of middle-class ladies, is far from applauded by working-class girls. Rows and arguments are seen as the normal channels of release for people who live in close proximity. To sort out a dispute by a face-to-face confrontation is considered appropriate and even laudable. Girls who 'bitch' behind each other's backs are rejected as not having the 'bottle' to take responsibility for themselves and their views. These themes will also be taken up later in the book. For the present the point must simply be made that no real understanding of female crimes can emerge without a much more detailed study than is currently available of the values of the working-class woman and the way in which they affect girls at a very crucial stage of their development.

The peer group

Delinquency is a social phenomenon. This seems to be one of the few 'facts' of criminology to which numerous studies have testified. For many years official police statistics have indicated that the majority of juveniles are picked up in groups, both in the United States (Erickson, 1971) and in Britain (Downes, 1966). Hindelang (1976) has suggested that police may be more likely to book, rather than merely to caution, delinquent groups, and that groups are more likely to be apprehended by the police than are lone offenders. However, further work using self-reported delinquency techniques has confirmed that the social nature of delinquency is not merely artefactual (Gold, 1970; Shapland, 1975). These facts have directed the attention of many criminologists towards the peer group as an important factor in delinquent behaviour.

Subcultural theorists unanimously view the delinquent solution as a collective one. Those who fail in the middle-class competition for success want to be able to attribute the blame to society rather than to personal deficiencies. Furthermore, they want to establish a subculture in which each member can achieve some measure of status. Since status is derived from implicit or explicit competition, the attempt to acquire it requires the active co-operation of like-minded others. These two reasons explain the importance of the group to the individual. It provides a source of self-esteem, a validation of a coherent world view, a consistent set of norms and an appropriate rationalization for antisocial acts. The group consciousness also offers strength and security against the critical assaults of family, school and social worker. Criminologists are unanimous in testifying to the positive attraction that the peer group exerts on individual members. A. K. Cohen (1955) writes:

> Relations with gang members tend to be intensely solidary and imperious. . . . the gang is a separate, distinct and often irresistible focus of attraction, loyalty and solidarity. (p. 31)

Sherif and Sherif (1967) note that

> those personal characteristics ordinarily prized in social life – friendliness, sociability, loyalty – are associated with longer and more serious participation in activities labelled anti-social. (p. 61)

Miller (1958), who views the gang as the testing ground for later manhood, similarly points to the social demands made of its members:

> The activity patterns of the group require a high level of intra-group solidarity; individual members must possess a good capacity for subordinating individual desires to general group interests as well as the capacity for intimate and persisting interaction. Thus highly 'disturbed' individuals, or those who cannot tolerate consistently imposed sanctions on 'deviant' behaviour, cannot remain accepted members. (p. 14)

Such writers, then, are in agreement about the quality of the friendship between the boys. However, discussion continues over the temporal relationship between delinquency and gang membership. Hirschi (1969) argues that 'birds of a feather flock together' after they have lost their ties with conformity, and that the groups that they form are made up of socially rejected individuals huddling desperately together for support. On the other hand, writers such as Patrick (1973) and Boyle (1977), who speak from first-hand experience, imply that delinquent groups are a highly respected part of the youth culture and that young boys aspire to membership from an early age. Discussion also continues over whether or not the term 'gang' should be used to describe these groups. The formal definition of a gang implies leadership, initiation rites, distinct identity, membership and endurance over time. Most recent writers have failed to find evidence of such highly structured units. In New York Yablonsky (1962) describes the 'near group', which shows no evidence of the above qualifications for the term 'gang'. He reports 'a mob-like collectivity that forms around violence in a spontaneous fashion'. Short and Strodtbeck (1965) in Chicago and Gannon (1966) in New York also report the absence of highly organized gangs, although they suggest a high degree of cohesion among very delinquent cliques. In Britain Fyvel (1963), Spencer (1964) and others similarly failed to find the classical gang. Patrick (1973) in Glasgow and White (1971) in Birmingham have reported groups of boys with names, definite territories, endurance over time and inter-gang battles. Specific initiation rites are not mentioned, and the gangs lack any very formal structure. Scott (1956) in London found that 86 per cent of teenage boys in his sample belonged to loosely structured and diffuse groups. Whether clearly structured or not, the quality and extent of the boys' positive tie to the group has been taken as axiomatic and, by its very nature, is a difficult thing to quantify in any 'objective' way. Klein and Crawford (1967) attempted to do this by asking detached youth workers to report the names of boys whom they saw around the city each day and to note particularly the frequency, location and groupings of the delinquent boys. The results indicated that the most delinquent boys interacted with each other more frequently, spent less time alone and were more tightly knit into distinctive cliques than less delinquent groups.

While this confirms statistically the close structure of the delinquent group, it fails to give any real picture of the quality of the boys' relationships. This can only be achieved by participant observation studies of youth groups. Such studies have been performed by Parker (1974) in Liverpool and Daniel and McGuire (1972) in London. By considering these accounts, it is possible to find evidence of the boys' friendship in their day-to-day interaction. If sheer amount of time spent together is an index, then these boys were extremely close. Not only had virtually all of them grown up together in the same streets, but they still continued to spend eight or nine hours a day in one another's company. In many cases the relationship was more like that of a family than a friendship. Since childhood they had eaten and slept at one another's houses and roamed the streets together after school, waiting for their parents to return from work. Their loyalty to one another was most apparent when it came to fights. Fairness 'rules' prevented a whole group of them from joining in with a friend against a single opponent, but members had no hesitation in extending a one-to-one fight into an inter-group brawl. At football matches loyalty was often put severely to the test. At away matches the 'nutter' of the group would prance about among the opposition, inviting trouble. His courage in doing this derived from his certainty that, in the event of his being set upon, his friends would rally to his support. (As Miller has noted, the execution of a delinquent act requires a close degree of co-operation from the team.) The Liverpool boys had perfected car radio theft to a fine art, which required the synchronized performance of at least three boys. Failure or cowardice on the part of any one of them meant detection for the rest. Their material generosity to one another was particularly striking. Those who were out of work could count on others for drinks. Spoils from illegal activities were shared with friends and family. In short, insiders' accounts of group dynamics unanimously applaud the quality of the friendships that the boys experience within the group.

The historical and evolutionary importance of male friendship groups has been discussed by animal behaviourists and anthropologists. Tiger (1969) suggests that the two primary social bonds in society are, first, that between mother and child and, second, that between co-operating males. He rejects the idea of an innate predisposition towards pair-bonding, arguing that the institution of marriage was constructed by society artificially to promote monogamy. For the survival of the group, the most important thing was to have a caretaker for the offspring, while males undertook the business of hunting to ensure an adequate food supply. The importance of male bonding has been taken up by Marsh (1978) to explain the behaviour of British football supporters. In the absence of the hunt, males today select new arenas in which they can demonstrate loyalty to their own group as well as fearlessness in the face of injury. Dominance and status among males in the group are decided by symbolic or ritualized aggressive encounters among themselves, which decide who will lead in inter-group battles. The behaviour of Dhani tribesmen, football supporters and gangs are used as evidence of the universal need for males to bond together. Females, by comparison, do not seem to need to select same-sex arenas in which to demonstrate their mutual loyalty against all comers.

Many of these evolutionary arguments are based on extrapolation from the behaviour of higher primates. The extent to which human social behaviour can be explained by recourse to the study of animals is an issue that provokes heated debate (Ardrey, 1976; Ashley-Montagu, 1976). It is a highly specula-tive area and one in which it is all too easy to simplify facts in order to support almost any position. Jolly (1972), for example, discusses the enormous variation between species in their social structure and dynamics. Even the same species under different ecological conditions will develop entirely new organizations and conventions to ensure survival. A key element in the con-tinuation of any group or species is its swift adaptability to new circumstances. Given this, it seems misguided to explain a dynamic process by recourse to appeals to biological necessity or genetics. Geneticists struggle to understand the determinants of hair or eye colour in humans, let alone more amorphous and complex questions such as the nature of pair-bonding or social groupings. Nevertheless, male bonding arguments do have an appeal when one considers the extent of all-male events and organizations compared with those of females.

In the area of animal behaviour, as well as that of human criminality, much less attention has been directed to the study of the female of the species. The evidence suggests that female primates neither compete ritually for dominance nor charac-teristically fight together in defence of territory. Their status in the group is dependent largely on whether they are sexually receptive, have young or are consorting with a high-status male – all of which are transient, situational criteria, over which they exert little personal control. Females are characterized as isolated from one another, linked either to their young or, temporarily, to a courting male. However, little mention is made of the enormous co-operation that is to be observed between females in the caretaking of offspring. Among chimpanzees childless females will beg to be allowed to hold the newborn, and a complex system develops of 'aunts' who support and help the mother to raise her young. Chimpanzees demonstrate none of the intra-sex jealousy for which the human female is famed. Males and females play rough-and-tumble games together when young and throughout life maintain cordial relations with one another. Females are sexually receptive for only 20 weeks out of a 20-year life span, and it would be quite wrong to characterize male–female relations as predominantly sexual (see Jolly, 1972). After oestrous and mating, male chimpanzees lose exclusive interest in one female, and the social structure resorts to a looser, more platonic grouping.

The economic dependence of women on the institution of marriage seems to have been largely responsible for the separation of human females from one another. The characteristic possessiveness and jealousy of females is founded on economics. Girls are set against one another in their competition to secure a man – preferably one who shows signs of achieving social and economic success. Through him, the female ensures not only her economic survival but also her status, since until recently she has been denied any means of attaining these on her own. The emotional concomitants of status – self-esteem and pride – have also become bound up in women's relationships with men. Historically, women have had only one arena in which to demonstrate their worth, and that was the attraction and retention of a high-status male. Failure in this endeavour – for instance, the loss of a man to a female rival – has provoked not only jealousy but also an abiding sense of personal failure. This view of females as highly competitive (fortunately, on the wane) has probably been responsible for the lack of interest in female friendship among adolescents.

The little work that has been done (McRobbie and Garber, 1975) views female friendship as essentially passive. In the culture of the bedroom girls talk rather than act. They speculate and reflect rather than generate. They fantasize about what may happen in relation to some pop star or local boy but do not put their speculations to the test. They are seen not only as marginal to male society but as parasites upon it. The company of males generates excitement and action – this experience is then used as material for discussion between themselves. It is as if access to life were gained via males. Once again, it is easy to see the societal pressures that led to such a state of affairs. Parental protection of girls was strong. Implicitly or explicitly, the fear of pregnancy caused parents to curtail their daughters' evening activities. Going out was a weekend luxury in an otherwise home-based life. In the restricted amount of time in which they had access to males girls rushed to prove their worth by attracting a boyfriend and experimenting sexually. This provided a talking-point for the long weekday evenings when they were allowed to spend time in other girls' houses, free from the threat of the rogue male. The increased freedom accorded to girls with the advent of contraception and sexual liberalism has certainly had the positive effect of allowing adolescents of both sexes to view each other in ways other than sexual. More time spent in mixed-sex groups is bound also to lead to a reduction in sex-role disparity and a more active role for girls in all activities – some of which may be 'delinquent'.

Recent work in female delinquency (particularly influenced by the women's movement) has directed attention to the search for the all-female gang. Hanson, a New York journalist, published a book in 1964 on female gangs in the Puerto Rican area of the city, based on street workers reports. The novelistic style of the book and its resemblance to *West Side Story* leaves the reader struggling to extract fact from dramatic licence. Adler (1975) also reports the existence of all-girl gangs in London and America. Reports from the United States estimate that about 10 per cent of all gang members are female, but that half of known male gangs have female branches (Miller, 1975). The New York Police Department in 1976 reported only six all-girl gangs who were not attached to a male group. The emerging pattern, however, seems to be one of heterosexual gangs. In Chicago and New York the enduring secondary and supportive function of females is perfectly in keeping with the classical female role (Marsh and Campbell, 1978a,b). They hide guns and knives in their clothing for the boys, as females cannot be searched by male officers. They buy beer and cigarettes, provide food, sex and support. Sexual relationships are flexible and unproblematic. Girls who sleep with different members are no longer characterized as cheap, although some monogamous pairings endure over a period of months. Certainly, the highly sexist attitude of the Hell's Angels to females, – as either 'sheep' or 'old ladies' – is beginning to die out (Thompson, 1967).

Brown (1977) offers an illuminating account of female involvement in black gangs in Philadelphia. He particularly notes the differences in initiation, role and criminality of girls who join heterosexual as opposed to all-female gangs. In primarily male gangs new boys have to be tested; they must have 'fair ones' (fist-fights) with specified gang members and prove that they have 'heart' (courage). Males who are simply 'drafted' or coerced into joining do not perform these tests and for this reason have no status within the gang. A girl need only express a desire to join in order to become a 'young girl'. As she gains experience, she graduates to become an 'old head', a term that refers to street experience, not age. These are the only two classifications for girls, although for male gang members there are many. To graduate, a girl must establish a reputation within the gang. This she may do in a number of ways. She is expected to participate in gang fights, although in general she will fight with female members of opposing gangs. She will use weapons herself, as well as carrying them for the boys. She can demonstrate 'gump' (courage) by taking on smaller fights with females from other gangs by herself at school and can progress through the gang ranks by challenging more senior gang members (usually, but not exclusively, female ones). She may also act as a spy by associating with males from other gangs or as a decoy to lure them into her own gang's territory. Her role within her own gang is not dependent on offering sexual favours to the males; Brown is quite clear on this point:

To be a female gang member in Philadelphia's black gang subculture does not have the automatic connotation of being a sexual object subject to the whims of the male gang members. Rather, it means that the female is an intrinsic part of that gang's group identity who participates in gang activities and is involved in various gang functions, rather than just ancillary activities such as sexual fulfilment. (p. 226)

Brown offers a contrasting description of an all-female black gang. The gang has between 20 and 30 members, mostly teenagers. Entry to the gang involves a fight with the gang's 'runner'. The initiate need not win but must display sufficient courage to satisfy the requirements of the aggressive philosophy of the gang. The gang's central activity is violence, and its members are reputed particularly to enjoy badly scarring and mutilating 'cute' girls. They use knives, hand guns, rifles and sawn-off shotguns. Their reputation is just as ferocious as that of any of the male gangs. In England Smith (1978) and Campbell (1978) have noted that girls seem to be taking a much more forceful role in adolescent delinquent groups. No longer content to remain in the background, girls are beginning to instigate and commit many previously 'male' crimes. Taking and driving away, burglary and grievous bodily harm are becoming as much female as male enterprises. In the area of violence girls were once content to provide an excuse for male fighting and occasionally even to engineer boys into aggressive encounters for vicarious excitement. Today girls increasingly fight their own battles and take pride in their ability to look after themselves (see chapter 5).

In the past, work on female delinquency has been notable for its failure to consider the peer group as an area of importance. Prominent texts such as Cowie et al. (1968) and Richardson (1969) make virtually no mention of it. Konopka (1966), in her series of case histories, clearly implies the social isolation of delinquent girls. Taking institutionalized samples, in which delinquents are mixed with girls suffering from clinical disorders, has certainly confounded the issue. But perhaps, at bottom, the lack of research on female friendships stems from the assumption that girls relate to one another competitively in the activity of attracting men. Because female delinquency has been equated with sexual promiscuity, it has been assumed that such girls are rejected by their own sex. Research showing the involvement of females in non-sexual crimes (Alder, 1975) and the social nature of that involvement (Smith, 1978) must at last direct attention to the effect of the peer group on female delinquency.

CHAPTER 4

Shoplifting

Shoplifting has always been considered to be the female offence *par excellence*. We all share a popular conception of the menopausal, middle-class housewife caught by the store detective, embarrassed and confused, with plenty of money in her purse. The available explanations for shoplifting are characteristically female too: they postulate pathological or clinical syndromes firmly rooted in childlessness or phallic envy. To arrive at a more factually based understanding of shoplifting, which may point to a more satisfactory explanation, the first step is to investigate the figures that are available on shoplifting and shoplifters.

Contrary to popular opinion, women do not outnumber men among those found guilty of shoplifting in current criminal statistics (Home Office, 1978). In 1978, for example, 46.8 per cent of all convicted shoplifters were women, and this figure is fairly typical of the ratio over the last twenty years. It is without doubt the offence in which women most nearly approximate to the rate of men. (As a contrast, only 8.2 per cent of those found guilty of violence against the person were women.) Since women characteristically have a much lower rate of criminality than do men, this 1:1 ratio has led to the idea that shoplifting is a female offence. It is possible to estimate the degree of change of female and male involvement in the offence over a period of 23 years by taking the proportions of female findings of guilt in 1955 and 1978 (in magistrates' courts), subtracting one from the other and dividing by the number of intervening years (23). This average rate of change gives a figure of +0.02, for shoplifting and +0.12 for violence (wounding). Clearly, shoplifting has maintained a very stable male–female distribution, while violence, for example, shows a substantial increase in female involvement.

We can establish the number of women criminals who are shoplifters by a simple ratio technique. In 1978 55.7 per cent of all female findings of guilt were shoplifters. Computing the average rate of change for these figures gives a much higher figure of +0.83. So while men and women participate equally in this kind of theft, as the years go by, with higher numbers of criminal convictions annually, more and more women are being found guilty of shoplifting.

Unfortunately, statistics from the United States do not give a breakdown of crimes as sensitive as that available in the United Kingdom. Simon (1975) notes that of all the offences for which women are arrested, larceny/theft ranks highest; 20.2 per cent of all female arrests are for this group of offences. Of all persons arrested in 1972 (male and female), 30.8 per cent of females were charged with larceny/theft. Just as in Britain, the average rate of change over 20 years for women's involvement in this offence, as opposed to other female offences, is high; +0.96 for larceny.

Among these global figures lie those that are our present concern: the number of juvenile girls who are participating in shoplifting. These figures are presented in table 4.1. For all three age groups the proportion of females to males involved in this offence is broadly on the increase. This is reflected in the figure for the sex ratio average rate of increase. The change is accelerating most markedly in the youngest age bracket, that of children under 14. Such a finding might be interpreted as evidence to support the cruder versions of the women's liberation argument: the more equality and freedom we give to females, the more we should expect them to participate in the traditionally male arena of crime. It is these younger girls who have grown up in a more liberal climate of opinion on matters female than have their 21 year old counterparts. However, later in the chapter, as we move on to consider the type of goods stolen by these girls and the motives involved, it will become clear that they have by no means escaped the sex-role trap. They may feel freer to break the law of the land but not necessarily the law of the female's position in a consumer society, where women themselves are still a commodity.

We may consider the 'popularity' of shoplifting among female offenders by returning to the ratio of findings of guilt for

TABLE 4.1 *Conviction rates for shoplifting in Great Britain by sex over a 22-year period*

		Under 14 years		14–17 years		17–21 years	
		number	%	number	%	number	%
1955	Male	2472	84	916	69	228	42
	Female	472	16	409	31	311	58
1960	Male	3355	78	1639	62	670	51
	Female	933	22	983	38	639	49
1966	Male	2779	66	2580	51	1542	49
	Female	1414	34	2495	49	1664	51
1970	Male	2232	65	2746	56	2739	52
	Female	1208	35	2184	44	2560	48
1976	Male	2249	70	4326	62	4796	52
	Female	969	30	2669	38	4338	48
1978	Male	2989	72	5654	63	5534	52
	Female	1172	28	3270	37	5067	48

SOURCE: Home Office, 1978, Criminal Statistics for England and Wales.

different offences by age groups; it is apparent that shoplifting among the older age group has been on the increase over the last 20 years. The average rate of change is high, at +1.03 per cent per year. It should also be noted, however, that the general increase in all forms of indictable crime has been highest in that group (an increase of 885 per cent over 23 years). Nevertheless, there is a preferential swing towards more shoplifting by females than by males. Just as with all official statistics, caution is necessary. Are more women really shoplifting, or is it simply that they are more frequently prosecuted? Or might it be that magistrates are becoming more willing to find them guilty? As a partial guide to this, we can look at self-reported delinquency data and at the reports of shop and store detectives on the quantity of unreported and unprosecuted shoplifting.

British self-report studies on boys give figures of between 19 per cent and 63 per cent. Low figures of 19.3 per cent ('I have taken things from big stores or supermarkets when the shop was open') and 36.8 per cent ('I have taken things from little shops when the shop was open') came from West and Farrington's (1973) study of boys aged 14–15. At the later age of 16–17 years these figures rose to 28.2 and 39.8 per cent respectively. A similar study by Shapland (1975) found an increase in shoplifting between the ages of 11–12 and 13–14 for these same two items; storelifting rose from 27.3 to 33.3 per cent and shoplifting in small shops from 41.8 to 47 per cent. Jamison's (1977) study gave a similar figure of 47 per cent for 13–16 year old boys. For girls the figures are lower. Jamison gives a figure of 21.6 per cent, compared with Campbell's (1976) 19.7 per cent of schoolgirls for the item 'I have taken things from little shops when the shop was open'. For the same item, 76.9 per cent of girls in an assessment centre gave a positive reply. Smith (1978) found that 37 per cent of 'normal' girls shoplifted, while 90 per cent of girls on probation admitted to this.

The sex ratio implied by these figures indicates a greater disparity than that actually found in official statistics. This impression is substantiated by American studies, which find that boys admit to theft in general with almost twice the frequency of girls. For theft by boys and girls Short and Nye (1958) give admission rates of 63 per cent and 36 per cent respectively. Wise (1967), in a sample of middle-class teenagers, reports 61 per cent of boys and 35 per cent of girls as thieving, and Hindelang (1971), in a Catholic high school, found that 53 per cent of boys and only 26 per cent of girls admitted to petty theft. This disparity must result either from differential concealment, or from exaggeration by girls and boys, or from disciminatory police and court proceedings, which penalize relatively more girl offenders than boys. The question of which is the source of the disparity is probably unanswerable, but Morris (1966) has produced indirect evidence that girls experience more guilt about misdemeanours than do boys and are less willing to admit involvement in criminal or 'naughty' acts. On the other hand, May (1977) investigated a Scottish juvenile court's handling of 126 girls who appeared before it. Girls were more likely than boys to receive institutional disposal or to be placed under supervision, while boys were more often fined for their misconduct. May concludes: 'with female offenders the courts were also somewhat more inclined to resort to severer disposal'

(p. 209). If girls do indeed receive harsher treatment than boys, this fact might be reflected in a higher rate of police prosecution as opposed to caution for girls and in the proportion of girls charged who are found guilty.

As long ago as 1937 Sellin undertook an investigation of three large Philadelphia stores to estimate the quantity of known but unprosecuted shoplifting. Although 4402 shoplifting offences were known to the police in that year, a further 5000 offences in these three stores alone went unreported. For 5314 thefts only 230 persons were prosecuted (about 4 per cent). Cameron (1964), in a similar study in Chicago, concludes that 12 department stores 'lost' $10,000,000 worth of stock in one year. It was estimated that two-thirds of this sum might be due to theft by employees, the rest to shoplifting. Store detectives reported that only 10 per cent of those apprehended were charged. The President's Commission on Law Enforcement (see Reiss, 1967) found that only 38 per cent of the stores they investigated kept inventory-control records good enough even to permit estimates of loss through theft, but where a theft was detected and the offender known, only 37 per cent of stores ever called the police. Taking into account all the information provided by store detectives, Reiss estimated that only 1 per cent of shoplifters would be known to the police. Robin (1963) studied shoplifting in Philadelphia and found that in 1579 cases in which disposition was known, only 14 per cent were prosecuted. Juveniles were at a particular advantage in escaping prosecution; only 5.5 per cent were charged, as compared with 25.8 per cent of adults. (It is important to note that such good will towards the young may have been mediated by the fact that juvenile thefts were worth on average only $5.98, as compared with $14 for adults.)

A study of British store policy was conducted by Dickens (1969). Questionnaires were sent to 250 leading groups of stores, resulting in information on 10,438 shops and supermarkets. Of these, 67.5 per cent kept records of offences by customers, numbering 18,263 cases of shoplifting, of which 45 per cent were reported to the police. In 80 per cent of these cases police proceeded with a prosecution. Once again, young people were at an advantage: 29.5 per cent of shops felt that young persons under the age of 17 should receive special consideration, and children under 14 received sympathetic treatment from 84.5

per cent of shops. Seventy-three per cent of shops felt that schoolchildren of any age should be dealt with leniently. At the same time, 22.8 per cent of shops gave lack of confidence in the processes of juvenile courts as a reason not to prosecute (as compared with 11.3 per cent for adult courts). This leniency may be related more to the feeling that prosecution would have no deterrent effect than to humanitarian motives. Special treatment of women offenders *per se* was not reported in the study, but shops tended to show sympathy to visibly pregnant women (60.5 per cent) and women of menopausal age (25 per cent).

To formulate any general conclusion in the light of the available data would be hazardous. Certainly, official criminal statistics must underestimate the true extent of shoplifting. The police themselves may have policies towards prosecutions for shoplifting that vary both regionally and temporally. Even store reports are underestimates, since store detectives must fail to detect some proportion of thefts, which later may be written off as 'stock shrinkage', perpetrated by delivery men or shop staff.

As May (1978) notes:

for these companies, occasional public rhetoric not withstanding, shoplifting *per se* is not a problem, or at least not the real problem. If this were not already apparent from the description provided of the measures designed to deal with shoplifting, it is clearly indicated in the general indifference as to the dimensions of the problem. Most companies seem to have only the roughest idea of their total 'shrinkage' (i.e., goods written off as 'lost'). And as to differentiating between the sources of the loss, it is clear that little effort is made in this direction. (pp. 141–2)

Certainly, juveniles are at a clear advantage. Stores themselves are reluctant to deal harshly with them, either through sympathy, lack of faith in the juvenile courts or fear of bad public relations. Since the 1969 Young Persons Act police too may have been reluctant to prosecute a juvenile, preferring to issue a caution, involve a Juvenile Liaison Bureau or bring a care order rather than a 'criminal' case. The younger the child, the less likely he is to be charged formally and therefore to appear in crime statistics. This is reflected in the big jump in shoplifting guilt findings between the two lower age groups of under 14 and 14–17 (see table 1.1). Similarly, the high figure (+1.06) for the average yearly rate of increase of girls' involvement in shoplifting between the ages of 17 and 21 probably results from a failure to prosecute the younger age groups. This may differentially affect girls, since the equivalent figure for boys aged 17–21 is only +0.15.

To put a figure on the true amount of shoplifting is nearly impossible. Sohier (1969) stresses the fact that most ordinary people have shoplifted at least once by the time they reach adulthood, a statement that could hardly be made about any other indictable offence. As he concludes:

> This basic fact – the ordinariness of shoplifting – has not been explored as it should. ... Shoplifting – this banal phenomenon – is found in a large proportion of the population and the offenders are mostly quite ordinary people who have only a vague awareness of the harmfulness of their actions. (pp. 162, 168)

Who shoplifts?

Before turning to some of the theories of shoplifting, it is important to consider some basic demographic facts about the population whose behaviour we are trying to understand. Many criminologists fail to do this and, as a result, end up with accounts that are relevant to only a small subset of offenders. Several studies have been undertaken of shop policy and incarcerated shoplifters. From such work we can obtain a more detailed view of the person behind the act than that available from criminal statistics.

Studies suggest varying degrees of female involvement in shoplifting. Sohier (1969) estimates that equal numbers of men and women are involved in Belgium, but his figures are based on conviction rates. Two studies that have worked within stores themselves put the female rate higher. Cameron (1964), in an American study, puts the figure for female involvement at as high as 80 per cent, whereas Robin (1963) offers a more modest 60.7 per cent. One clue as to why the official figures show more parity may lie in the value of the goods stolen. Small-scale pilfering is less likely to result in a court appearance and subsequent conviction. Robin investigated the relationship between size of theft and subsequent disposition. Out of 416 shoplifters studied, 'lifters' of goods valued at under $20 were prosecuted on only 6.07 per cent of occasions; $20–30 thefts were prosecuted at a rate of 29.79 per cent; $30–40 thefts, at 73.33 per cent; $40–60, at 78.57 per cent; and where the goods were valued at over $60, 93.55 per cent of the offenders were prosecuted. Whereas the mean value of goods stolen by women was $16.40, men were more ambitious, taking goods with an average value of $28.36. In Britain too the value of the goods seems to be an important factor. Dickens's (1969) survey of shops showed that 54 per cent of shops would take no action if the item stolen were worth less than 25 pence. However, where several small items were lifted, even if the total value was less than £1, 98 per cent of shops reported that they would take up proceedings. It should be noted, however, that Robin's study was of the shops' action, not of their expressed attitudes or policy; stores may respond to a questionnaire more zealously than they would ever act. The size of the theft interacts with both age and sex in determining a shop's disposal of a case. In Dickens's study 86 per cent of shops said that they would take no action on a 25p theft if the culprit were aged 14 or less. Robin reports that in his study of three American stores juveniles (under 18 years) accounted for 58.1 per cent of all known shoplifters. The mean value of goods stolen by juveniles ranged from $6 to $8, while merchandise stolen by adults was valued at between $14 and $15. Of $12,172 worth of recovered merchandise from shoplifters, only one-third had been lifted by juveniles. Shoplifting is a much more petty affair among juveniles than among adults, and consequently it is unlikely to be as energetically pursued to court. Indeed, the Philadelphia Juvenile Aid Division pressed charges against only 5 per cent of the minors turned over to them by the stores.

The true extent of juvenile involvement in shoplifting is hard to establish. Sohier (1969), presents a graph comparing the age distribution of offenders with that of the general population. The similarity is very marked indeed. He notes that an age graph not only of convicted shoplifters but also of those caught by store detectives shows a similar relationship. He therefore rejects any pathological explanation of the crime, suggesting that it should be treated as a misdemeanour, not an offence, because of its frequency and generality in the normal population. He does note, however, the surprisingly 'social' nature of the crime. Often two or three people are involved in perpetrating a theft. Robin considers this particularly true of juveniles; 75 per cent of them (compared with 23 per cent of adults) worked in groups, the vast majority in dyads. He also looked at aiders and abetters – those who acted as look-outs and attracted attention to themselves, while their companion escaped with the goods or received the stolen merchandise from the lifter. Twenty-seven per cent of juveniles (5 per cent of adults) were aiders and abetters. In a British study (Gibbens and Prince 1962) juvenile shoplifters were split almost exactly equally by sex. The peak age for both sexes was 13–15 years. Juveniles' thefts were usually of low value (25p to £1) and, once again, shoplifting was a group activity. In this study only 16 per cent of juveniles stole on their own, as compared with 35 per cent of lone juveniles apprehended for all indictable offences in the Metropolitan Police District.

Whatever the truth of the matter it is clear from May's (1978) excellent study of store security and shop policy that store detectives themselves certainly believe groups of unescorted juveniles to be up to no good. Their attitude was summed up by one detective.

> Children stick out like a sore thumb, particularly when they haven't got parents with them. They usually walk around in twos and threes, with their hair all over the place, and their shirt tails hanging out. (May, 1978, p. 150)

The subtle blending of age with implied social class was made even more explicit by another detective, who was asked what kind of children most frequently shoplifted. He replied:

> Those from the poorer-class homes, dirty-looking, poorly clad, often both parents out working, a lack of control . . . the raggly muffins, those poorly put on, untidy, unkempt. (p. 150)

One detective reported how a group of beautifully dressed

children entered the store and no one suspected them of dishonesty until they were caught red-handed. On investigation, it was discovered that all their beautiful clothes had been lifted, and their dirty old clothes were in the polythene bags they were holding. As soon as their true social class was revealed (in the bags), the uncomfortable paradox was resolved and the class-related criminal stereotype could be reinstated.

While store detectives seem quite clear about the class composition of shoplifters, this clarity is not always reflected in the available academic literature, nor in the popular imagination. This results indirectly from the many psychoanalytic interpretations of shoplifting (for example, Neustatter, 1953). These will be considered later in more detail, but it should be noted in passing that psychiatrists are not regularly employed to treat criminals. Psychiatric case histories are characteristically derived from middle-class women who, the courts feel, need medical rather than social help. For this reason they are far from typical, but they have contributed to our everyday idealization of the well-off, middle-class housewife who shoplifts for no apparent economic reason. To balance such an idea, we must also take into account studies that have actively looked at social class as a factor.

Gibbens and Prince (1962) investigated women appearing before the courts on shoplifting charges. They compared them with data obtained from other types of female thieves and, where possible, with data from surveys and censuses of the general population. It is these latter comparisons that are of most interest to the present argument. Shoplifters were more often single (46.9 per cent, compared with 21.8 per cent in the normal population) and in 32 per cent of cases were the chief wage-earner (normals in London, 20.3 per cent). Among shoplifters the weekly housekeeping budget was under £10 in 66.3 per cent of cases as compared with the London norm of 33 per cent. More shoplifters were in receipt of National Assistance Benefit and yet most paid higher rent than their 'normal' counterparts; rent of under £3 a week was paid by 97.8 per cent of normals and by only 38.5 per cent of shoplifters. Unfortunately, the most direct measure, weekly income, was omitted from the study, while factors such as promiscuity were carefully recorded. Gibbens and Prince did a separate analysis of female juvenile shoplifters. Regrettably, the results are largely uninterpretable, due to the lack of a 'normal' control group. Comparisons were made instead with non-shoplifting but delinquent girls admitted to Cumberlow Lodge Assessment Centre. Generally, shoplifters appeared to have a less disturbed background – they more often lived with both parents, experienced less family conflict and, in 44 per cent of cases, had 'suitable' mothers. Shoplifting girls' mothers worked about as much as was normal in the general population, although such girls probably lived in more over-crowded homes. The most relevant variable for the present argument is the social class of the father's occupation. Data from 36.5 per cent of the sample was unavailable, since they were either not known or not applicable. Even with this taken into account, their distribution maps well on to data from the national sample used in the Ministry of Labour Household Inquiry. The missing responses would probably have fallen into the manual or unemployed category.

Certainly, there is no statistical evidence to suggest that shoplifting is a particularly middle-class activity. And there can be no justification for the assumption that economics is an irrelevant factor. The evidence strongly suggests that lack of money plays a part (see Arboleda-Florez et al., 1977). On the other hand, it would be romantic and inaccurate to paint a Dickensian picture of shoeless orphans stealing loaves of bread. Sixty-six per cent of girls in 1959, for example, stole clothes or cosmetics – luxury items. Sohier (1969) plotted socio-professional categories of shoplifters, and this showed a good fit with distribution in the general population. The issue seems to be not genuine need but greed at all social class levels. Living in a consumer-orientated society as we do, this is hardly surprising, and we shall turn to this 'temptation factor' in the next section.

The shop asks for it?

Although shoplifting may cause concern to moralists, criminologists and courts, it appears to cause very much less concern to the shops themselves. Obviously, shops are in business to make a profit – in other words, to ensure that turn-over exceeds overheads (and overheads include theft). As May (1978) notes, large stores that employ sophisticated managerial and retailing practices would certainly be aware of losses due to theft if such losses significantly affected profit. However, stock-loss estimates are so erratic that the Shrinkage Working Party of the Institute of Grocery Distribution (Home Office, 1973) put the percentage of shrinkage attributable to dishonesty at between 15 and 90 per cent! Gibbens and Prince (1962) similarly found that the stores they studied were unable to value the losses that resulted from shoplifting. Loss of stock is not necessarily the consequence of customer theft; Dickens found that in the stores he studied 18,263 cases of customer theft were detected, as well as an additional 1728 offences by staff. As he notes: 'Differences in the figures must be seen in the light of the fact that detection of offences by staff was considered to be rather rare, especially concerning smaller and less expensive items' (pp. 468–9). Dickens notes that Section 5(1) of the Criminal Law Act 1967 states that no further criminal proceed-ings need to be instituted if the offender returns the stolen goods or pays for them. While this legislation is as applicable to customers as to staff, this route is usually taken only when managers or delivery men are found to be involved in theft. Again, to put precise figures on shoplifting losses is nearly impossible – an indication of company attitude to the 'problem' – but Robin reports in his study of American stores that the sales volume per annum ranged between $24,000,000 and $64,000,000, while recovered shoplifted goods amounted to between $6,152 and $12,172. This means that detected shoplifted goods amounted to between 0.19 and 0.02 per cent of sales turnover.

The management faces a dilemma; shoplifting might be cut down by reintroducing counter service, but the outlay for staff salaries would be prohibitive, and the public prefers self-service stores. Also, goods are openly displayed in a way that invites people to touch or handle them before purchase. Sweets and candy are purposely displayed at children's height, and cosmetics often have 'testers' to encourage customers to sample the goods. All these devices designed to tempt the buyer also tempt the shoplifter. To contain the problem, store detectives are employed, but technological devices such as closed-circuit television, one-way mirrors and observation panels are more talked about as deterrents than used. In May's study most detectives were either housewives picking up pin-money or retired policemen. Few had any specific training for the job, and most learned it as they went along. The detectives patrolled selectively at 'high-risk' periods – Saturdays, the pre-Christmas rush, lunchtime and late afternoon. Many shops had no security personnel at mid-week 'slow-sales' periods. Because store managers are a highly mobile group, remaining in their posts for only a year or so, detectives had a high degree of autonomy in the execution of their job. The head offices of shops checked up by means of occasional one-day visits and by requiring periodic reports on apprehensions. Most detectives had no idea of what happened to these reports after they reached head office.

Sohier (1969) points out the dangers of employing private security companies in large stores. Debuyst et al. (1960) warn that store detectives operate as a 'miniature public prosecutor's office' in deciding which offenders should be turned over to the police and note that they may be tempted to use rather questionable methods of intimidation. In Robin's United States study detectives routinely demanded and got information on the suspect's occupation, marital status, family situation and so on. The protection manager then produced a confession form to be signed, and failure to sign it automatically resulted in prosecution. Robin also notes the three main lines of psychological attack that are made on a suspect; reference is made to the inherent wrongness of the act, the disgrace to the family and the threat of legal punishment. In Gibbens and Prince no mention is made of the arrest and interrogation procedures used by detectives, but the list of excuses offered by suspects implies that they were certainly highly distressed and inconsistent in their accounts. In Belgium various Government agencies have carried out 'police wars' on security services suspected of illegal practice. Juveniles are particularly vulnerable to intimidation. The fact that the public police force cannot be diverted to the detection of shoplifters leaves stores with private organizations as their only possible protection. Because such organizations are not subject to close police scrutiny, and because they are staffed by relatively untrained personnel, wide variation in performance results. Also, shops have different attitudes to shoplifting, ranging from tolerant to severe, and these are reflected in the *modus operandi* of detectives. At bottom, the detection system is one that rests heavily on human factors, an understanding of which can only be gained as May (1978) did, through observation of, and interviews with the detectives themselves.

Shops are unwilling actually to exclude any section of the public from entering. As one manager explained, 'You know, children eventually will become our best customers. So it would be bad policy, you know, to ban them from coming in altogether. So we try to keep them under control really' (May, 1978, p. 146). This 'control' may take the form of simply stopping all suspected juveniles at the door whenever they are seen leaving the shop and searching them. Children and young people on Saturdays hang around large stores, often using them as meeting places, playgrounds or places to 'chat up' girls. While they are in the stores they are subject to the temptations around them, and many may 'drift' into shoplifting. Detectives have clear stereotypes about shoplifting 'types', as we have seen. May's analysis clearly shows that young people without adults are highly suspect. In addition, and compounding this, working-class customers receive special attention. These preconceptions are not guided by store policy or the size of losses attributed to these groups. They arise out of detectives' (and indeed the public's) ideas of which sector of the population produces the criminal 'type'. As with most categories of crime, the rate of detection for the middle classes is substantially lower than for the working class, partly because they may engage in less visible crime and partly because they are under less rigorous surveillance and are consequently detected less frequently. Detection rates also vary according to the time of day and the places to which the energies of the security staff are directed: young children at sweet counters and teenage girls near cosmetic counters or clothing departments arouse suspicion. A female detective (and many detectives are women) would look obvious hanging around a menswear section alone and would perhaps be more apprehensive about arresting a male than a female or a juvenile. These facts may contribute to the large number of girls arrested for shoplifting. Many detectives realize that arrests may create bad feeling towards the store on the part of other customers, and that the local press may give such events wide publicity. Some stores, however, welcome the focusing of local media attention on detected shoplifters, as it has a deterrent effect on further crime. As a general rule, the larger the store or the bigger the chain, the less it will be afraid of newspaper coverage. Smaller stores depend more heavily on the individual good will of customers.

The behaviour of potential shoplifters is also monitored by detectives. Suspicion will be alleviated by the possession of a store-provided wire basket, the obvious possession of money or attempts to attract the attention of sales staff. On the other hand, young people wearing baggy sweaters or large coats, carrying carrier bags or large holdalls and hanging around an area too long without making a purchase draw attention to themselves.

Apprehension of a suspect is a problematic step. The officer must be quite sure of his guilt, for the fear always exists that an accused innocent might sue the shop. Robin cites the case of a woman who sued a shop for false arrest for stealing a hankerchief. A barely visible laundry mark proved her case and she was awarded $2000. To establish adequate proof, the detective himself must witness the theft, and preferably the theft of more than one article. The theft must also be corroborated by another witness, usually a member of the sales staff. Finally, the suspect must be allowed to leave the premises to forestall any claim that he was 'going to pay'. Apparently, in the United States a few states demand only that the suspect carry the item 200 feet or more away from the counter on which it was displayed. The moment of apprehension may be difficult and embarrassing for the detective himself as well as for the suspect. Women and juveniles often become hysterical and make such a scene that the detective may wish to drop the issue if the goods are worth only a few pence. The subsequent interview in the manager's office will usually decide if the case is to be dropped or pursued. Gibbens and Prince (1962) found that in 11 per cent of cases suspects explained that they had insufficient money or wanted something for nothing. Nine per cent seemed confused and mystified, and another 9 per cent apologized and offered to pay. It seems likely that the class, appearance, attitude and general demeanour of the suspect may influence the decision among store detectives, as has been shown to be the case with policemen (Piliavin and Briar, 1964).

In summary, shops and stores take inadequate preventative or detective measures against shoplifters. Probably only a fraction of the true number are ever caught, let alone prosecuted, and even the stores themselves are unaware of the scale of their losses through shoplifting. The individual detectives are free to operate without intervention or surveillance by either internal management or the police. Their lack of training leads to stereotypical perceptions about the types of people who shoplift, which in turn leads to the perpetuation of such stereotypes in the official statistics resulting from prosecutions. The lackadaisical attitude of the shops is a consequence not only of economic considerations but also of an awareness of their own implication in the crime. The Working Party on Internal Shop Security (Home Office, 1973) reported:

> Most of the retailers' representatives with which we discussed the matter agreed that layout could make a substantial contribution to the prevention of losses. It was agreed that those high displays and blind corners which impeded observation by staff, those unattended low counters and shelves which facilitated shoplifting, the stacking of displays close to or in entrances and at exits were all to be avoided. It was also agreed that offices overlooking the shopping area and (in supermarkets) the check-out points were aids to security. Yet in every case we were told that management took little, if any, account of these points when planning the lay-out of shops and display areas. The sole criterion was the effect it would have upon sales. (para 3.13)

Since shops are so indifferent to shoplifting, and since shoplifters themselves show so little consistent sign of pathology but rather mirror the demography of the general population, the burden of responsibility must to a large extent lie with the shops themselves. They invite petty theft by people who would never dream of normally becoming involved in any other form of criminal behaviour. Gibbens and Prince list the justifications offered by detected shoplifters: they blame the assistants, claim that they were impatient at having been kept waiting and make other 'ludicrous excuses'. Perhaps they are not so ludicrous as they might at first sight appear.

Shoplifting and mental illness

From the facts, figures and descriptions of shoplifting and shop policy, we turn now to the theories that have been proposed to account for shoplifting. To the layman, shoplifting is *par excellence* the psychoanalytical offence. Almost immediately ideas of kleptomania, obsessive neurotics and women spring to mind. Although workers such as Gibbens and Prince (1962) discuss the material and social circumstances of shoplifters, such vulgar considerations are forgotten when they move on to account for the behaviour itself. Suddenly psychiatric jargon springs up everywhere – depression, over-compensation for inferiority, penis envy, hysteria and masochism. Gibbens et al. (1971) admit that of the 886 women shoplifters they followed-up ten years after their initial offence, only 8.4 per cent were admitted to a mental hospital. Comparable figures are not available for women previously involved in violence, prostitution and robbery, but if they were, it is doubtful if the proportion of mentally ill would be any lower. Why is it, then, that this small proportion of shoplifters has succeeded in convincing academics, practitioners and laymen alike that shoplifting is a sign of mental illness?

Shoplifting is the crime that is performed by proportionately more women than any other. It has come to be considered the female offence. The involvement of women in most crimes has been explained by recourse to personal maladjustment rather than social circumstance. However, in most cases women comprise only a small proportion of the convicted. When the number of women involved increases, the crime itself takes on the trappings of femininity – it becomes a crime requiring psychiatric (and therefore usually psychoanalytic) interpretation. This has happened to such an extent that male shoplifters have had to be reinterpreted as homosexuals to keep in line with the kinds of explanation psychiatrists wish to offer. Gibbens and Prince note:

If we examine the [shoplifting] boys as a group, certain

recurring themes are made evident. Firstly, they were frequently very intelligent. ... The second unexpected feature was that homosexual difficulties were rather frequently mentioned. (p. 118)

And again in reporting interviews with store detectives: 'Several detectives thought there was a high correlation between homosexuality and shoplifting in men' (p. 149). It is hard to think of any characteristically male crime that has received such a singularly psychoanalytical interpretation as the 'female' crime of shoplifting. The sexual basis of the explanation is even more surprising in the light of the fact that it is not, in itself, a sexual crime. Even the most sexually criminal act, that of rape – a 100 per cent male offence – is often characterized as a fundamentally 'natural' biological response to deliberate or unwitting sexual provocation by a female. The man's motivation is more often ascribed to sexual frustration or drink than to unresolved Oedipal complexes.

The reasons why women have received such monolithically clinical explanations of their criminal behaviour probably stems from three major sources. First, since women are statistically under-represented in crime figures, this fact might lead naturally to the assumption that female crime requires a different kind of explanation from that which accounts for male crime. Since so few women commit crimes, the few that do must be disturbed. Whereas it is 'normal', to some extent, for a certain percentage of men to be criminal (a natural extention of their aggressiveness and competition), it is certainly abnormal for a woman, whose passive and co-operative nature should in general inhibit such antisocial impulses. This statistical explanation must also include these values of sex-role appropriateness, since we do not give 'special' explanations to the under-representation of other minority groups in crime (for example, Asians or Jews). Second, by treating criminal women as sick society can write off any serious statement that such crime figures make about women's increasing dissatisfaction with their position and lifestyle. Third, Smart (1977) has drawn attention to the fact that stereotypical views of women's personality and character make them, even in a healthy psychological condition, a natural target for psychiatric attention. I. K. Broverman et al. (1970) asked clinicians to rate bipolar trait scales to represent healthy male, female and adult (sex unspecified) behaviour. Results showed that for male and female clinicians the concept of healthy male much more nearly approximated to that of healthy adult than did healthy woman. This latter was seen as more excitable, more easily hurt, more emotional and more submissive. Thus even healthy women fit more easily with the mental illness model than do men. Phillips and Segal (1969) also note that women are more expressive about physical and mental illness than are men. Whereas it might be seen as weakness for a man to admit to illness, the same is not true of women. Women are far more amenable to psychoanalytic 'treatment' both in and out of prison because they are more willing to accept a 'sick' label and because they are willing to discuss their problems openly rather than deny or minimize them. Their subordinate position *vis-à-vis* males gears them to a submissive acceptance of such labels by experts, especially when the experts agree with the social *mores* of society and the family, who all demand with one voice to know, 'What is the matter with you?' Often treatment consists of resocializing women into their rejected female role. Hart (1975), among others, notes with concern the increasing 'boyishness' of female delinquents; social skills training programmes in Borstals provide ample opportunity to 'rehabilitate' their blunt assertiveness or 'deviance'.

A brief historical analysis of the clinical interpretations of shoplifters parallels general fashions and movements in psychiatry. Throughout the last 100 years the motivational base has shifted in line with current thought about the nature of mental illness. It should be remembered, however, that these theories derive not from broad empirical studies but from clinicians' own experiences in treating and interpreting particular cases. The extent to which such cases are in any sense typical is open to speculation. The following account is taken very largely from Gibbens and Prince (1962). In Paris Esquirol described certain behaviours, such as alcoholism, murder and arson, as resulting from 'instinctive monomania'; the individual is driven by an involuntary, instinctive impulse. This idea was taken up by Mathey, who first referred to 'kleptomania'. The notion of a pathological rather than a social or material problem was understandable in the light of the cases of King Victor of

Sardinia and Henry IV of France, who regularly stole petty objects but frequently confessed and returned them. Similarly, the class of society treated by such writers could have had little material need for theft. This notion of a highly specific mental disturbance was taken up by phrenologists, who claimed to have found among thieves an enlarged area on the temporal bone, the theft organ. By the beginning of this century, however, attempts were being made to integrate petty theft into a more general theory of mental disturbance by viewing the criminal act only as a by-product or symptom of the real intra-psychic problem. It was the beginning of the use of a medical model in criminology. Guddens, in 1906, viewed kleptomania as an aspect of obsessive-compulsive neurosis, a pathological desire for order that in some cases may entail the acquisition and hoarding of seemingly irrelevant objects. Another form of neurosis, curiously described by Gibbens and Prince as hysteria, some-times results from intense anxiety on the patient's part that he may one day involuntarily shoplift. Sargeant has noted that such patients will often feel driven to do the very thing they most fear in order to allay their apprehension. As long ago as 1801 Lichtenberg had stressed the sexual aspects of thieving, but he concerned himself largely with fetishism, the stealing of women's underwear by men being the classic example. However, among women this kind of theft is rare, and shoplifters rarely steal clearly sexual objects. Yet sexuality remained an important focus among women shoplifters, not in terms of the object stolen but in terms of the motivational aspects of theft. This view was, of course, heavily stressed by the psychoanalytic school. Stekel stated: 'Kleptomania is ungratified sexual instinct ... to take something forbidden secretly is common to both motives – to the sexual desire and the impulse to steal which then meets a much slighter mental resistance'. Feniche mentions a woman who experienced real sexual excitement when shoplifting and fantasized about shoplifting during masturbation. Of course, such ideas sprang up in an era of extreme sexual repression, and even if psychoanalytic thought were correct, today we would expect considerably less ego-blocking of sexual motivations. Among current generations pre- or extramarital sex would be unlikely to arouse as much anxiety as being detected in the act of shoplifting. It also seems probable that the somatic bodily reactions to fear and stress – increased heart rate, sweating, respiratory changes – might easily have been interpreted as sexual, especially in an era that took so much prurient interest in sexual urges. However, even in the 1950s and 1960s sexual frustration was thought to be implicated, due to the number of single, divorced or widowed women who shoplifted. Unfortunately, theorists ignored the economic stresses on this particular group of women.

Other writers, particularly Fore, linked shoplifting with masochism. Detection of the offence was thought to correspond to detection of sexual activity, provoking feelings of both shame and satisfaction. Women were seen as masochistically requiring punishment by males in the form of policemen or husbands. Once again, male involvement could only be explained by postulating at least covert or subconscious homosexuality.

The high involvement of women in the crime almost inescapably led from concern with the 'natural' female psyche to the study of the biological aspects of femininity – most especially the pre-menstrual tension syndrome. The relationship between such a factor and crime has never been very clearly explicated at a theoretical level, but this has not deterred researchers who regularly collect data on the subject. With respect to shoplifting. Epps (1962) considered 200 women shoplifters remanded or sentenced to Holloway Prison. Only 27 women (13.5 per cent) admitted to pre-menstrual depression, irritability or tension. Of these 27, only 10 stole in the pre-menstrual phase, and Epps concludes: 'any evidence of a connection between pre-menstrual tension and acquisitive crime appeared slender' (p. 134). She went on to chart all pre-menopausal women (45.4 per cent of the sample) on the time of their offence (regardless of whether they reported any psychological symptoms). Only 12 per cent stole in the pre-menstrual phase, 9.5 per cent during the menstrual week and 14 and 16 per cent in the remaining two weeks. She also notes that 31.5 per cent of the sample were post-menopausal, compared with 9.5 per cent undergoing the menopause. She therefore also rejects the menopause itself as playing a significant part in female shoplifting.

In 1922 Alexander offered a more clearly articulated psychoanalytical interpretation of shoplifting. Among males shoplifting was seen as resulting from an unresolved Oedipal jealousy of the father, which found expression in the theft of a symbolically larger penis by which ideationally to castrate the father figure. The women's penis envy took a more diffuse form, resulting from their sense of 'cosmic injustice'. Their attempts to steal substitutes were often directed at the world in general. However, a less sexual interpretation is now current among those dealing particularly with juveniles; they see shoplifting as an attempt to find a substitute for love withheld by the parents, originally at the mother's breast. This view is operationalized in the various studies of delinquency that 'measure' parental affection expressed to the child.

The Adlerian school emphasized that neurotic theft resulted from over-compensation for feelings of inferiority – a view that meshes well with the broader Freudian view but whose validity is equally hard to prove. Studies of self-concept, even those that succeed in showing it to be lower in delinquents, always measure it after detection, court appearance and disposal, by which time even the most robust self-concept might be expected to have been damaged.

A more recent study of the psychopathology of shoplifting comes from Epps (1962) and Gibbens and Prince (1962). Epps's study of Holloway shoplifters found a reassuringly simple dichotomy between professionals (23.5 per cent) and pathological cases (76.4 per cent). Of this latter group, 17.5 were psychotic; 12.5 per cent were neurotic; and 46.5 per cent had a 'personality disorder'. The fact that her table of diagnoses shows no classification for normals arouses some suspicion of the results. Surely not everyone could have been professional or pathological? She is happy to assume that the criminal justice system sees fit to remand and sentence only the mad and the bad *in general*, since she notes: 'These figures would not apply to shoplifters as a whole but only to those who passed through prison' (p. 136). The majority of women were classed as 'mildly unstable' (75 out of 200 women), although we are not informed of the criteria for such a judgement, nor the behavioural implications of such a condition.

This rag-bag labelling approach was also adopted by Arieff and Bowie in 1947. They studied 313 cases of shoplifters referred to psychiatrists by the courts. Of these 77 per cent had some nervous disorder (hardly surprising, in view of the selection criterion of the sample). These disorders included depressive and anxiety states, mental defectiveness, psychosis, psychopathy, organic disorder and compulsive behaviour. There seems to be no reliable association between any particular psychiatric condition and shoplifting, even in the small proportion of cases (25 per cent) that were referred to a psychiatrist.

Gibbens and Prince's study favoured depression as the most common causal factor in shoplifting among women. They see the act of shoplifting as a 'cry for help', although we have no evidence that shoplifters want to be caught, and indeed most take elaborate precautions to ensure that they are not. It is equally unclear why such women should turn to shoplifting as opposed to more direct appeals, such as suicidal gestures. They also cite resentment as a motivation, but once again we are given no clue as to why this resentment should express itself as theft, or why it is not more clearly directed at those individuals who the women believe have abused them. The last two categories are 'keeping up appearances' and 'meanness', presumably not related to any clinical condition. Such motives, related more charitably to capitalist competition and poverty, may have a much wider currency than the more psychoanalytical alternatives, and they will be considered in the next section.

Gibbens and Prince addressed themselves to the issue of juvenile shoplifters, and the now familiar double standard of explanation for boys and girls appeared. Boy shoplifters were 'not a serious problem', at least not from a clinical standpoint. In 57 per cent of the boys 'it appeared to be a typical marauding offence, a group of very young boys wandering through the shops and picking up a selection of articles of little use to them, often under the influence of a delinquent leader' (p. 120). In the remainder of cases the authors were surprised to find a high proportion of middle-class boys, who apparently require a different explanation: 'machismo' seems to be the prerogative of the working-class boy. These grammar-school boys were of high intelligence, 'more often than is usual with delinquents', but had homosexual tendencies. After effectively demasculinizing this group, the 'female' mediators of depression and guilt now become applicable and account for their 'deviant' behaviour.

The girls are the target of the bizarre double-think recognizable in the writings of Lombroso and Ferrero (1959) and Cowie et al. (1968). While eliciting more paternal concern – 43 per cent were 'liable to produce more serious maladjustment if not suitably treated' – they were also seen as more robust and better able to survive than boys. This idea seems to be related to the ancient notion of the hardy, child-bearing, working-class woman, combined with the well-known plasticity and lack of enduring 'character' among females. For example:

> The social role in which they are cast, however (not to mention any possible temperamental differences), inclines them to tolerate hardship far better than boys, to make internal psychological adjustments to make life tolerable, rather than to select or alter their external environment. (p. 120)

This kind of benign rationalization has been used again and again to justify the oppression of minority groups. The major source of concern, as far as Gibbens and Prince are concerned, once again lies with the girl's sexual morality, not her criminality.

> The maladjusted girl is more likely to gain what she wants by wayward behaviour – staying out late, running away, going with undesirable boys or being promiscuous – than by crime, which is by comparison so unrewarding. Crime, if it occurs, is largely limited to . . . secondary crime due to being involved with delinquent boys and is likely to be abandoned in as far as waywardness proves more rewarding. (p. 121)

At one blow the issue of girls' shoplifting is dispensed with in favour of their sexuality. Any motivational account is reduced to the search for boyfriends. Any analysis of character is redundant, since they are merely *tabulae rasae* led on by 'bad' boys. Girls in themselves are never bad, only weak, having a 'passive, timid personality'. Once again, the middle-class female stereotype is used as a template for working-class female 'deviance'. Since girls are female, they cannot act autonomously or instigate for themselves any antisocial act. Since they have male providers (fathers, boyfriends, husbands), their material requirements are not their concern. There is no evidence whatever of any consideration of the contribution made by working-class life or culture to the girls' view of their opportunities or lifestyle. The fact that so many of these girls face a future of poorly paid, menial employment until they marry, and very often beyond that, is ignored. The fact that their *economic* well-being rests largely on the calibre of the husband they will attract is forgotten, as is the fact that in Western society such attractiveness costs money.

A new approach to shoplifting

Studies of shoplifting have in the main concentrated either on the pathological individual personality of the offender or on shop policy that promotes this kind of behaviour. Very few studies have sought to position shoplifting within a broader social and political sphere, where women in particular are vulnerable to a consumer fetishism that drives them to law-breaking. A coherent account must view the phenomenon as a particular response to economic and social factors, a response that can be embedded in a set of values and attitudes that justify the behaviour within a subculture.

The 1960s in Britain saw the rise of the teenage consumer. As a developmental period, adolescence took on a new autonomy. Prior to this time the teen years were dealt with by a single step from childhood to adulthood; girls mimicked adult appearance by buying their first pair of stockings, high heels and twinset. Only the Teddy Boys made any real effort to set themselves apart in appearance from the adult world. But in the sixties many firms (often picking up young people's initiative) realized the buying power of teenagers in relation to luxury goods, particularly clothes, records and cosmetics. To some extent Mary Quant and Biba began the movement by offering a selection of clothes aimed exclusively and directly at the teen market. Within a few years such styles had been copied and were on sale nationally in chainstore boutiques. In the early sixties 'style' was dictated by Swinging London's young designers and was relatively homogeneous. Most teenagers aspired to a fairly similar prototype of geometric haircuts, false eylashes and white boots. Before long teenagers themselves formed factions and began to generate their own style, based on selections made from the alternatives offered by the now burgeoning fashion market (see Willis, 1978). This movement was primarily among working-class teenagers, who established, most notably, the image of Mods and Rockers. Although the Rocker uniform was fairly tightly defined and invariant (requiring a substantial initial outlay for leather jackets and boots), the Mods were more keenly consumer-minded and Mod style could accommodate a number of permutations, providing it adhered to certain basic tenets.

The stimulus for such a market was the affluence of the 1960s, when Britain was told it had 'never had it so good'. Working-class kids – photographers, actors, musicians, models, artists – were in vogue and gave the impression that anyone could make it if they only had enough 'style'. It was the short-lived era of the illusory 'British dream'. Later came the backlash. Hippies – members of a predominantly middle-class movement – rejected materialism in favour of a *mélange* of Eastern culture, supernatural beliefs and whole foods. It is perhaps no accident that such a movement came as the economic nirvana began to vanish. With less surplus money available, style could be bought cheaply at second-hand shops and jumble sales. Hippiedom was a very adaptive economic movement for the less wealthy, grant-dependent student. Working-class teenagers moved on to become Skinheads, a more extreme and more acerbic group than Mods in terms not only of appearance but also of attitudes. Skinheadism still cost money – crombies and Doc Marten boots did not come cheaply (see Daniel and McGuire, 1972). After a quiet hiatus, both musically and subculturally, Punks grew up. The wheel had turned full circle in one sense; the affluent consumerism of the Mods had become the bitter nihilism and anarchy of disillusionment. There were no jobs, no money; the working class had been put back in their places now that the rich had moved on. As economic conditions declined, it was no longer trendy to come from Bermondsey. The working-class teenagers were angry and resentful; still children in the sixties, they had expected much, only to find that they had missed the tide. But Punk was, for all its cynicism, a style. And, once again, the chained trousers, the hair dye, the black boots cost money. As the style was rapidly distorted and glamorized by the media, the rich began to be affected. Zandra Rhodes designed safety-pin evening dresses for £150. But this was different from the sixties. The art-school middle classes aped Punks but did not join them. They wanted the look but not the dole to go with it. Although bands sang 'Poor little rich boy', Punk was not a Marxist movement. Punks wanted a bigger share of the cake; they did not want it equally divided. Trades unions demanded more money but still respected wage differentials. The working-class attitude was hostile, angry and economically short-sighted. The whole structure could stay intact as long as they could have more money. The greed for consumables remained; only the hippies (who could afford to reject it because Mummy's and Daddy's detached house proved that they were only playing the poverty game) resisted the continuing demand for luxury goods.

The crime statistics for shoplifting reflect the rapid increase in the affluence and materialism of the sixties. Figure 4.1 shows the

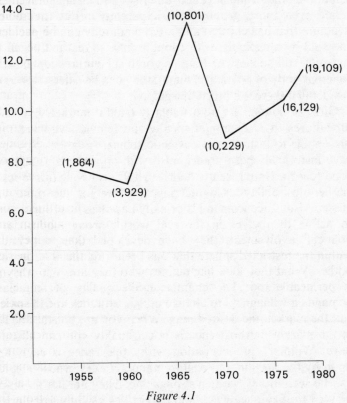

Figure 4.1

SOURCE: Home Office, Criminal Statistics for England and Wales.

proportion of all juvenile offenders committing indictable offences who were shoplifters during the period 1955 to 1978. The highest jump on the graph is between 1960 and 1966, when male and female shoplifting, as a proportion of all offences, increased by 6.3 per cent. In absolute terms it increased by 274 per cent in those years. No subsequent increase has been so great. Of course, such concomitant changes in economic, sub-cultural and crime indexes do not prove any causal relationship, but they are suggestive. Put bluntly, teenagers whose style and self-concept have come to depend on buying power and sub-cultural knowledge of the right thing to buy will be driven to theft when economic circumstances demand it. It is not a simple case of capitalist greed; the issue is consumables as self-definition. And, ironically, consumerism and fashion continue to define even those groups who apparently reject the societal structure that has cheated them. Even anarchy can be packaged and sold by a capitalist with enough sense to realize that 'divide and rule' still applies. As long as youth subcultures represent no coherent body of political thought, they can be catered for to the last detail if there is a profit margin in it.

Girls, of course, are a particularly fruitful market. Even with subcultures, it is characteristically the females who are most susceptible to fashion and cosmetic selling. As a group, women have historically been preoccupied with appearance – and with good reason. Until recently a girl's whole economic future rested on her desirability as a marriage partner for the right male buyer. Also, since women historically have had little opportunity to define themselves in the real world through industrial or political involvement, they have developed their self-concept within the restricted sphere that has been truly theirs – their own bodies. What they look like defines who they are. Who they are is permeable too. The chameleon-like quality of female life demands a willingness to change image, attitudes and lifestyle to suit the market, the desired man. When you are bought and sold in the market, intransigence is not a quality you can afford to have. Women's preoccupation with appearance is capitalized upon by the fashion and beauty manufacturers, whose methods can be seen in any women's magazine. They are not as simple-minded as they once were, and magazines aimed particularly at the adult market incorporate 'women's lib' at the most trivial level while still firmly holding the reigns of power. Woman is encouraged to enjoy her body and appearance not merely to get her man but for her own sake too; because it is fun. As Butcher et al. (1974) point out:

> Both magazines [*Honey* and *Cosmopolitan*] portray women as 'more liberated', but they also portray them as more materialistic. It is they who buy and take advantage of all the trivia that capitalist society has successfully delivered to us. But it is they also who are concerned about their sexuality in a living way. We see that the independent female image still wears her capitalist dress like the *Honey* November covers; the plastic women, not smiling, but sullenly aggressive and independent. ... Fashion and make-up are supremely run according to capitalist practice – obsolescence built into their definitions, but as we see the representation of women and their fashion in the magazine context at one level it makes a mockery of the world – that world embodied by men – which produces it. (p. 20)

Magazines that cater for younger girls are less sophisticated in their approach. They propose a dual message. One is social: looking 'right' is the passport to social success, a positive self-image and, best of all, a boyfriend. The second message is more moralistic, stressing the need for tidiness, cleanliness and 'taste'. This second theme is dropped in adult magazines; such basic female qualities are assumed to have been learned already. The common theme is still the necessity of spending money to look good, and since fashions change, this requires a never-ending outlay of cash. As McRobbie (1978a) notes:

> The fashion industry requires that new clothes are constantly being bought, regardless of 'need'. This is guaranteed at least partly by seasonal innovation and 'style'. Fashion depends on its consumer wanting to be 'up-to-date'; so, for example, the sweater is advertised for autumnal walks; but the language of fashion indicates that it is not for *all* autumnal walks but for this season's rambles in the country. Likewise the same sweater is not designed for *all* Sundays but for *these present* Sundays. (p. 37, original author's emphasis)

While presenting this strongly commercial message, out of all proportion to teenagers' income, such magazines as *Jackie* are strongly censorious of shoplifting. McRobbie again picks out moralistic overtones in *Jackie*'s presentation of the temptations of theft:

> In 'I made him hate me' the girl describes how, to keep her boy, she joined in with a group of girls who stole from shops. She then presented him with an expensive birthday present which he realized was stolen. Disgusted by her actions, he went off with another girl at his party! (p. 34)

While 'keeping your man' and consumerism are the two major themes of the magazine, both are condemned when they involve illegimate or illegal practices. We see, then, how such publications present a dual message; they encourage material acquisition while condemning the illegitimate expression of the needs that they encourage. A similar double-bind is seen in the layout of the shops themselves.

The greater proportion of shoppers are female. This is no less true today than 50 years ago. Girls feel at home in a store, whereas for men it remains an alien environment. Characteristically, the male shopper has a clear idea of his intended purchase when he leaves home – he goes out to buy a suit or a record. The purchase is made with a minimum of delay and he retires, relieved, to the pub to wait while his girlfriend 'looks around'. In menswear departments, even in more informal male boutiques, customers are attended to by individual assistants. The reason for this is probably partly historical, stemming from the tradition of the tailor-made suit, requiring direct interaction between customer and tradesman. These days the practice often has the effect of capturing a customer who might otherwise escape nervously from the ordeal of publicly choosing clothes (a 'sissy' preoccupation; real men do not bother about their appearance). It also speeds up the customer's choice by directing him immediately to the range of possibilities. The personal attention given to male clothes purchasers probably militates against the successful shoplifting of clothing. Gibbens and Prince (1962) noted the less frequent stealing of clothes by boys. Even in 1979 security officers in a large department store chain remarked on the lower rate of clothes theft by men (personal communication from store detective, 1979).

Women, on the other hand, are frequently exposed to more temptation. The greater time spent by a woman in shops for the necessary purchasing of food and household items renders her more likely to 'drift' into unnecessary purchases. The repetitive nature of food buying leads to boredom and susceptibility to the lure of something 'new'. Often she may have little idea of what she will buy; she merely knows that she needs something for the evening meal. Stores quite blatantly capitalize on this uncertainty by using open layouts in food halls and by placing special offers in large baskets at hand height. Shops encourage customers to pick items up – a half-way step to purchasing. This is particularly true of cosmetics and clothing. Prospective customers are encouraged to 'test' perfumes and skin preparations. Dresses are left on open racks to be picked up, carried around and tried on, with the idea that once it has been worn in the fitting-room the customer will become firmly attached to a dress and buy it. Unattended fitting-rooms and easily accessible goods clearly encourage theft as well as legitimate purchase, but, as previously noted, stores are unwilling to change their layouts, as such a move would deter *bona fide* customers.

The materialism of subcultures (and of the fashion market that lies both within them and outside them) extends beyond the simple business of greed. Possessions exert a twofold influence. First, everyone's choice of possessions makes particular statements about the kind of person he or she is. In the case of subcultures this is fairly easy to see, since style is dictated either by the central London scene or by manufacturers with a stake in the movement. But even for those who do not subscribe to a received style, magazines and advertisements encourage a more classical style or even persuade the reader to develop her own. This aim can be achieved by a never-before-attempted combination of pre-packaged 'looks' or products. One perfume sells itself on the claim: 'A thousand girls can wear it. It won't be the same on any two' – clearly supporting the individual style notion. Other manufacturers are less confident of the consumer's initiative where individuality is concerned and so provide a pre-packaged style, of which their product forms a part. For example, a trendy restaurant that claims to be 'the most civilized place in London for afternoon tea' clearly relates to an audience of blasé, cosmopolitan young aristocrats. Some products select individuals to promote their image; one perfume offers a picture of a smart Parisian girl who leaves no doubt as to her personal identity by listing her idiosyncrasies: 'I like horror films, playing the guitar, spending money... I hate public transport, young girls. ... My perfume is not too strong, fresh....' Although much has been written about women and the consumer 'self', men are not exempt. Cars, hi-fi equipment and clothes confer class, and even in fashion pages men are 'made over' into new images of themselves. Butcher et al.'s comments on the subject are as applicable to men as to women:

> We have to agree that though there is not one image for women to be bonded by, the several can just as well be bondage. She still must perform the delicate task of presenting to the world an image that conforms to the images of the moment, and yet also expresses individual 'taste'. In one article the magazine suggests just that. On 'style':

>> It is a sense, a touch – nothing more. Something between a talent and a commitment. It is nothing more than a way of expressing yourself, your style. It shows in the way you choose clothes and put them together, in the way you interpret yourself through make-up and your hair, the way you decorate the place you live in. More than anything else style comes out of conviction in expressing your personal tastes, fantasies, wishes and your self.

> Three young women and one young man are helped by the magazine to find their 'style'. They emerge at the end of the day as plastic people – lifeless. (p. 21)

The second aspect of materialism is what has been called 'consumer fetishism'. The object may remain quite separate from the self and form no obvious part of self-presentation, yet the owning of it becomes almost an obsession. Even if never used or worn, the possession of a Gucci bag or a Dior scarf fulfils a need in itself. It is the act of ownership – the translation of an object from the world to the individual – that satisfies the craving to own and accumulate. Some shoplifters who hoard stolen objects without ever using them may be responding to this need. It is even acknowledged in advertising when we see a middle-aged man sneaking down to the garage at midnight merely to sit in his expensive new car. Admiring the object and furnishing lavish attention on its maintenance and beauty seems to satisfy a desire that is related not merely to the preservation of its resale value. The possession of an object of power or beauty becomes its own end, something that is particularly noticeable in the world of antiques and art.

In the face of the enormous machinery of advertising and selling, we have to look at the opposite side of the coin − the importance of labour in generating the means of material acquisition. The differential attitude of the social classes to the role and value of work has been documented extremely widely (A. K. Cohen 1955; Marx and Engels, 1977; Willis 1975). What follows is no more than a paraphrase of such writers. For the member of the middle class (the professional, the entrepreneur, the factory owner, the academic) work is an integral part of self-worth. His relationship to the means of production is one of relative power and confers high prestige. As training for such a position, public school, university and the family endorse notions of responsibility and conscientiousness. The well-being of less fortunate members of society rests on his prudence in providing jobs, investing money, distributing justice or interpreting facts. Wages depend in our society not on the physical or mental demands of a job, nor on its centrality to society's survival, but to the amount of 'responsibility' that it entails. Responsibility generally equates with power over others' livelihoods. Since income is related to control, then for the middle class buying power is related to prestige. What is owned is a measure of society's evaluation of the individual. Such a statement of course, holds true only to the extent that the illegitimate acquisition of these status symbols is severely sanctioned. In capitalist society it is property crimes that are penalized even more heavily than crimes against the person. The buying of visible luxury goods is a barometer of social success and of personal worth for the middle classes, and cultural pressures against crime are strong enough to deter the majority from shoplifting. The stigma of conviction is double-edged; the rules of the capitalist game have not only been broken, but broken in a petty fashion, and petty concerns are not the arena of the middle class. Large-scale fraud, embezzlement and tax evasion can be tolerated, however, as only the middle classes have access to such rewarding crimes. Racketeers even elicit a degree of respect for their skilful manipulation of loopholes in property laws. Thus criminal activity in the middle classes takes a particular form, which incorporates the prestige of business know-how and therefore misuses the rules of wealth acquisition without really challenging them. For the majority the relationship between work and consumerism is mediated by self-worth.

The working class is traditionally alienated from the means of production. The labour of its members is sold in the market place to the highest bidder, resulting in little sense of loyalty to any particular employer. Such loyalty is often considered a 'mug's game', for when retirement comes, 25 years' labour is rewarded with a digital clock and forgotten. The worker exercises no control or power over others' livelihoods and sees little possibility of ever doing so legitimately. There are no 'career structures' on a production line (except within the union), and the possibility of escaping from manual or clerical work is negligible without the academic qualifications that most abandoned at sixteen. Wages depend not on individual skill but on the going rate for the job, argued out by unions and management. The money that the worker earns is for his labour, not for his self-worth. As Rowbotham (1973) clearly expresses it:

A man's capacity to make something can be exchanged as a finished product for things made by other men. Through wages, a man's capacity to labour is exchanged for money. His work turns itself into money. The money represents the measure of time and possibility which has been subtracted from his life. Time is a measure of what he has lost, money represents the measure of what he is allowed. The worker bargains his life away. (p. 50)

In his free time the worker is encouraged to spend his money by the leisure industry (pubs, cinemas, holidays, clubs) and by the consumer industry (houses, cars, clothes, hardware). These goods are both ends in themselves and, for the aspiring proletariat, the symbols of success. Yet the success they symbolize is not middle-class 'worth' but rather the capacity to make a fast buck, the initiative to set up as self-employed, the wit to play the game and perhaps cheat a little. In general, work and the money that results from it are separate from the self. Money is not hoarded or invested as an end in itself; it is used as spending power to buy leisure time that will compensate for the time 'lost' at work. Its value lies in consumption (alcohol, cigarettes, music, fun) or the possession of objects that give meaning, excitement and identity – fast cars and motor bikes, guitars, hi-fi equipment, clothes and hairstyles. As Cloward and Ohlin (1960) argue, working-class kids endorse the desire for the material goods that society as a whole is taught to want; what they reject is the 'legitimate' means to attain them. The possession of goods *per se* confers status and provides fun, whether the goods are acquired out of wages or from shoplifting. To get something 'that fell off the back of a lorry' carries no stigma even among rigorously law-abiding people – it is one of the 'perks' of having friends 'in the trade'. Because the middle-class equation of power with money and goods does not hold so strongly among the working class, goods in themselves, however acquired, are valued. When the demands of fashion or subcultures move too swiftly for wages to keep up, then shoplifting is a viable alternative. No stigma is attached to looking good and having fun, and no questions are asked about where the money came from.

The impetus to shoplift, then, is a product of the interaction between self and possessions, between work and fun. Why is it a crime in which girls participate in greater numbers than in any other offence? The answer given by many writers is solely in terms of the greater exposure among women to goods and shops; the simple opportunity thesis (Hoffman-Bustamente, 1973; Pollak, 1961; Simon, 1975). But as well as this, it is important to consider the extent to which self-representation and appearance are particularly important to girls economically and therefore psychologically.

The motive for shoplifting in boys is probably twofold. First, there are the same pressures towards ownership, self-image and status as among girls. The right clothes, the expensive record collection and so on not only provide fun and enhance peer-group approval but may also provide greater access to girls. In a recent musical teen film a group of boys discussing their friend's performance on a date sing, 'Did you get very far?', while the girl's friends simultaneously chorus, 'But does he have a car?' The refrain is recognized as a reflection of the time-honoured bargaining of sexual favours for economic security through the relationship of dating and marriage. If you cannot be the toughest or most popular boy, you can at least improve your sexual chances with affluence. So access to girlfriends may be a concrete result of the ownership of material goods. However, the act of shoplifting is not one that *per se* is likely to confer the respect of other male peers. It is a girl's crime; the risks and possible penalties are not severe; and it represents no open challenge to authority. Boys may boast of their spoils but not of the act itself. A great deal more kudos still attaches to the machismo activities of drinking, fast driving and fighting. Shoplifting is, for most boys, primarily a functional act, not an end in itself (see Parker, 1974). Some boys, however, as noted by Gibbens and Prince (1962), engage in shoplifting episodes that do not seem related to the material benefits. They acquire collections of seemingly random objects, which are either hoarded or dumped, and they seem to gain satisfaction from the risk-taking alone. It is interesting to speculate about the type of boy who steals in this way. Gibbens and Prince note that among their sample many were of higher than average intelligence, were at grammar schools and seemed socially isolated. Many did it as a result of a 'dare' by other boys who were regularly involved in shoplifting. For boys who find it difficult to relate to peers, this kind of activity may be thought to confer status, and its function may be to prove masculinity, both to the boy himself and to others. The homosexual attributions made by detectives and researchers alike could quite plausibly result from these 'effeminate' aspects of the boy's character, which both cause his social isolation and determine the nature of his attempted solution. It is less terrifying to shoplift than to risk a head-on fight as a means of establishing self-worth.

Girls' preoccupation with physical appearance has been inculcated historically, and in each girl's own development, through family, school and the media. Its purpose is not merely to fill up time in a fundamentally pointless existence (*Jackie* magazine: 'When you're all alone you can have a great time making yourself up . . . trying out different hairstyles and seeing what suits you best'), nor is it simply aesthetic. As McRobbie (1978a) points out:

> The messages stemming from these images are clear. First, if you look good, you feel good and are guaranteed to have a good time. Second, looking as good as this, you can expect to be treated as something special, even precious. And third, beauty like this is the girl's passport to happiness and success. (p. 39)

The success at which the girl aims is marriage. Marriage to the right man guarantees economic security for life. Her future financial well-being rests on her looks. She may be a humble typist, but if she is beautiful, she could be married to a millionaire tomorrow. Success stories such as these are carried by the newspapers all the time. Butcher et al. (1974) analysed the appearance of women in a selection of British newspapers over a one-week period. One of the main reasons for females being in the news was as a result of 'borrowed status'; that is, they are the wives or mothers of famous men. A recent newspaper article on a 'fortunate' nurse began:

> Fun-loving nurse Lorna Kirk staged a wild party prank and captured a millionaire's heart. A whirlwind romance followed and they will be married next Monday. Lorna, 22, will then be the new Lady of Hickstead. (*Daily Mirror*, 6 March 1979)

The message is clear: men want beauty not brains. The function of women is decorative. Every minute spent in physical self-improvement is an investment, not only materially but in terms of emotional adjustment too. To be old and unmarried still represents a fearful cloud on a teenage girl's horizon. Even an unhappy marriage is better than none at all. As one woman writes of her marriage:

> If he stops loving me, I'm sunk; I won't have any purpose in life, or be sure I exist any more. I must efface myself in order to avoid this and not make any demands on him, or do anything that might offend him. I feel dead now, but if he stops

loving me I am really dead, because I am nothing by myself. I have to be noticed to know I exist. But if I efface myself, how can I be noticed? It is a basic contradiction. (Tax, 1970)

Work is seen as a temporary stop-gap before marriage. Of course, in reality millionaires are thin on the ground, and a woman's marriage partner may rely on her income as well as his own. Even then, work will be of secondary importance, representing nothing more than pin-money. This fundamental lack of commitment to work as a lifetime's activity has led to the failure of women to unionize and to demand better conditions and wages. In magazines the heroines are usually vaguely defined office workers, but work itself is merely a backdrop to the real business of husband hunting. As McRobbie (1978a) says:

The characters speak without an accent and are usually without family or community ties. They have all left school, but 'work' hovers invisibly in the background as a necessary time-filler between one evening and the next or can sometimes be a pathway to glamour, fame or romance. ... Thus the train, supermarket, and office have meaning, to the extent that they represent potential meeting-places where the girl could well bump into the prospective boyfriend, who lurks round every corner. (pp. 16, 19)

Work may take a secondary place in their values, but it does in reality absorb a large proportion of teenagers' time. Sharpe (1976) looked at job preferences among a group of London girl school-leavers. Four girls in every 10 chose office work, and, by including the jobs of teachers, nurses, shop assistants, bank clerks, receptionists, telephonists, hairdressers and nannies, three-quarters of the choices were accounted for. These selections were probably realistic in terms of the sort of work that is available to average 16-year-old school-leavers. With the exception of teaching and nursing, these jobs require little specialized training, and for most a good physical appearance is a distinct advantage. The importance of looks becomes even more pronounced when considering the types of occupations to which girls, often unrealistically, aspire – the glamour jobs. The role of air hostesses, models, actresses, public relations officers, sales representatives, promotion girls and personal assistants is often one of sexual window-dressing and male ego-boosting. At worst, it can be a kind of social prostitution, through which the girl is selling her 'sexiness' rather than her ability. Within large firms bosses choose their personal secretaries from the typing pool or steal them from one another. The criterion is often physical attractiveness and good grooming – she is a perk and a status symbol to go with the company car. So even if a husband is not immediately forthcoming, a girl's financial security within a job is also bound up with her appearance and, once again, the magazines advise her prudently to impress the boss: 'Appearance is of paramount importance to the girl; it should be designed to please both boyfriend and boss alike and threaten the authority of neither' (McRobbie, 1978a, p. 44).

With so many demands on incomes that are often quite low, it is hardly surprising that girls are heavily involved in shoplifting. The pressures – material, psychological, social, romantic – assault them from every side. The shops invite them to touch, smell, feel and wear everything that they need for instant success in all these spheres. When the temptations are all weighed up and the chances of detection calculated, it is remarkable that so few girls do it.

CHAPTER 5

Aggression

That females are the gentler sex is a popular belief to which criminal statistics, cross-cultural studies and common sense have in the main testified. Over the last 10 years, however, the rate of female juvenile involvement in crimes against the person has increased even more dramatically than that of males, in both England and the United States. In the academic world new impetus has been given to attempts to understand more thoroughly the basis of aggression in both sexes and its origins particularly in the female. The media have capitalized on this by giving their attention to the 'problem' of female violence. The aggression of girls, the potential mothers of future generations, has taken on a new dimension of concern. The women's movement oscillates uncomfortably between applauding and decrying this 'new' aspect of female behaviour. In all the politicizing and popularizing, few people have taken the trouble to consider the facts of female aggression and the research that has been done to date.

Brain mechanisms and hormones

At a physiological level work has been performed that has located the apparent brain site of aggressive behaviour. The pioneering work of Klüver and Bucy (1939) suggested that the removal of the temporal lobe, including the limbic system and amygdala, produced a state of placidness in normally vicious rhesus monkeys. Further work using brain stimulation (Mark and Ervin, 1970) suggests that the amygdala plays an important part in aggressive behaviour. It is now also believed to be implicated in sexual behaviour in some animals, affecting the timing of puberty, ovulation and maternal behaviour (see Weitz, 1977). Raisman and Feld (1971) have suggested that the junction of the amygdala with the preoptic area of the hypothalmus may be particularly sensitive to the male hormone, androgen, and as such may be the anatomical site of sex differences in aggression. They say, 'It is tempting to speculate that it may be this connection of the preoptic region which is affected by neonatal androgen and is therefore sexually dimorphic' (p. 14).

The specific site at which hormones have their sexually differentiating effect is still far from proved. That they do have an effect is argued forcibly by both clinicians and those involved in animal behaviour. Gray (1971) reviews a body of literature that strongly suggests a reliable sex difference in aggression in many species, from mice (Lagerspetz, 1969), and rats (Conner and Levine, 1969) to chimpanzees (Van Lawick-Goodall, 1968). This sex difference occurs in *one form* of aggression only: within-species aggression that controls dominance ranking. Differences have not yet been found with respect to between-species or predatory aggression. These two behaviours are in turn controlled by separate brain sites – inter-specific aggression by the lateral hypothalmus (also responsible for food-seeking behaviour), and intra-specific aggression by the corticomedial amygdala, the hypothalmus and the central grey matter of the mid-brain (Gray and Drewett, 1977). Such a finding also supports the view that the two sites may indeed be differentially responsive to male and female sex hormones.

The dependence of sex differences in aggression on the sexual endocrine system in rodents has been well documented. The castration of adult males reduces their aggression level, while injections of testosterone restore it (Tollman and King, 1956). Androgen facilitates aggression only in males. Female aggressiveness is affected neither by testosterone injection nor by ovariectomy (Conner and Levine, 1969). However, testosterone administered to neonatal female mice does increase adult aggressiveness (Conner and Levine, 1969). So it appears that the facilitative effect of testosterone on intra-specific aggression works only on an animal that is already sexually differentiated as male. Goy (1968) has demonstrated a similar effect in rhesus monkeys: a pre-natal injection of testosterone in a pregnant monkey produces masculinized female offspring, which display male levels of rough-and-tumble play and chasing during childhood.

For the present purposes the most relevant data has come from hormonally imbalanced girls described by Money and Erhardt (1972). Two clinical syndromes were investigated: progestin-induced hermaphroditism (PI) and the adreno-genital syndrome (AGS). PI results from the administration of progestin to pregnant women, causing any females born to have masculinized genitals while leaving intact both female organs and a female hormonal system (the effect of the progestin medication being confined to the foetal period of sexual differentiation). AGS babies have defective adrenal glands, which release excessive amounts of androgen instead of cortisol during the critical period of sexual differentiation before birth. The adreno-cortical function does not correct itself post-natally. It is necessary for children with this condition to be regulated on cortisone therapy throughout adulthood. Ten PI girls and fifteen AGS girls were matched individually with 25 controls for age, IQ, socio-economic status and race. Dependent measures of the subjects' childhood behaviour were taken by means of interviews with both mother and daughter. Although both PI and AGS girls differed from controls in being known as tomboys, having strong athletic interests and skills, preferring male playmates and preferring trousers to dresses, there were no differences on several indices, including fighting.

The absence of significant aspects of foetal androgenization on fighting in particular is discussed by the authors. They suggest that a better measure would perhaps have been the striving for position in childhood dominance hierarchies. However, the data available on this suggest that the two diagnostic groups did not strive for dominance in competition with boys, and that they were not interested in the rivalries of other girls. It is important to note that very many studies of sex differences in aggression in both primates and humans do not take fighting as their main dependent variable. Because of its rarity of occurrence, they substitute instead rough-and-tumble play and activities involving 'high energy expenditure' (see for example, Goy, 1968). Tomboyism and athletic interests would be included in such a working definition and might lead to the erroneous conclusion that such girls would be more belligerent.

Conflicting results from different studies may often be explained by differences in operational definitions employed.

A further study by Erhardt and Baker (1974) compared male and female AGS patients with their normal sisters and brothers. If tomboyish behaviour were found to be generally above average in the families of AGS girls, the exclusive contribution of the hormonal input could be ruled out in favour of more general socialization effects on all the children in the family. AGS girls, when compared with their sisters, were found to have high energy expenditure, to prefer male playmates, to be tomboyish and to show little interest in dolls, infant care and marriage. Once again, no significant differences appeared with respect to fighting. It has been suggested (Quadagno et al., 1977) that high energy expenditure may be a by-product either of the adreno-genital syndrome *per se* or of the cortisone replacement therapy used to treat the condition. Similarly, both the patients' and parents' knowledge of their condition may have generated a perceptual set towards attending to and remembering particularly 'male' aspects of the patients' behaviour.

In interpreting results such as these, it is important to remember that what is being considered is the *relative level* of aggression displayed by normal and hormonally disturbed girls or by males and females. No one would deny that females can and do respond aggressively, but physiologists argue that the provocation for such action must be greater for girls and possibly of a different quality. The contribution of both ethologists and anthropologists has been to document the naturally occurring rate of aggression by males and females in different species and cultures and to speculate upon its functional significance within a social context.

Cross-species and cross-cultural aspects of aggression

Lorenz (1966) has noted the evolutionary value of aggression among many animal species. Predatory aggression is obviously required to ensure food supply. Intra-species aggression also serves important functions; it distributes individuals or groups over the available habitat, for example. By creating territories, it selects out the strongest animals as defenders of the group against intruders or predators, and it allows for the establishment of dominance hierarchies within the group for purposes of mating and leadership. In order to ensure that rival fighting within the group does not end in fatalities, certain rituals have evolved to ensure the containing of such encounters. Fighting is often directed towards relatively robust parts of the opponent's anatomy, and assaults are rarely made with the most dangerous parts of the body, such as teeth or claws. In many species the fighting itself is so highly ritualized that no physical attack takes place. In Spiny-rayed fish, for example, the protagonists position themselves broadside to one another (thus creating the illusion of greater physical bulk) and the water disturbance caused by ritual tail-beating may be sufficient to end the encounter before it begins.

Animals have developed relatively non-injurious ways of settling internal disputes, and to some extent these rituals seem to be transmitted genetically to the offspring. Further up the evolutionary scale, at the level of monkeys and apes, these predispositions are encouraged and modified by socialization and learning within the group (see Harlow and Harlow, 1962). Initially through play young animals practice and perfect their fighting behaviour while at the same time learning their own strength and capacity to inflict damage.

Although our knowledge of behavioural genetics among humans is still rudimentary, it is widely believed that culture has taken over the role of genetics with respect to the expression of aggression (Fulker, 1979). Cultures develop their own means of channelling and containing agonistic attacks in order to minimize the number of fatalities. Thus aggressive behaviour can be finely tuned to the particular social or ecological circumstances in which a society lives. For further information on these kinds of limiting rules, data from anthropologists must be considered.

Gardner and Heider (1968) wrote of the Dani people who inhabit the New Guinea plains. The Dani fight regularly and consider it to be an integral part of life. Battles frequently occur between different tribes, but adherence to rituals contains the amount of damage that occurs. Challenges are issued, and the battle is convened with proper consideration of the weather and time of day. The battle consists of a number of minor skirmishes and is called off when all the combatants become too exhausted to continue. Although the Dani use feathers in many aspects of their day-to-day life, they do not use them as flights on their arrows. This ensures that the level of accuracy in firing is low and the chances of a bad wound relatively slight. When a spear has been thrown, the warrior must retreat, since he is defenceless, and this ensures the rather leisurely pace of the battle. In a whole year's fighting, only between 10 and 20 warriors die, but the battle serves as an arena for the demonstration of masculine bravery. The authors sum up the mood of the whole battle thus:

> By noon, most of the warriors have arrived and the various formations have taken more or less final positions. Some are armed with bows and arrows, some with spears. The opposing armies are deployed so that between the most forward elements of each there lies a battle ground of perhaps five hundred yards. A mood of silent but excited expectation pervades all ranks. From this point on, the day will bring the pleasures of the fight to several hundred of both sides, momentary terror for the handful who will feel the sudden pain of an enemy arrow, and, rarely, the unmentionable shock of death to someone who acts stupidly or clumsily. (p. 138)

The Maring cultures (Harris, 1974) also engage in frequent skirmishes for territory, but victory in battle does not result in the victor's taking possession of the land. Instead the hard-won land is left empty by both sides; thus it lies fallow and the forest regenerates itself. In this way the cut-and-burn agricultural system is maintained without wholesale ecological destruction. Such studies indicate that fighting does indeed have functional value and that it is not the destructive and chaotic affair that we often imagine.

Nearer to home, Fox (1977) has written of the inhabitants of Tory Island, which lies off the Irish coast. Fighting in this community of 300 people has lost none of its ritual aspects. The two combatants choose to fight in public places where intervention by friends and relatives is bound to occur. Each has a number of allies on his side, who attempt to talk him out of further action.

The fight itself is composed largely of insults, with occasional sallies forward toward the opponent. It escalates in seriousness when coats are taken off. Following this, the men shout that they will surely commit murder unless someone holds them back. Their allies obligingly restrain them. At worst, there are a few bruises and grazes, but the main point is that honour has been satisfied. The rules are implicitly understood; they do not exist in any overt from:

> What I've described here is something that's interesting because there are no explicit rules. If two Tory men have a quarrel, they don't go and appeal to the duelling master. What happens seems to be spontaneous. There are no written sets of rules and yet it falls into this pattern of fighting which everybody enjoys thoroughly and through which the men can make their point without affecting too much damage. (p. 46)

It would be misleading to imply that all anthropologists share this relatively benign view of human aggression. Washburn (1959), for example, states: 'Man has a carnivorous psychology. It is easy to teach people to kill and it is hard to develop customs which avoid killing. Many human beings enjoy seeing other human beings suffer, or enjoy the killing of animals' (p. 26). Similarly, Freeman (1964) seems to present a very pessimistic view of human nature in his historical analysis of aggression. However, both these authors confuse several issues. First, large-scale international war has little to do with human aggression. It is better analysed with respect to politics and economics. People who drop bombs rarely experience the emotions concomitant with aggressive behaviour, rage, anger or a desire to dominate another person. Second, it is particularly important to distinguish predatory aggression (such as the killing or slaughtering of animals) and intra-specific aggression. They correspond to different psychological and social-functional systems. Third, the point should be made that accounts of ritual aggression do not attempt to explain individual pathology or disturbance, which may cause deviance from such rules and result in particularly bloodthirsty crimes.

In most cultures anthropologists have indicated that it is the males who participate most fully in aggression. Some psychological and ethological studies have investigated children's behaviour in different cultures in an attempt to understand whether this universal sex difference in aggression is learned or innate.

The etiology of sex differences in aggression

Since the 1930s over 150 studies have investigated developmental sex differences in aggresive behaviour. Attempts to summarize the results must of necessity involve simplification. Studies have looked at behavioural indices (in the context of observational and experimental situations), as well as ratings and questionnaires (by children and related adult supervisors) and 'subconscious' factors such as guilt and repression, via projective tests. Operational definitions used range from attacks on inanimate objects, through verbal hostility toward peers, to the administration of electric shocks to other people. Of the 130 studies undertaken that have relied on behaviour indices, Rohner (1976) concludes that 71 per cent show boys to be more aggressive; 23 per cent show no significant sex differences; and only 6 per cent show girls to be more aggressive. This is particularly striking since the range of techniques used is so broad. Maccoby and Jacklin (1974) point out that the variability in modes of expression, interpersonal differences, social contexts and stimuli provoking violence in everyday life are so great as to make even more surprising the finding of a consistent sex difference.

The bulk of the evidence suggests that there are no significant fluctuations in this sex difference over age. Children from 2 to 17 years old have been studied. Only Rohner (1976) suggests that such sex differences diminish with age. In a survey of 31 societies he reports that 65 per cent show no sex differences in aggression among adults. While the mean aggression score for males drops slightly in adulthood, the female increases by the same amount. Whiting and Pope (cited in Maccoby and Jacklin, 1974), took time-sampled behaviour observations in seven cultures of two age cohorts (3–6 years and 6–10 years). In all cultures physical assault of one child upon another was so rare as to make it impossible to test the sex differences statistically. However, boys engaged in more 'mock fighting', verbal abuse and counter-attacking. Omark et al. (1973) studied three cultures (the United States, Switzerland and Ethiopia). Aggression was defined as pushing or hitting without smiling, and a greater incidence of this was found for boys in all three samples. Rohner (1976) sampled 101 cultures, instructing investigators to code all aggressive behaviour (verbal and physical) on a nine-point scale from low to high aggression. The operational definition of aggression was not given. He concluded that while cross-cultural variations in children's aggression are substantial, variations in sex differences are usually slight. The results table shows a perfect pattern: girls fall almost exactly one point lower than boys in every culture. In spite of disparate (and sometimes inadequately described) methodology, these studies, by virtue of their consensus, do suggest the universality of sex differences. However, this in itself does not demand any genetic interpretation.

Over the last few years researchers have realized the futility of extreme polarities in the nature–nurture debate. Clearly, broad tendencies or predispositions may be capitalized upon, enhanced or given new forms by culture. The interaction of genes and culture is complex and a number of explanations for disparities are possible. Originally, small morphological differences between the sexes may have cast males in the role of fighters and predators (especially since females were often incapacitated by pregnancy or dependent infants). Subsequently, the weakest males would have died, thus ensuring that the larger and more aggressive males would reproduce and so exaggerate the originally minimal sex differences. Culture clearly exerted its effect on such predispositions by generating the ritualization of male dominance struggles so that this necessary aggression would not take the form of intra-group bloodshed. Gray (1971) and Maccoby and Jacklin (1974) suggest that both female fearfulness and the reluctance of males to be violent towards females may have evolutionary value.

For the survival of a bisexual species, it is more important for a higher proportion of females than males to survive to maturity; hence a low level of aggression toward them by the more powerful male would have value from an evolutionary perspective. (Maccoby and Jacklin 1974, p. 239)

A second genetic explanation suggests that aggression is only one part of a sex-linked gene for higher activity level among males. Hutt (1972) suggests that androgens may be the *fons at origo* of all drives, including sex and aggression. Money (1965) suggests that 'androgen is the libido hormone for both men and women.' Women who are deprived of adrenal androgens suffer a great or complete loss of libido. Testosterone has also been shown to be linked not only to aggression but also to improved focusing of attention on, and persistence with, a number of tasks (D. M. Broverman et al., 1968; Hamburg, 1971). Patterson et al. (1967) explicitly tested the link between activity level and aggression with children. Three measures of activity were used: distance covered per unit time, vigour in physical activity and vigour in verbal activity. The correlations between the first two measures and aggression were low (0.23 and 0.10 respectively) but verbal vigour and aggression gave a value of 0.66. The authors concluded: 'The child who interacts at a high level with his peers is not only an active child but he is also an individual who has been conditioned to be highly responsive to peer-dispensed reinforcers' (p. 35). Once again, 'genetic' predispositions are seen in interaction with particular social and cultural factors.

Extreme environmentalists (and feminists) argue that the visible sex differences in aggression arise exclusively from different socialization practices among the two sexes. Such a position is cogently argued by Mischel (1966), who takes a social learning standpoint. He argues not only that boys and girls are differentially rewarded and punished for aggression, but also that the demonstrable preference of children for imitating the behaviour of same-sex adults works to maintain these differences within the culture. A strong piece of evidence comes from a study by Bandura et al. (1961). Boys and girls observed an aggressive adult whose behaviour was either rewarded, punished or accepted without consequence. Predictably, post-exposure tests showed that response contingencies to the adult model produced differential amounts of imitative behaviour, and that boys were more reluctant to imitate a woman than were girls. In the next phase of the experiment, all the children were offered attractive incentives for displaying aggressive behaviour. This effectively eradicated previous sex differences. Clearly, females have the capacity for such behaviour in their repertoire and, in these unusual conditions, will manifest it. If environmentalists are right (and few people would argue with the modifiability of most human behaviour), the questions still remain of why so many cultures have systematically discouraged the expression of aggression in females, and why this socialization practice has been so success-ful. Two studies, (Sears, 1961; Rothaus and Worchel, 1964) have found that girls demonstrate more guilt and anxiety over aggression than do boys, which would suggest the use of strong negative socialization pressures on them in the past. Direct evidence of whether boys and girls are differentially punished for aggressive behaviour is very hard to collect; however, Maccoby and Jacklin (1974), present evidence that in the early years at least boys receive as much punishment for aggressive acts as do girls.

A small body of work has addressed itself to the issue of qualitative differences between the sexes in the behavioural expression of aggression. The distinction between verbal and physical modes has been explored, based on the hypothesis that boys rather than girls would tend to employ physical forms of aggression. Both Bandura et al. (1961) and McIntyre (1972) claim to have found such a difference. However, Whiting and Pope (see Maccoby and Jacklin, 1974) found that in seven cultures boys more frequently used both forms, and this finding was in agreement with that of Hatfield et al. (1967), who observed the behaviour of nursery-school children towards their mothers. Sears et al. (1965), however, using the same sample of children, reported no sex differences with respect to verbal aggression. This line of work to date has proved inconclusive. It is important to note that physical aggression is almost always preceded by some form of verbal abuse or challenge, however minimal. The relationship between verbal and physical measure then is non-reciprocal. Verbal confrontation or abuse may go no further than that, but physical aggression will almost always involve some verbal exchange.

Related to the verbal/physical dichotomy is that of direct/indirect forms of aggression. Fesbach (1969), in a study of five-year old children, observed the reaction of same-sex dyads to the arrival of a third child who wanted to 'join their club'. Ignoring, refusing and excluding were coded as indirect aggression, while physical, verbal and expressive behaviour (sneering, gesturing) were coded as direct aggression. Although indirect forms were more frequent for both male and female dyads, the latter demonstrated significantly more instances of indirect aggression. Both male and female dyads displayed most aggression (of both kinds) to the arrival of boys rather than girls.

Maccoby and Jacklin (1974) have given further attention to the targets of aggression. Hutt (1972) presents data from nursery-school children that confirms that the biggest sex difference occurs in aggression toward members of the same sex. Cross-sex aggressive encounters, in fact, show that attacks by girls are somewhat more frequent. Attacks on teachers or inanimate objects show no difference. This finding is supported by Fesbach's study. Shortell and Biller (1970) on 10-year-olds and Taylor and Epstein (1967) on adults also show that more frequent and more intense aggression is displayed toward males. Patterson et al. (1967), undertook a study of nursery-school children in order to investigate the hypothesis that positive reinforcement by the victim increases the likelihood of further attack by the aggressor. Positively reinforcing responses were: target does not respond, gives up toy, cries, assumes defensive posture or protests verbally. Negatively reinforcing responses were: target tells teacher, recovers property or retaliates. While their hypothesis was confirmed overall, girls as targets were no more positively or negatively reinforcing than were boys.

This reinforcement explanation *per se* does not account for the difference. Whiting and Pope (1974) report that in seven cultures boys as targets were more likely to retaliate than were girls but were still more often chosen as victims. The evolutionary value of the morphologically stronger male restraining his attacks on weaker females is doubtless upheld not by genetic factors but through culturally transmitted social taboos on such behaviour, which are learned during socialization.

The aggressive personality

A body of work in both psychiatry and criminology has focused on the characteristics of particular individuals that make them predisposed to be aggressive. Such studies give scant attention either to subcultural support or to social and situational factors in incidences of violence. In regarding subjects as independent of their peers and social context, the studies often present a clinical picture of isolated and disturbed personalities.

The term 'psychopathy' came into current usage after Cleckley's *The Mask of Sanity* (1964). He described the typical psychopath as neither neurotic nor psychotic but as superficially charming, intelligent, remorseless, free of guilt, unreliable, untruthful, insincere, incapable of love and highly egocentric. Much concern has been expressed at the relatively loose clustering of such symptom descriptions and at the imprecision with which the term is applied by psychiatrists. Buss (1961) suggested that a series of behavioural descriptions be offered instead, which would avoid the necessity of inferring or attributing internal states. Work on psychopathy has been conducted from both personality trait and physiological standpoints. Hare and Shalling (1978) have emphasized some of the prominent biological correlates of psychopathy as follows (although by no means all diagnosed psychopaths display these malfunctions):

1 The EEG (brain-wave) patterns of some psychopaths resemble children's, and some investigators have hypothesized delayed maturation of some cortical neuronal mechanisms.
2 Limbic system disfunction has also been implicated.
3 Psychopathy may depend on a decreased state of cortical excitability and on an attenuation of sensory input.
4 Some psychopaths display symptoms of sensory deprivation.
5 Many demonstrate an intense need for stimulation.
6 Psychopaths seem to improve with age, thus supporting the concept of delayed maturation.

Other researchers have used clinical tests such as the MMPI in order to find objective paper-and-pencil measures with which to pinpoint more precisely those behavioural scales that inter-correlate to form the elusive psychopathic personality. Quay and his associates (Peterson et al. 1959) factor-analysed behaviour ratings, self-report data and case histories. The first factor was psychopathic delinquency, followed by neurotic sub-cultural delinquency. This distinction has also been found by Blackburn (1974a) and Hare (1970). Widom (1978) cluster-analysed the responses of incarcerated women to 10 scales of the Special Hospitals Assessment of Personality and Socializa-tion (SHAPS) inventory. She found a first cluster of psy-chopathy that accounted for only 6 per cent of her total sample. Other estimates of the incidence of psychopathy in female offenders vary between 2 per cent (Woodside, 1962) to 65 per cent (Cloninger and Guze, 1970), probably reflecting the different diagnostic criteria and tests that were used. Although comparable figures are not available for male prisoners, Widom (1978) concludes, 'the frequency of this syndrome in the female offender population seems to be smaller than the frequency of psychopathy in male offender populations' (pp. 293–4). Widom suggests that this pathology may have different manifestations or symptoms in males and females.

The implications of this kind of research are far from clear. Many writers are pessimistic about finding any 'cure' for psy-chopathy. Patients respond to punishment with aggression rather than behaviour modification, and attempts to control their behaviour by chemotherapy or surgery have been fairly unsuccessful – to leave aside the ethical issues involved (see Hare and Shalling, 1978). Even now many psychologists are reluctant to use psychopathy as a clinical diagnosis because of its rather ill-defined symptomatology. A clustering of response tendencies of itself does not imply any single, homogeneous clinical category. Nor can we conclude that a syndrome of questionnaire responses or even antisocial behaviour must be caused by an underlying organic disorder.

Many psychological studies of aggression have been hampered by a failure to define aggressive behaviour systematically in operational terms. Play-fighting is not aggres-sion, nor is pressing a button to deliver an electric shock at a superior's instigation, yet both have been taken as dependent measures. Responses to questionnaires and the use of car horns by motorists have also been used. In general, psychologists have been in such a rush to find the 'cause' of aggression that working definitions are set up and abandoned again at the drop of a research grant. It is little wonder that so few reliable findings have emerged. The obsession with quantification in the social sciences has militated against careful, descriptive studies of the phenomenon that is under investigation. The ease with which laboratory studies can be performed by comparison with the slow process of data collection of naturally occurring aggression has similarly encouraged the growth of one-off studies. In this unsatisfactory state of affairs, concern with female aggression has always been an afterthought in studies predominantly concerned with males. The dependent measures of aggression are nominated, and the sexes are compared on the relative frequency of their performance of various aggressive acts. If aggression does serve a social function however, then it is time to ask what the function is for females today. Are the social goals of aggression realized in the same way for boys and girls? Before we can conjecture about function or cause, it is important to arrive at some understanding of the particular form and management of female aggression.

Virtually no empirical research has been undertaken on adolescent girls and fighting in a community situation. Deutsch et al. (1978) have investigated agonistic behaviour within an American female reformatory. Hart (1975), in Britain, has written on the social and personal backgrounds of girls who are referred to assessment centres, charged with violence. Hanson (1964) has written a so-called 'fact-based' novel on New York girl gangs. Research into violence among adult women has largely concentrated on the more spectacular crimes of manslaughter and murder (see, for example, Ward et al. 1968; Rosenblatt and Greenland, 1974). In the light of this deficit, I recently completed a study of British adolescent girls and their experiences of fighting. The general orientation and methodology were influenced by ethnographic approaches, and the results were considered in relation to work on the social 'rules' of male fighting. The study was concerned primarily with interpersonal conflicts and their resolution, *not* with instrumental violence carried out for material gain. Instrumental violence does not seem to show evidence of constraining rules and perhaps corresponds more to predatory aggression than to the intra-specific aggression by which personal status is established. This study will be described in the next section.

Social rules and fighting: males and females

Marsh (1978) and Fox (1977) have both offered very similar descriptive accounts of male fights, although the populations studied were quite disparate (a group of football supporters and a small island off the coast of Ireland). Both view the expression of aggression as essentially rule-governed; that is, the parties involved share a tacit, common understanding of the limits and boundaries of a fair fight. Such rules are seen as the cultural and learned equivalent of the rituals of aggression that we have already discussed in connection with animal species. The rules allow dominance to be established within the male group while ensuring that damage is kept to a minimum. Such rules state, for example, that fights should involve equal numbers of pro-tagonists on each side, that some verbal negotiation should precede the introduction of weapons, that certain bodily areas are not legitimate targets for attack, and that attack should be in accord with wrestling and boxing traditions – scratching, spit-ting, hair pulling and biting are 'out of order'. A second important feature of male aggression lies in the way in which it is reported and discussed. Although males are aware of these tacit rules, which limit effective injury, nevertheless in reporting fights a certain level of exaggeration is accepted and even expected. This two-level system has been termed the 'dual rhetoric' of fighting talk (Marsh, 1978). On one level boys report feats of amazing brutality while at the same time admitting that nobody really gets hurt. Ideally, in order to gain adequate access to both the rules and the 'dual rhetoric', the researcher should observe the fight in question directly. In this way, the operationalization of the stated rules can be seen and the ambiguity of the two-level rhetoric resolved. Among males it is relatively easy to gain access to fights. Both Marsh (1978) and Miller (1958) express the view that adolescent males actually seek opportunities to display their courage and belligerence. The football match is the most popular arena for this kind of activity in England. Among females direct observation is much more difficult, as they do not commonly gather together with this kind of aggressive behaviour in mind.

One aim of this study was to investigate the extent to which girls also subscribe to some commonly held set of rules about fighting. While historically and ethologically males commonly engage in intra-specific struggles for dominance, the issue is less clear-cut among females. In primates, for example, the dominance ranking of the female is established largely by oestrus, the rank of her consort and the nursing of offspring. These bio-social factors exert the strongest effect (Jolly, 1972). However, at other times females have been reported to engage in ritual fights among themselves to establish dominance. The parallel with human societies is fairly clear. Biological and economic constraints have forced women in most cultures to seek partnership with males to ensure survival. In most cultures the wife becomes the male's property, and he must not only provide for her but also fight off rivals. Her social position depends on that of her husband. Consequently, she has little need to fight on her own behalf against other females. However, returning to animals, many studies have shown that both sexes demonstrate similar degrees and types of inter-specific aggression. When attacked or when in search of prey, females stalk, attack and kill just as ferociously as males. In inter-specific aggression there is no ritualization, since there is no need to ensure that the victim remains unharmed. It may be that women, even today, understand only this system of fighting – one that recognizes no rules. Such a statement should not in any sense be read as a genetic argument. On the contrary, while little boys are socialized into acknowledging the values and behaviour of fair fighting, girls are strongly discouraged from displaying any aggression. For this reason, they have little opportunity to learn rule-governed fighting in childhood. In adulthood society in general and husbands in particular discourage women from engaging in aggression. The virtues of passivity and nurturance are extolled, and women are sanctioned for any open display of violence. This has probably resulted in the legendary deviousness and 'bitchiness' of women, since verbal and indirect hostility are the only channels of attack allowed to them. Such an argument would posit that when females do fight, they do so without adherence to any limiting rules. Certainly, the media would have us believe that 'cat' fights are tooth-and-nail affairs in which anything goes.

However, two further factors must be taken into account. The first is an historical perspective on female violence. It is virtually impossible to demonstrate an increase in female aggression empirically. Criminal statistics can often be misleading, and the rate of increase over the last decade may either be an artefactual result of changes in police or judicial attitudes towards the arrest of women or may indicate that women have simply begun to fight in more public places where they are more liable to detection. Nevertheless, reports from girls' home superintendents (Hart, 1975), as well as from police, social workers and academics (Adler, 1975; Smith, 1978), tend to suggest a less inhibited attitude among girls to overt aggression in the post-war years. The reasons are likely to be economic and social. Increases in employment opportunities and in wages have given females greater economic independence from men. Social changes have altered prevailing attitudes to women's visibility in the community, so that a woman drinking alone in a pub causes less and less concern. Freedom from unwanted pregnancy has prolonged the 'single' years of girls who were previously married by eighteen. Changes in the education system have meant that boys and girls grow up together and view each other in contexts other than purely romantic or sexual ones. It is not that the women's movement (a predominantly middle-class organization) *per se* has changed women's lives, but that economic and material conditions have opened up new possibilities for work and leisure. Females are enjoying a new and more equitable relationship with males, in which each sex learns from the other. The adolescent girl who spends her teenage years with a heterosexual group may be more likely to learn the rules of 'aggro' at first-hand now than a decade ago, when teenage girls sat in each other's bedrooms reading magazines and dreaming of rock stars. According to such an explanation, girls would be hypothesized to have absorbed some, but not all, of the 'rules' of aggression and perhaps to show less consensus about them than would a group of males.

The other important factor is social class. Virtually all our ideas of femininity, as we have already noted, are derived from the middle-class 'lady'. To be pampered, egotistical, passive, nurturant, care-taking requires a certain level of economic security. In the archetypal working-class family the women takes a far more assertive stance (see Hoggart, 1958). Quite often she is in charge of the family budget and must struggle to feed and clothe husband and children. Often she holds down a full-time job as well as fulfilling her other duties. In Young's and Willmott's (1957) description of working-class life in London it is the females who are the focal point of the family and the neighbourhood. Coping with the stresses and strains of such a lifestyle involves the occasional eruption of antagonism into outright fighting, either verbal or physical. 'Loose' women who might walk off with the economic base of the family (the husband), 'bad' friends who might turn a son's attention from his hard-won apprenticeship are subject to a very direct 'mouthful'. There is also a positive moral value attached to such a stance. While such women are often joked about, they are also respected and accorded the status of those who don't stand for any nonsense. Many writers have drawn attention to the enduring and supportive relationship between women (particularly mother and daughter) in working-class neighbourhoods. The strong bond between the women might find expression in a set of tacit rules that are parallel to, but not isomorphic with, male rules for fighting.

To look further at these various hypotheses, I gave questionnaires to 251 16-year-old schoolgirls from working-class areas of London, Liverpool, Oxford and two areas of Glasgow (a central urban location and a satellite council estate). In addition, I surveyed a group of 60 girls from a Borstal. In order to get more sensitive, qualitative material, I also interviewed a subset of each sample. The discussions were held in groups of about eight girls at a time and they were tape-recorded. The girls did most of the talking, often between themselves, and I intervened (as little as possible) to redirect attention to the topic if it began to stray too far away.

Every single one of the 251 schoolgirls had seen a fight, and 89 per cent had been in at least one themselves. This certainly promotes confidence in their statements about the circumstances and management of fights. The majority of the girls (58 per cent) had begun fighting in childhood, when they were under 10 years old, and 43 per cent had fought within the preceding year. Fights were not very frequent, however. The majority had been in a total of less than five fights, although 26 per cent had fought more than six times in their lives. The schoolgirls were split quite evenly between those who spent most of their time in mixed-sex groups, and those who went around exclusively with girls. Only 3 per cent claimed to hang around only with boys. Those girls who went around with groups of boys and girls were much more likely to have had a number of fights than were girls who spent their time mainly with other girls ($\chi^2 = 6.54$, p < 0.05). In spite of what seemed to me a surprisingly high rate of involvement in fighting among ordinary adolescent girls, only 6 per cent had ever experienced police involvement in a fight, and only 1 per cent had been prosecuted for any violent offence. The girls believed that minor personal disputes that erupted in fights were none of the police's business, although if weapons were involved, the fight became legitimately 'criminal'. This is what some London girls said:

AC   Are you glad when the police arrive?

–   I think it's none of their business.

–   It is none of their business, but it's their duty really, isn't it? That's what they're paid for, to go round and make sure there's no trouble.

–   If it's a fist-fight, it's none of their business. If it's a weapon fight, then it's their duty to stop it. If it's a fist-fight, it's none of their business.

The questionnaire began by asking about the girls' general attitude to fighting. The response was surprisingly negative. On only two of the 10 questions did the majority of girls give a reply that was in any sense favourable towards fighting; 59 per cent of them disagreed with the view that 'fighting is only for boys', and the same number rejected the idea that 'it is only for people who can't argue with words.' Although on most items the girls were equally divided between positive and negative views, they were quite forceful in their opinion that fighting was 'not a laugh' (89 per cent), and that it was 'not the best way to settle disputes' (79 per cent). Overall they held as negative an opinion of male fighting as of female fights. There was no indication at all that girls were contravening their sex role or jeopardizing their femininity by fighting. Far from condemning them for it, boys often encouraged the girls to fight. However, the girls generally agreed that it was immature, quite suitable for kids but not for their soon-to-be-assumed adult status at work. It was interesting to see the contradictions that arose later in the discussion, when they considered, in more detail, the social context of fights. Their restrained moral tone, which had been easy enough to assume in answering abstract questions, revealed much more confusion when looked at in detail.

AC   What would you think of somebody who backed out of having a fight? Would you think, 'Oh, they're very mature and intelligent, and they realize there's no point,' or would you think...?

– Chicken (laughs).

– If you come to think of it like now, it's mature really. After a while you get older, you get to think 'Oh, it's mature,' but before, you think it's chicken. At the time, you think it's chicken.

– If you back out, you think to yourself, 'I should have fought anyway because I'd have shown everyone then that I could have duffed her anyway. So it would have been all right.' So you think 'Maybe I should have done it.'

– If you back out, the other person will get more confidence and then she might try it again and think you're going to chicken out.

– They keep on picking on you if you've given up, so you've just got to show them.

The contradictions indicated that the girls were in a period of transition, not simply from childhood to adulthood, but also from schoolgirl to career girl. A veneer of sophistication had been assumed in tune with their projected entry into 'glamour' jobs; many wanted to be models, receptionists, air hostesses and journalists. All were socially aspiring. They wanted to leave the estates and 'make it'. So to some extent their rather superior attitude to fighting was part of a social-class contradiction. Quite what would happen to this attitude when the darker realities of unemployment and factory jobs intervened is open to speculation.

Boys were frequently accused of 'showing off', both in the amount of damage that they claimed to inflict and in the current fashion for carrying weapons.

- They think it's really good to carry a knife.
- I think they'd use it if they were with friends just to show off.
- They say 'You need it,' but they just carry it to show off.

One of the girls was particularly scathing about a boy who had capitalized on being in prison in order to improve his 'hard' reputation.

- We know this boy. He got nicked – he was using a knife. And when he was in prison, his Mum came to see him like and he said 'Mum, get me out of here' – you know, when he was with his Mum. But when his mates came, he was really big-headed. Now he's outside, you think, 'Oh, he's been inside,' so he goes, 'Don't muck about with me, else I'll go back. I'm not afraid. I've seen it – its nothing.' But when he was with his Mum he was saying, 'Oh, get me out. I hate it in here.'

There was a healthy scepticism about boys' accounts of fights. The girls certainly gave every indication that they were as fully aware of the 'dual rhetoric' as the boys themselves. The difference was that girls openly expressed their cynicism about the machismo male (at least among themselves), while boys on the whole conspired with each other to maintain the illusion of violence by mutually supporting exaggerations. As we shall see later on, the 'bullshit factor' of aggressive talk was far more evident in the Borstal girls than among the schoolgirls, who on the whole admitted that rather little real damage ever occurred in girls' fights.

Although one London girl described a fairly violent fight that she had witnessed between a boy and his girlfriend, there was surprisingly little mention of violence between boys and girls in the context of romantic relationships. Their talk about this kind of domestic violence sounded distinctly theoretical rather than practical. The girls endorsed the idea of a dominant and decisive male; nobody wanted to go out with a 'drip'. The question of whether or not the male should demonstrate his dominance by the use of brute force was the focus of some dissent.

AC   What about when you get married? Will you fight with your husband?

–   Not all the time.

–   But I wouldn't expect it to be right if we didn't. Once in a blue moon.

–   I'd never fight.

–   No, not fighting-punching. Just verbal arguments.

AC   What if he hit you?

–   I'd like that.

–   No, if a guy ever hit me, I'd walk away and never see him again.

–   Like if I was going out with a guy and I was keeping on at him, I'd like him to turn round and slap me. I wouldn't like him to just stand there and take it.

–   If he told me to shut up, that'd be all right but I wouldn't like a guy to hit me.

It would be fair to say that the old idea of the 'original sin' of females lingers on. Given half a chance, the girls suggested, they would try to dominate or to take advantage of males. In order to prevent this, they seemed to feel that they needed chastisement and should show repentance. This was seen as the duty of any red-blooded male. Being 'in love' seemed to embody notions of dependence, fear and respect – for females only. Miller's (1958) paper on working-class male 'focal concerns' or values meshes well with the kinds of statements made by these girls. The male must be tough, straightforward and superior; to complement husband or boyfriend in this precarious and demanding role, the girl must comply by being weak, devious and inferior. Such qualities, if carried over to the same girl's relationships with friends of either sex, would be very negatively viewed.

The girls more often (especially in Glasgow) spoke of being hit by males who were not boyfriends. Their attitude here seemed to be different. They certainly did not enjoy being hit, but they were willing to accept that if they could belt boys, the converse should also hold. There was a reluctant egalitarianism about it, in spite of the obvious physical superiority of males. However, the girls were not above playing to male gallantry if it might deter a punch.

AC   What about fights between blokes and girls?

– That's the best kind.

– Sometimes a boy wouldn't hit a lassie, would they?

– That's what happened to me. There was this guy with the yellow suit, he thinks he'd dead good. He was standing talking about my big brother and I told him to shut up. There was about nine or ten guys there and there was me and my pal. And he went to hit me and I know if he'd hit me he would have killed me 'cos I was really being dead cheeky and I said, 'Ay, on you go – prove yourself to your pals.' It was the only thing I could think of to say. As soon as I said that his pals said, 'You're not going to hit a lassie are you?' He says 'No.' Then I just walked away. Sometimes guys, if they're not thinking, turn round and belt you. But a lot of lassies deserve it. I mean, I know I deserved it a couple of times and I've been lucky not to get it. I wouldn't blame a guy for hitting a lassie.

– I think it's all fair.

- If a lassie can go up and slap a boy in the jaw for saying something, why can't he go up and slap her for saying the same thing?

AC A guy wouldn't put all his weight behind it?

- The guy who punched me did.

- It was a different thing. That wasn't – he wasn't coming to get you.

- He was going for someone else but he just took me instead.

- You were just standing there so he punched you, but probably if he'd have thought about it, he wouldn't have done it so sore.

AC Do they hold back at all if you're a girl?

- I think they do.

- If it's a square-go, I don't think so.

- I think they would.

Several cases were discussed in which girls who attempted to interfere in fights were hit by boys. Fox (1977), in his discussion of Tory Island fighting, suggests that women play a key role in preventing fights:

> someone was bringing wee Johnny's weeping mother forward; the crowd parted for the old lady. With prayers and admonitions she pleaded with wee Johnny to come home and not disgrace her like this in front of friends and neighbours. Saints were liberally invoked and the Blessed Virgin implored often. People hung their heads. Johnny, looking dazed, told her to quiet herself – and hurled himself at Paddy and his group: 'I'd have had your blood if me mother hadn't come. Ye can thenk her that you're not in pieces on the road, ye scum.' (p. 142)

It would seem that the placating and intermediary role of the inviolable female is now a thing of the past, however.

By far the most common form of fighting was between girls. Out of all the fights that the 251 girls described, 73 per cent were against other girls. Fights mostly commonly happened either in the street (74 per cent) or at school (29 per cent). Only 9 per cent of female fights happened in a pub or a discotheque. Of course, it is quite likely that any incipient trouble would be taken outside on to the street, either at the manager's suggestion or by the girls themselves. In perfect support of the importance of the peer group in aggression, 88 per cent of the girls were with friends when the fights occurred. In examining the reasons that the girls offered for the fights, issues of public status and integrity emerged often, and, like males, the girls were keen to impress the assembled audience of acquaintances with their courage. In 75 per cent of cases the girl fought just one other girl, although a surprising number suggested that their friends had intervened to help them out (52 per cent). Questions about who had made the last remark before the fight and who had struck the first blow revealed no consistent pattern. Many of the girls were reluctant to state precisely what was said before the fight began, perhaps for fear of offending the researcher's delicate sensibilities. Those who did reply most commonly offered as causes slurs on their sexual reputation, such as 'slag', 'tart', 'scrubber' (18 per cent), or remarks directly related to the topic of the dispute – for example, 'You nicked my boyfriend' or 'You told her I was a liar' (18 per cent). In 12 per cent of cases there was a straightforward piece of abuse ('Sod off', 'Fuck you'), and in a further 10 per cent, a direct challenge to fight ('Make me', 'Go on, hit me'). Instances of racial insult were so low as to be negligible.

By far the majority of the fights happened over issues of personal integrity. False accusations gainst a girl, gossip behind her back and suggestions of a pejorative nature about sexual morality, delinquency and intelligence all fell into this category. Attacks on personal integrity included all abuse of a girl's private and public self-concept. Failure to retaliate would inevitably have meant a loss of face. Such provocations accounted for 35 per cent of all fights. A further 10 per cent involved issues of loyalty (that is, where the personal integrity of any friend or relative was at stake). In their absence, the girls stepped in to defend their friends' good name. Nine per cent of fights occurred as a result of jealousy of another girl who was flirting with a boyfriend, and a further 9 per cent over minor frustrations, such as being in a bad mood, feeling irritated by another girl's stupidity and so on. Only 2 per cent of fights were about race, and only 1 per cent were instrumental acts of violence to gain money.

The girls believed that boys and girls fought for much the same reasons.

AC What do girls fight about?

– Boys.

– Ripping up one another's clothes and calling each other names.

– Jealousy.

– Breaking up best friends.

AC What sort of names?

– Slag, things like that.

AC What do boys fight about?

– Girls.

– Who's better than who.

– 'I've seen you with her.'

– Chickening out – they say, 'Oh, you chickened out of that,' and fight about it to show they're tough.

AC Does machismo work for girls too?

– Yeah, yeah.

– It does.

– There's always some girl you say, 'I wouldn't have a fight with her,' but when it comes to it you do.

AC So, do they fight about the same thing or not?

– Boils down to the same thing, really, 'cos girls fight over boys, boys fight over girls. Fight for their pride, things like that, and boys fight about the same things.

- A girl that's been called a slag is the same as a boy that's been called a chicken.

- But they [boys] never fight when they're by themselves. They've always got to have a crowd.

- *Groups of boys will fight for the sake of just being groups.*

- *Girls don't do that really, do they?*

- I don't think girls just go round in a group and fight another girl group.

- You get some – it's usually individuals talking to another group – fighting and then they'll all join in, but it's not like that with boys.

Although fundamental motives for the fight might be common to both sexes, the girls suggested the group basis of male fighting was distinctive. This seemed to be a common theme among the schoolgirls' accounts. Boys' involvement in fighting seemed closely linked with maintaining loyalty in the group and a sense of solidarity between members. Girls' fights were most often of a personal nature between individuals, although friends were nearly always present to lend moral support and to provide an appreciative audience. Boys, on the other hand, were seen to fight not only over personal grievances, but also merely because they were part of a distinctive group, whose reputation for toughness had to be maintained. This group basis of male fighting finds expression in the football supporters (described by Marsh, 1978), as well as in the gangs that Miller has investigated. In both cases the male group provides opportunities for individual members to demonstrate their toughness.

Male gangs were talked about by the inner-city schoolgirls. They were most evident in Glasgow, where they have a long history (see Patrick, 1973). In Glasgow the gangs were predominantly all-male, although girls would join in where it was necessary.

AC Do you mean a real gang with a proper name? Or just a group of people?

- No, real gang.

- In the town you've got the Cowards, the Cumby, the Tongs. . . .

- Hundreds of them.

- Blue Angels.

- It's more or less the names of the places they come from.

- Drummie team.

- There's a lot of people from Drumchapel. Then you've got lots of people from Posel.

- The Carlton Tongs and all that.

- They don't fight or anything. It's just, 'Right, that crowd come from Carlton. Call them Carlton Tongs.' It doesn't mean they're going to go out and start trouble. It's just to separate them out.

AC   They don't wear similar clothes?

- No.

- They all wear polo necks and V-necks and anoraks.

- Things like that – knocked off.

- If one of them's got a new sweater, they've all got a new sweater.

AC   Do you consider yourself part of the team?

- No.

- But say we were up the town and there was a crowd of guys, and there was a crowd of lassies jumping in. Just say Drumchapel were fighting Carlton and then the lassies jumped in, I think it would be really necessary to jump in. But I wouldn't consider us part of a team.

- If someone came up and said, 'We need you, you've got to help us out,' then we'd jump in.

AC   Would they do it for you?

- Aye, they've done it many a time.

AC Would you bring a bloke in to help you fight a girl?

- No.

- No, but see there's a lot of lassies that'll say . . . If I say, 'Right, I'll see you outside,' they'll not know whether I'm going to go out and get a team. I mean one night somebody was fighting me, there was this big team waiting for me. It was someone I knew and there was this big team of guys and lassies standing there, and I took a couple of pals and this lassie who'd a big team felt dead stupid 'cos we just toddled out ourselves. It was funny.

AC What happens if you change areas? Do you change teams?

- No.

- Depends what age you're at.

- Say if somebody gets a doing or they're jumped or something like that – our team will help us out, then you get one team fighting with another.

- I'd be scared to go up that hill at night, because I'm terrified of that place.

- If you were up there and say someone was digging you up, saying 'Where do you stay?', you say 'Pure Glen,' they'd say 'PGB' – two opposite teams. They'd get their team to fight yours.

The gangs were based on area and any trouble that might happen seemed to be restricted to the gangs themselves when they met, often in the neutral territory of the town centre. The gangs did seem loyal to girls and children in their own area, and the extent of criminal activity seemed quite low, restricted to petty theft and vandalism. The impact of the gang on the community did not seem very marked. Although their names were often emblazoned with aerosol paint on walls and tenements, they did not have distinctive uniforms and strictly defined territories. These features in the United States seem most pertinent to the levels of violence (Marsh and Campbell, 1978b). In New York a territory is rigidly defined and adhered to. To venture out of it wearing 'colours' is to invite trouble. Things had not reached such a level in Glasgow, although knives were being carried and used. Within the gangs or 'teams', nutters were tolerated with good humour.

- He's daft, he's crazy. This crowd – Posel. He wanted to fight with the Posel. He says, 'I'm going to have you.' So they expected a big great team all to be standing there. So they go away and get all this team – hundreds of them. And there he is, all by himself, saying, 'C'mon, I'll have you all' – millions of them.
- The thing is, I don't think anyone of them would have touched him.

- He's daft.

- He's a grand guy but he's mental.

Discussion with the teaching staff, social workers and lawyers in Glasgow did nothing to convince me that the girls' stories of 'chibbings' were fictitious. Many incidents were known to the staff, who had occasionally tried to prevent serious fights by involving parents who knew little of their sons' extra-curricular activities.

In London too 'gangs' were mentioned. In addition, the girls were convinced that all-female gangs existed.

AC Are there girl gangs in London?

- Yeah, Drapsey.

AC What do they do?

- Take your jewellery or just frighten you, take your money, things like that.

AC Just on the street?

- Yeah.

AC   Has this happened to you around here, around South London?

–   Most of it is South London. This side and Lambeth, East End, Poplar Way.

–   My cousin went to a club and all these girls come up and said, 'Oh, that's a nice ring, can we see it?' So my cousin just showed them and they said, 'We're not going to give it to you now.' So my cousin called over all her friends and they said, 'You'd better give her back that ring,' and they gave it her back. (Laughs)

AC   But they were going to take it, were they?

–   If you're going to school, you know, everyone's got sovereigns and gate bracelets these days. You never come home with them if you get in a gang. That's the sort of thing they do.

AC   Do you think some girls have got real reputations for fighting – who are known as really tough girls?

–   Coxwell Manor – they think they have, always going round fighting. Until they get beaten up, then they shut up.

–   But girls with reputations usually go round in gangs.

–   Yeah.

–   Then there's the gang leader. The one with the best reputation is the gang leader.

AC   So, in these gangs they actually have a sort of leader and she's like the toughest?

–   Yeah.

AC   How does somebody get to be leader?

–   Being toughest, having the most fights.

–   They probably usually go round picking fights just to be leader.

–   Standing up to teachers and things like that at school.

     –   Cheeking teachers – that's meant to be big.

AC   You know these girls that go round just in the female groups, what's their attitude to blokes? Do they go out with blokes as well?

     –   They do, yeah.

The girls themselves, however, suggested that gang fighting was far from typical of their own fights, particularly with respect to two factors. First, their experience with aggression, unlike that of the gangs, was unconnected with economic gain; second, most of their fights occurred on the basis of a one-to-one confrontation, at least initially. It was considered the boys' prerogative to get into group fights.

In order to investigate the extent to which female fights are constrained by rules, the questionnaire offered 18 examples of various actions that might be performed in a fight, and the girls were asked to indicate whether or not it would be 'OK' to do any or all of them. The notion of social rule not only implies a behavioural imperative but also carries with it a moral statement. It suggests that a course of action should not be taken because it would be wrong – it would break certain subculturally agreed conventions about personal conduct and integrity. In a perfectly rule-governed world one would, of course, anticipate 100 per cent consensus on the composition of the rules. However, this is rarely achieved, either because some individuals (peripherals or non-members) may be ignorant of the rules or because the rules themselves may be in a state of change, of which only some members are aware. Similarly, some rules are conditional; they state that X may not be done *unless* Y. Inadequate specification of the situational constraints may then lead to disagreement. In the present material, however, a rule was said to exist when it received endorsement by at least 75 per cent of the population. Such a criterion is more stringent than has been usually accepted (see Argyle et al., 1979) and is particularly so as the present sample was drawn from five different geographical and social locations.

Proscriptive rules (those that state what *must not* be done) are more common in this sample than prescriptive rules (which state what *should be* done). Eleven proscriptive rules emerged, of which seven showed the required level of consensus. Five of these were related to the social setting and stage management aspects of the fight: you should not take on more than one person at a time, ask you friends to join in, get your friends to call the police or report the fight to the police or school yourself. These rules clearly have the effect of withholding access to agents of the adult world and of limiting the fight to a fair one-to-one situation. The proscribed behaviours related to the use of either bottles or knives, thus limiting the extent of possible damage. The two significant prescriptive rules that emerged stated that it was OK to punch and slap. Kicking very nearly met the 75 per cent consensus criterion.

Items were included that, it was presumed, boys would have ruled as 'out of order'. These were biting, using handbags, scratching, tearing clothing and carrying on fighting after the opponent is on the ground. In every case except scratching, the majority of girls also ruled them as 'not OK'. They did not, however, achieve 75 per cent consensus. (Tearing clothing was most strongly rejected by 72.9 per cent of girls.) The results suggest that female rules operate at a macro-level to prevent detection and to limit damage. They are not as finely tuned as those of boys to disqualify behaviours that might result in the drawing of blood (scratching, biting and fighting opponents who can no longer defend themselves).

Some of the girls disagreed with their peers and rejected many of the accepted rules. Taking three of the most universally endorsed rules, it was possible to see their interrelation with other rules by performing χ^2 tests across items. What emerged from such an analysis was that those same 'black sheep' who were prepared to tell the school about the fight were also likely to break other proscriptive rules by telling the police and parents and by getting friends to stop the fight or call in the police. Those girls who believed it was OK to use knives in a fight were also likely to endorse their tough image by breaking other rules of fair fighting; they were more likely than the other girls to take on more than one person at a time, to use abusive names, to bite an opponent, to use a bottle and to carry on fighting when the other person is on the ground.

These two types of subcultural 'deviant' are quite distinct. The first is a goody-goody who rushes to adults when things get too rough for her. Such behaviour is likely to isolate her even further from her peer group. The second type of girl tries to aggrandize her tough image by ignoring all limits within a fight. She may be ignorant of the rules either through inexperience or because her habitual peer group is composed of individuals whose behaviour would be condemned even by their contemporaries. As we shall see later, many of the tougher Borstal girls seemed to project this anomic image.

So, girls do have rules for fair fighting, at least in the abstract. Because the last section of the questionnaire asked each girl to describe a specific fight in which she had been involved, it was possible to look at the relationships between the rules to which she personally subscribed and at the behaviour of her opponent and herself as she reported it. This was done by a χ^2 analysis for each rule and its corresponding behaviour.

In virtually all cases there was a significant correspondence between rule and behaviour. Thus even though all girls may not agree on the existence of any given rule, each girl fights with respect to what she believes the rule to be. Not too much should be made of this result, however, since there is an obvious demand for consistency within the questionnaire itself. Girls may have lied about their own behaviour in the fight in order to make it congruent with their previous statements about rules. But it is noteworthy that their opponents were seen as adhering to the rules of fighting as closely as they themselves did. Opponents who fought 'dirty' were, in fact, acting within the boundaries of the less stringent rules to which some of the girls adhered.

The questionnaire results produced some anomalies and inconsistencies that were explored, though not always resolved, in discussion with the girls. 'Fair fights' or 'square-gos' were essentially one-to-one fights with limiting rules. But the business of establishing how strict this one-on-one rule was proved puzzling. Most girls initially endorsed it at an abstract level but then proceeded to offer examples of its breakage and suggested some conditions under which it would no longer hold.

> *AC* What about something like more than one person picking on someone?

- I've had that.

- I've had that happen to me. I've never been in a fight where I've asked someone else to come in, I just wouldn't do it. I wouldn't like no one to do it to me, so I wouldn't do it back to no one – even if I was losing.

AC So it should be just one person to one and you wouldn't want your friends coming in to help you?

- No, I wouldn't.

AC Even if you got beaten, you wouldn't want them to come in and help?

- It wouldn't be you, would it? They'd say that you hide behind your friends.

- It's not your fight, it's a gang fight, isn't it?

- Say, if there's three of them and one of you and they start picking on you, so I go, 'Yeah, you're really big when there's three of you, let one of you come.' And they say, 'You go, I go, I go,' and I say, 'Anyone, it doesn't matter, just one of you.'

AC What do you think about more than one person on one person?

- I think it's better to fight with one person – more than one person if you can handle it – but if you can't there's no point in trying, is there?

AC Would you feel outraged if, say, three girls picked on you all at once?

- I think even if you've got some mates and they've got some mates, not all of them would start on you, it would be one-to-one.

- Mainly they'll only start 'cos there's one person they're picking on.

- They'll always jump in if they think you're losing, like, 'She ain't going to say that our gang's the weakest.' They always jump in and say, 'We bashed the rest of them.' Even if some of them lose, the majority of them won.

- It's the gang.

- It's the gang's name, not yours.

A similar pattern was described in another location, where just as much confusion was apparent.

- She walked outside. All night she had been putting on an English accent. It sounded dead convincing. And we called her 'Sassanach' – words worse than that. She turned to walk away and Marian booted her so she turned round and skudded the whole five. Then she ran away and got all of us. 'Cos there were five of us and five of them, so it was fair. But her pals went off. . . .

- There were two of us onto her.

- The way we were fighting. I was trying to get her down but the others were trying to keep her up to kick her so I just left her to fight, and I'm crawling about the floor . . . and these three guys were standing about, holding our coats and bags. So this guy dumped them and he dived in as well.

AC What about two people fighting one?

- No.

- It really depends where you are, though. If you're in school or something, it's sort of like . . . most of the time it's one-to-one.

- If a person's stronger than you and you're getting a doing – you expect your pal to jump in.

- Even if you don't expect it, she does it anyway.

AC If she came to help you, would you stop fighting?

- No.

- It depends if she's stronger than you, right?

 −   If you were down and your pal just dived in, helped
     you. Just saving you getting a doing.

AC   Would you start a fight – two of you against one?

 −   No, start it a square-go, and if you're getting a doing,
     somebody else jumps in.

The rule at best seem flexible. Other girls do come in to help if
one of their friends is losing, and in the second example two
Glasgow girls picked on one girl without any qualms. In fact, the
girl they fought was so badly hurt that she couldn't get up and
had 'blood coming out of her head'. The girls were sufficiently
worried (either about her well-being or about the involvement of
the police) to return to the alley, pick her up and walk her down
to the station.

Group fights are acknowledged to be qualitatively different
from fair fights. The involvement of girls in these fights seems to
occur only if there are also girls fighting on the other side.
Otherwise group fighting remains an exclusively male affair.
Negotiating the size of the encounter can be a problem, as can
be seen from the Glasgow 'nutter' example. Clearly, a large gang
will not pick on two or three girls, and negotiations, sometimes
explicit, have to be entered into as to who will or will not be
involved in the fight.

Fights are usually ended by the participants (25 per cent), by
bystanders (18 per cent), or by adults in authority (34 per cent).
The girls suggested that to go on fighting someone who was
incapable of defending herself was 'out of order'.

AC   When do you stop a fight? When do you say, 'OK,
       that's enough'?

 −   You don't.

 −   When you feel you've made your point, really. Some-
     times if you back out in the middle of a fight, they think
     maybe they should run after you, and it starts all over
     at the beginning.

 −   If you've got someone up in a corner or on the floor,
     then you say 'Had enough?' and then back off.

AC   So you'd ask them that?

–   Yeah.

–   Or when you see that they're going down. 'Cos there's no use getting someone on the floor and keep beating and beating them.

–   You just sort of give them a last warning and say, 'You do it again and you know what you'll get.'

AC   How do fights usually end? Are they often broken up by people coming in?

–   In school they are.

AC   What about other places?

–   I suppose it's the same.

–   I suppose it's the same. You always get a crowd when there's a fight. Then someone's got the sense to break it up.

AC   Do you think all that's changing, people's willingness to intervene?

–   Yeah.

–   It's none of your business no more.

AC   Why's that?

–   You get clobbered.

–   You don't get involved because you don't know if they're fighting with friends or anything like that. You've got your life in danger, right, and then again you've got people who say, 'Those nosey parkers, I saw it, they started it and now they're trying to stop it.' Know what I mean? And you can get into trouble. It's more of a risk trying to stop a fight than it is to have a fight, I think.

–   Any other times, to stop a fight, you was the hero.

–   Yeah.

– You was good, but now they say, 'Oh troublesome, nosey cow, you should have left it alone, it was getting good, it was.' (Laughter)

AC Really, you think things are changing that much?

– Yeah, they do.

– Yeah, I think they do.

– People have got more violent.

– If you try and stop a fight, you end up in it. You'll probably end up the worse one.

– Or the watchers will knock you back and say, 'Get out of it.'

– Yeah, 'cos they're really enjoying it.

– Most of them seem to enjoy it.

AC Have you ever had a fight in a place where it couldn't be stopped? What I mean is, have you ever had it in the sort of place that nobody would ever come to?

– (Pause) No.

– (Pause) No.

AC Maybe it's partly because people are willing to fight, because in a way they know that sooner or later it's got to be stopped? Because if something didn't happen to stop it, there'd be murders on the street everyday. That's why you've got to have some sort of mechanism to stop it going too far.

– There's always someone to stop it, 'cos if you have a fight and you started the argument in public then the public's going to follow you, aren't they?

– Yeah, unless someone's watching them and they say, 'Oh look, we were just going.'

– Or it's stopped when the police come or something. Everybody legs it.

- Yeah, or they just want so see more, they just want to see how far they can go. How far it takes them to see blood. They're more vicious.

- You say they're more vicious and you have to fight back but they've got violent and vicious somehow.

AC But do you think it's something to do with the sight of blood?

- Yeah.

AC Do you imagine if you actually saw blood, you'd probably stop and think, 'Oh, my God, what have I done?'?

- Yeah, you do.

- Yeah, if you saw blood on somebody else you're more likely to stop than if you saw blood on yourself.

There is a suggestion here that community involvement in limiting fights is beginning to break down. Onlookers don't want to become involved, although at the same time they get a vicarious pleasure from watching the fight. Control over the amount of damage then has to come from the fighters themselves by limiting the seriousness of their own attacks.

When we discussed the rules of behaviour within the fight itself, the initial response from most samples was that scratching, biting and so on were 'out of order'. Kudos was gained by approximating as closely as possible to male fights. As one London girl said, 'Some of the tough girls punch.' The Glasgow girls' reaction was fairly typical:

AC How did you fight?

- Same way as usual. I pulled her by the hair and kicked her in the face.

AC What did you kick her with?

- My foot and my knee.

AC What do you think about scratching and biting?

- It's a cat's game.

- I think it's stupid. There's no point in it. It's not really square. It's not a square-go then.

AC   What's a square-go?

- Well, fists and feet and no like using weapons or anything like that.

AC   You've never been involved in scratching or hair pulling?

- When I was a wain I was.

Almost immediately after statements such as these followed a series of completely contradictory stories of admitted cat-fighting.

AC   How much damage was done in the fight?

- None, really, she might have scratched – that's it.

AC   And slapping?

- There was some slapping but she couldn't catch me.

AC   Would slapping be all right?

- Yeah, I'd do it back.

AC   Have you ever seen blokes slap?

- No, punch mainly.

AC   Do you think girls fight differently?

- Yeah, some.

- They scratch, bite.

AC   You don't think a bloke would do that?

- No.

- Yeah.

- I've seen blokes do that.

- Some of the tough girls punch.

- I've been in lots of different fights 'cos I've got a quick temper. One of the fights was 'cos this girl, she's younger than me but every time I passed her, she used to give me dirty looks. And one time, I was in the shop and she give me a really dirty look and when she was walking out, she knocked my book out of my hand. And all my friends told me I should do something about it, but I didn't do anything about it and when we came to school, I threw my drink at her and messed her clothes up, and I asked her if she's going to waste her drink. She'd just opened a tin – she threw the whole tin at me and I had a fight then. And there was a lot of scratching and that. She got most of it and I just got a scratch on my hand.

AC   And how did you fight then?

- Kicked her, bit, slapped.

- I never used to pull anyone's hair.

- I used to bite a lot.

- If they had long hair. I used to grab some of that.

The girls generally applauded male fighting behaviour and believed that more kudos accrued to girls who emulated 'clean' fights. Nevertheless, they were not above resorting to dirty tactics if their opponent did.

AC   Do you think that there are limits – that, say, you don't use knives and you don't kick people when you're on the floor?

- I think there is.

- Unless you're really out for blood. If you just want to show them that you can fight them, you just give them a good duffing that they'll remember – a few bruises or such, don't give them concussion or punch in their ribs.

- Yeah, but you get more respect if you fight and you fight cleanly, than if you fight dirty.

- If they've beaten up your little sister and they've put her in hospital for cracked ribs, you're going to come out and get blood off them, aren't you?

- Yeah, but that's fighting dirty, because if you fight dirty you're going to fight ... the other person's going to fight dirty, aren't they?

- Yeah, if they know you fight dirty, then you're going to get dirty fighting back because they're going to be prepared as well. If you're someone who fights with a knife, they're going to come with a knife, or something else, you know.

The general opinion was that it was better to receive rather than give the first punch.

- If the other person punches you first, you feel really angry but it's harder to do the first punch, in a way.

- Also, you've got something to haggle against, you know. She hit me, it's self-defence – I hit her back.

- If you hit the first punch and you get beat up, they say, 'Oh, look, she started fighting,' and you couldn't take care of yourself.

This was quite opposed to the more aggressive view of the Borstal girls. The general pattern, however, seemed to be that when the girls really lost their temper, they abandoned rules completely. Scratching and biting were endorsed as OK if you were 'stuck and going down'. However, the girls generally saw weapon fighting by females as 'out or order'. Some suggested that they might employ weapons if they were in a tight spot, but most said they would not use a weapon under any conditions. Although some said that they feared the amount of damage they might inflict, nobody suggested that she was personally afraid of being hurt.

AC   Would you be prepared to use weapons under certain circumstances?

- Yeah, you'd be prepared to use them, yeah.

- Yeah.

- I wouldn't fight if there was going to be weapons.

- I don't think I'd use them.

AC   Why?

- I've got a quick temper. I'd probably kill someone. So I would never try to fight with a weapon.

AC   You don't really trust yourself, then?

- Yeah, I'd try and back out, I would.

The use of weapons among girls seemed to be one of the critical differences between those in Borstal and those in school. While it is possible that this was only one aspect of the Borstal girls' tendency to exaggerate, this seems improbable, since some of the schoolgirls also tended to exaggerate the injury that they had caused in fights. But the damage of which they boasted was always inflicted by fists, not knives.

In the next extract one girl boasts of the extensive damage she inflicted on a male classmate. Her claims are followed by a contradiction – an immediate denial that anyone ever really got hurt. Then the girl quickly offers various examples of knifings in the area. (These allegations were checked with teachers who assured me that they were, in fact, accurate.)

- The teacher went out of the class and I started fighting with this boy. So teacher came in and he was sitting with his face burst open and blood all over his face. So I said, 'Sir, George Best fell off his chair and hit his head on the radiator,' and the teacher looked at him and there was no radiator near him. And he said, 'Was that you?' and I said, 'No.' Then I said, 'Aye, it was.' So he sent us down to Mrs Lavery, but I wouldn't go. So he says, 'Come down with me to Mr Docherty,' so I went down to the boys' headmaster and he says, 'Take George down and give him a wash but give her 300 lines.' But I wouldn't do it.

AC How much damage gets done in fights?

– Not that much.

– Black eyes.

– The worst thing I've ever had is a black eye – that's when I was fighting a lassie and her pal kicked me in the face.

AC You've never had stitches?

– Aye, my big sister had 18 stitches.

AC So fights aren't really that dangerous?

– No.

– It depends who's in it.

– It just starts off a wee fight and somebody can't handle it. They get a doing, they get someone else and you get two teams fighting each other – somebody always gets hurt.

– They shows off when they're in a big crowd.

– We're talking about fights saying there's no damage, but a man got murdered the other week, on his birthday.

– John Duglash got done in.

– And Mal got done in as well.

– Dougie got done in.

AC What do you mean by 'done in'?

– Stabbed, not killed.

– That was the same guys that done it. That happened that night two guys were out on the rampage for anything and we were on the bus. The bus got really packed. My big brother was on it. There was this guy Miff and your big brother was on it and we were all just sitting. And they were carrying the joke a bit too far and all shouting and bawling. Then the guy finally says,

'Look, the bus is stopping, the police are coming on the bus.' And someone set the alarm off but he got off the bus at his own stop, the guy that had done it. So I went down the stairs and some people came down and the doors wouldn't open so somebody opened the doors and we all bailed out and the police came running across the street. Me and Leslie just walked up the road. They never said anything to us. My big brother ran right up the stairs. The next day we hear that Miff had got stabbed. Him and George ran down the road and there were these two guys and they walked up to them and says, 'What are you doing? Jumping off the bus to chase us?' And my brother says, 'No, we weren't, we jumped off 'cos the police were coming on the bus.' Next minute George saw the guy had a knife and he said to Miff, 'Run quick.' and George started to run but Miff didn't catch on. The guy just stuck it in his back. The same night they slashed a guy, slashed all his face.

– His face was all wired up.

However, no examples were given of female 'chibbings'. These seemed to be an exclusively male activity. The same pattern was evident in the other urban locations. In London, for example, there were some descriptions of the damage that the girls had allegedly inflicted, which sounded fairly exaggerated.

– I just hit him and he fell off his bike and I busted his nose, gave him a thick lip, black eye. That was all.

AC   How did you hit him?

– Punching him. He pushed me against the wall and so I stuck my knee up and pulled his face to my knee, that's about it.

AC   You're a professional.

– I am. (Laughs)

– I just started with her, and then the police and her Ma came and her Ma started shouting at me, 'Look at the state of my daughter's face. Look at her knees.'

AC   How did you fight?

–   Same way as usual – I pulled her hair and kicked her in the face.

This method of attack occurred fairly regularly in the interviews among the 'hard' girls in different locations. Instrumental hair-pulling of this kind was considered well within the rules of the fight.

In spite of the aggressive-sounding tactics, by far the majority of the schoolgirls had fought with a friend or acquaintance. In practically all cases there was no lasting grudge; and girls later reunited and remained friends. Very little serious damage occurred during the fights described. Among most schoolgirls there was a tendency to say that the opponent came off the worst; in only 15.1 per cent of cases did the opponents sustain no damage at all. The most common injuries to the opponent were bruises (46.2 per cent), cuts (24.7 per cent) and scratches (20.3 per cent). With respect to themselves, schoolgirls admitted to sustaining bruises (41.0 per cent) and scratches (21.9 per cent), but 25.5 per cent said they had received no injuries at all. A very small proportion claimed to have knocked out the other person's teeth (2 per cent) or broken her bones (6.8 per cent).

It seems that girls are more willing than boys to acknowledge the relative harmlessness of fighting. Machismo seems to be gained by girls merely by virtue of being *willing* to fight, rather than by 'bullshitting' about the devastation caused to the opponent's face. This was borne out in the items relating to who had won the fight. There was a surprisingly low response rate to the questions about why the fight was stopped, who won and how victory was recognized. While this may be because such facts are too well understood to be made explicit, it is equally plausible that the girls were genuinely unable to answer such questions. Since 51.8 per cent of schoolgirls did not seem to know who had won, and 55 per cent had no idea how to tell who had won, it is hard to determine what they see as the point of fighting. It may be no more that a demonstration of certain qualities (toughness, determination, positive self-concept), which are confirmed merely by participation in the fight rather than necessarily winning. Perhaps a large number of respondents lost fights and were unwilling to admit it. Of those that did reply, the vast majority claimed that they had won. Among the schoolgirls the victor was determined by the submission of the opponent. Fights were believed to stop because they were becoming too dangerous, although the small amount of serious injury sustained and the ability to recognize and respond to a submission gesture probably both militated against any real danger of physical damage.

The picture that emerges of adolescent girls' fighting is remarkably similar to that of fights among males. Unfortunately, there are no directly comparable data with respect to boys, since most accounts are impressionistic and interpretative. Boys verbal accounts of fights to each other are available, but the public setting in which such material was gathered probably encouraged individual exaggeration. Perhaps on an anonymous questionnaire such as this one boys too would be more likely to admit openly to the relatively safe nature of teenage fighting. Certainly, in the interviews girls were somewhat more prone to tell tales of heroics and brutality than they had been on paper. Girls do seem to have rules, many of which are common to boys also. The rules are easier to voice in the abstract than to apply, however. 'Dirty' tactics were used by some girls and had a contagious effect: if one girl began scratching, the other would do it too. On the whole, clean fights were most applauded, although rules could be broken if the cause of the fight were sufficiently serious or if a girl lost her temper because she was injured or unfairly attacked. Even so, serious injury was very rare. The adult world was refused access to fights by virtue of the commonly agreed proscription against telling parents, teachers or police. The girls, even in the tougher areas, condemned the use of knives and deplored the fact that more and more boys were carrying and sometimes using them.

Contrary to popular opinion, rather few female fights were over boys. Most girls agreed that it just was not worth it. Fights were about keeping 'face' in front of friends and were triggered, as with boys, by issues of personal integrity. Willingness to fight was generally seen as sufficient testament to a girl's integrity, regardless of whether she ultimately won. The girls did not give any indication of fighting for the sake of it. They did not fight as groups to defend either reputation or territory, nor did they seek out public arenas in which to demonstrate their bravery. This kind of behaviour was seen as the prerogative (and foolishness) of males.

The Borstal girls

The girls to whom I spoke in Borstal were somewhat older than the schoolgirls; 32 per cent were over eighteen. Their degree of criminal involvement was also very much higher. An astonishing 75 per cent reported that the police had been involved in at least one of their fights, and 58.3 per cent had been brought before a court. The involvement of the police is hard to interpret: it may be that police come down heavily on those who fight more frequently and at an older age. On the other hand, the girls may already be known to the police and social services, so that their behaviour is under particular scrutiny. The police may also take a particularly negative view of female violence while tolerating other more 'acceptable' forms of female delinquency (for example, prostitution, shoplifting). The large proportion of Borstal girls who had been involved in drugs or prostitution may have incidentally been involved in violent subcultures through their day-to-day life. These high figures could be nothing more than products of gross exaggeration on the girls' part, inspired either by a sense of personal grievance against police or by a desire to appear 'hard'.

Although the differences between the schoolgirls and the Borstal girls in terms of age and criminal association might be responsible for the very different pattern of responses each group gave, it seems most likely that the age factor is not of great relevance. Most of the Borstal girls had begun fighting as early as the schoolgirls. Their involvement in fighting was more frequent (65 per cent had been in more than six fights) and were protracted (90 per cent had fought within the last year).

The Borstal girls showed a far more positive attitude towards fighting than the schoolgirls. In addition to disagreeing with the idea that fighting was a boys' activity and only for those who couldn't use words, they also rejected the idea that fighting was unfeminine and childish. They believed that fighting was a good way of releasing anger and of settling some disputes and agreed that it did succeed in solving problems. In general, the Borstal girls took a sympathetic view of fighting. They did not believe that fighting was always necessary for survival, nor that they wanted to have a reputation as fighters. They certainly did not consider it to be just 'a laugh'. But they did endorse items that indicated that they saw it as a legitimate means of settling conflicts and one that was quite in keeping with their sex role.

Such an attitude constellation has to be seen in terms of the social background of the girls. Many of them talked of the aggression to which they had been subjected in their homes as children.

> — My father used to get me and turn the gas on and hold my head over it, and my hair used to singe and I used to scream and scream. If I screamed, he used to sort of give me the mit, if you know what I mean.
>
> — I remember, I was calling Mum everything under the sun, and I remember my Dad coming and he held a burning iron up to my face. He was going to burn me — if it wasn't for my other sister, I think he would have done it.
>
> AC How did your father hit you?
>
> — Well, he didn't slap me round the arse. He used to batter my face in. All I had to do to get hit was the littlest thing. If I coughed or sneezed, which you can't help, when one of his operas was on, he used to batter me. He used to really batter me for that. I used to get battered nearly every day. That's no exaggeration. I used to be a right little bastard.
>
> — My father — he took my arm, right, and he really hammered me. He didn't just smack me, he really laid into me. He got my head and he was sort of punching it.

The girls almost unanimously affirmed that their parents had positively encouraged them to fight back in self-defence against other children who fought them, and many said that they were punished if they did not win fights against their peers.

> — When I was little, I used to always fight and I used to always go for the throat, try to strangle them. But when

I was little, I didn't pull hair and that because I suppose, like, I got it off my father. And now I still do the same – I batter.

– Last time my dad hit me he broke my collar bone. 'Cos my dad used to say to me, 'If you get beaten up, I'll give you worse than what they did.' So all the time I was fighting, I was thinking, 'Don't go in and be beat,' 'cos my dad knows as soon as something has happened. There's a right atmosphere in the house.

– If I got into a fight at school, I'd get battered, but if I got in a fight and I went home crying about it. I'd get battered twice as hard.

Fights between siblings were often very vicious, and many of the girls said that they learned to fight from older brothers and sisters.

– When my brother goes, he goes mad. Sometimes he has blackouts and he don't know what he's doing. . . . He's done it to me, he stabbed me in the tit once. It bloody hurt.

– Our Tony stabbed a fork in my knee. . . . He's got a temper like me. It's bad when he gets really roused. I was sat like that and he stuck it right in, and I couldn't bend my knee 'cos he put it in my joint, like, 'cos I wouldn't iron his pants.

– I remember my sister getting me, and she was put away in a mental home for violence, right? She used to work [as a prostitute] and take drugs. She used to come home and my dad he was a really big stout Irish bloke, and my sister could put him on the floor with one punch and fight with him. She's a nutter, man, she was. When I think back when I was younger. I used to say I'd never turn out like that, but here I am.

Although some of the girls were involved with men (some as prostitutes), the majority were not. They exhibited a contempt for men in general, although a few were singled out as tolerable.

– It's more of a strain when you fight with a bloke.

- You're more tempered, you know what I mean? You're more annoyed.
- They're meant to be the stronger sex and you're determined to prove they're not . . . you're really battling.

AC   What do you think of men on the whole?
- I hate them. (Laughs)
- I like them. I like men on the whole. (Laughter)
- You've got a one-track mind.
- No, there's one I'd like to kill.
- And the rest aren't too bad.
- I've got one whose in prison now for the charge that I'm in for. And he's dead good. He's really great. We're really good spars and everything. And I like him, you know what I mean? I love him in a funny sort of way. Not love-love – brotherly love, you know what I mean? But as for the rest of them, they can go to hell as far as I'm concerned.

Unlike the schoolgirls, they were unanimously contemptuous of girls who tolerated beatings from boyfriends.

AC   What about getting belted by boyfriends?
- If I ever had one, I'd punch him back. My mate's boyfriend – I was going out with him and now I hate him, I'd love to kill him, so I used to cut him. I used a knife and just did it for the fun of it. Or if I had it in my hand and he said, 'You wouldn't dare,' I'd just throw it. Because he said that.
- If a lad ever hit me, he'd get it back and he'd never see me again.

The feeling against men ran very high. Some of the girls were homosexual. Many simply had an exploitative attitude towards males – they turned to them only for sex and money. The story told by one girl is far from typical, but it illustrates the extent of the girls' hatred for males. The details of her story were corroborated by the police report on the incident for which she was sent to Borstal.

– That bloke that I'm in for. he picked me up at a bus
   stop and we went, and he had a shop, and at the time I
   was really bad on drugs and everything and I really
   needed money. Money, that's what I was thinking
   about. And he was really drunk at the time, and this
   bloke, he'd said, 'Do him' – you know what I mean? I
   got a monkey wrench and I bashed him over the head,
   and this bloke turned round and said, 'What are you
   trying to do?' So I hit him again, a bit harder and it was
   a mistake, and he fell on the floor. And this bloke was
   smashing and smashing him in the head. Blood was just
   spurting everywhere, and then the bloke got the better
   of this other bloke and then I thought (laughs), 'It's my
   turn now,' so I had to pick it up and hit him. But at the
   time it was really nice, you know, to give other people
   some pain, you know what I mean? And this bloke, his
   head was just. . . . When Jeff hit him I saw his skin split
   right across, you know what I mean? And then I ripped
   the telephone wire out of the wall and I put it round his
   neck, and I really had it up tight and he couldn't even
   speak because I was choking him but I didn't think – I
   was pulling it, you know? And then I got the hammer,
   one of them big heavy ones, and smashed it three times
   on his leg, and he was just in a complete state. It was
   like a slaughter movie.

The girls rejected the idea that limiting rules applied to any of
the fighting that they had witnessed among the males they knew.

AC   Is it true, all this stuff about boys having rules for fight-
     ing?
–   Is it heck.
AC   They'd use weapons?
–   Yeah. I think if someone is mad enough and there's a
     weapon there and someone else has got a weapon, the
     other person is bound to pick it up to show they're not
     frightened.
–   If I've got the opportunity to put a glass or a knife in
     someone if they get the better of me, I'd do it, I reckon,

if I was right in a temper. Most blokes that I know, they wouldn't even think about it, they'd do it anyway. You know what I mean? But they're all horrible blokes, East-Enders and that.

— [My brother] punches, and if they're on the ground, he kicks and stamps on their faces. Like, they're fighting and the other fella had a bottle, he just got this knife out and stabbed him.

The extent of the gratuitous violence engaged in by the boys is perfectly illustrated in one girl's example.

— I remember I was in this club and it was a straight club and all the guys — we was having a right laugh. And I was dancing with this bloke Mick, and this bloke bumped into him and the bloke turned round and says, 'Can't you say sorry?' And this bloke I was with, he was a bit paralytic, and this bloke said something cocky and next thing I knew, blood literally from there to there on me, and this bloke had split has neck from there to there with a bottle. I just saw his neck and I looked at it and I nearly collapsed, you know what I mean? But I just ripped my T-shirt off in the middle of the dance floor and put it round his neck to stop the blood. But that's the first time it's been so close up and I've seen it really just come out. I've never seen blood come out so fast.

When the girls were asked why they fought, they gave a fairly concise and exhaustive set of replies, beginning with the ubiquitous male.

AC   What do girls fight about?
— Anything and everything.
— Jealousy.
— Boyfriends.
— Jealousy, boyfriends, girlfriends — you name it and we fight about it. If you were in the right mood, you could argue over the colour of the wallpaper.
— I'd fight to protect my family.

- Oh yeah, yeah.
- Personal insults, things like that, if someone slags you
  down.

The most prominent reason for fighting seemed to be personal
integrity and, especially, the safeguarding of their tough reputation. They noted that they had often gained this reputation more
through luck than judgement but, once labelled, they felt com-
pelled to live up to it. Many described how in their first physical
confrontations they felt frightened but quickly realized that
attack and bluff were the best forms of defence.

- I remember this girl once. She was really big, she was
  tall and she was fat, and she was meant to be getting
  me. I was shitting myself, 'I'll make a good paste for the
  wall.' Then one day I was in a good mood, and I went
  up to this girl 'cos I saw her, right, and said, 'Well,
  you're going to get me are you? 'Cos you'd better get
  on with it because I won't be able to fight in a minute,'
  and she says, 'No, I wasn't going to get you, no.' I
  thought, 'Christ,' you know, 'this is good.'
- I had a good few drinks in me – that's the only time I
  can fight, when I've had a good few drinks in me and I
  think, 'Cor, I'm hard.' And I says, 'You either want us
  in your pub or you don't.' My mum says, 'Shut up, it's
  my job,' you know. And I went into hysterics and I was
  screaming and shouting like a right little idiot, and she
  goes up to my mum and she says, 'Will you go and ask
  your daughter what's wrong? She's putting the shits up
  me,' and if anything, I'm scared of everyone else,
  they're not scared of me. And I felt really great when
  she said this and of course I carried it on and on, until it
  finally blew up.
- I was sitting there and it was like all the coloured girls,
  and they used to gang up on one girl and it was a really
  horrible feeling – you thought, 'My mates, where are
  they now?' So anyway I was sitting there and they were
  all standing there calling me every name under the sun
  but it didn't really bother me that much, and then I said,
  'So where's this girl then?' And she said, 'Oh, she's

going to get you.' And I said, 'Well, my sister's waiting,' and she said, 'She don't fight slags.' And then that was it. Christ Almighty. I don't know what come over me 'cos there was a chair and I just kicked every single one of them out of my way and I got hold of her, and she was right in the middle, and I knocked the girls out of my way and pulled her. And we started struggling and I was really banging her, and my mind just went blank and all I could think of was really to kill her.

After these initial incidences demonstrating toughness (often born out of fear), the girls acquired reputations that they had to defend. They were often challenged to fights or expected to help out younger girls who were being threatened. In one girl's school there was a definite pecking order, which was established by physical fighting.

-   At our school you had to be tough to survive, 'cos it was a horrible school, really. You had to be. Well, the fights I had at school, nobody ever beat me so you're automatically pushed up to the top – cock of the school, like. And it was just me and this other girl, all the way through, but we never battled until the fifth year. That's when it happened.

AC Why did it come to a fight then?
-   Because we'd been arguing outside the youth club and she'd been going on ... and she lives on this estate called Berryshore, which is really tough. Rats running about and everything. It's really bad. And I says, 'Fuck off back to Berryshore,' and she says, 'Fuck off back to Leeds.' By that time we'd been arguing that long I'd been getting sick. So then I just let fly, 'cos I thought, 'In a minute she's really going to hit me and she's bigger than me,' so I thought, 'Sod you,' and I just hit her.

AC What would have happened if you'd lost that fight?
-   I'd be picked on at school. She'd have really shown me up. And all the time we were fighting, I were thinking, 'Don't let her beat you,' and I was going berserk.

AC   Do you think once you start getting a reputation, you've got to keep that reputation? You can't disappoint people – you've got to keep showing that you can do it?

–   Well, at school I was fighting anybody who wanted to fight – they'd come up to me and say, 'You're meant to be cock of the school,' and I'd say, Yeah,' and they'd say, 'Fight me at ten to four when we finish school.' So I'd fight them and I'd beat them, and their mates would come and it was going on like that. I was continually fighting. But when I left school I didn't have half as many fights when I started work, 'cos nobody knew I was a fighter at work. I only fight when it's necessary now.

AC   Do you think you fought more than you needed to?

–   Yeah. It is ... in our school, there's second, third, fourth and fifth year. Well, when the second years are running up to you and saying, 'She's battering me,' you feel really horrible when your mates are saying, 'Go and stop it.' And I'm saying, 'No, leave them, let them fight. They've got to fight their own battles.' They looked on me like a big sister and quite a few others – all my friends, like. There was a bad crowd and a good crowd in my school. The bad crowd used to batter the little ones, where our crowd used to stop them from battering the little ones. So we had to really put on a bit of a front, like.

AC   Did you ever use the fact of being tough for anything else other than just fighting?

–   No, not really, because I don't think I'm tough. I'm not chicken. If someone wanted to fight me and they were six foot tall, I'd have to fight them because I just can't turn round and say no.

These fights were often particularly motivated by a need for excitement, and many girls mentioned the thrill of the fight itself.

–   It's great while it's going on. The excitement, you know what I mean? You're wondering how much is she going

> to hurt you? Is she going to win you? You're really
> giving everything you've got in the middle of a fight –
> it's great.

The Borstal girls were very concerned with maintaining their self-esteem within the community and among their friends. They had to demonstrate publicly their willingness to fight. Within the Borstal, however, they felt they had no reputation to defend, since the population was transient and unknown to them.

> – If someone showed me up in the front of my friends, it'd
> make me so mad. In here, I wouldn't give a monkeys,
> so whatever anyone says to me, I just take it. Fair
> enough, you know. They don't know the truth and I do.
> But outside if I'm in the pub, especially if it's my local
> and some girl starts slagging me down in front of my
> friends, saying, 'You split up a family, this that and the
> other,' I'm not going to stand there and take it.

This kind of fighting was seen as an integral part of their lives. The concise answer given by one girl summed it all up.

> *AC* What do you feel about your own fighting? Do you
> wish you could grow out of it?
> – No, because you wouldn't be able to survive, would
> you?

Borstal girls, like schoolgirls, often fought in the street (28 per cent), but they were much more likely to fight in pubs (23 per cent) and in private houses (30 per cent). The fact that such a high proportion of the fights described happened in houses may account for the much higher levels of physical damage inflicted. As well as cuts and bruises, 32 per cent said that they had broken the bones of their opponent. While this may be no more than 'bullshit', it may also reflect the fact that there were no outsiders to intervene in these private disputes, as well as the absence of limiting rules. As with the schoolgirls, most of the girls had been with friends at the time of the fights. The Borstal girls were much more likely to take on more than one person (52 per cent) and were less likely to have other people fighting on their side (48 per cent). Borstal girls fought predominantly other females, but a higher proportion (27 per cent) had fought with men. Once again, this indicates a higher level of domestic violence and a greater chance of severe injury. The provocative remarks before the fight were very largely direct abuse ('Fuck off!') or insults to the girl's sexual reputation ('Slag!', 'Tart!'). These two categories accounted for 58 per cent of all verbal provocations. In the Borstal groups there was a more distinct tendency to strike the first blow (68 per cent).

The Borstal sample was numerically less rule-governed than the schoolgirls. They achieved greater than 75 per cent consensus on five proscriptive rules; it is not OK to ask friends to join in or to call the police, to tell the school or police yourself, or to use a handbag. These rules do little to limit the possible damage of the fight. The proscription on handbag use relates to the seriousness and machismo of the fight rather than to damage. Most of the Borstal girls thought this item quite absurd and could not imagine any self-respecting person using anything so ridiculous. They were more unanimous than the schoolgirls in prescriptively endorsing punching and kicking. Slapping was favoured much less than among the schoolgirls. Of the items among which clear sex differences would be expected, the Borstal girls *did* tend to reject biting, scratching, using handbags and tearing clothing. Unlike the schoolgirls, however, the majority believed it was OK to go on fighting someone who was on the ground. Certainly, according to their own reports, Borstal girls' fights are more likely to result in serious damage. The taboo on intervention by authorities, coupled with a much less consensual rejection of the admissibility of weapons and a tendency to go on fighting even after submission, may lead generally to a more serious outcome.

In discussion with the Borstal girls it was equally hard to find any evidence of rules of fighting. There were some points of agreement between the girls that might at best be considered norms, but on the whole there were simply individual preferences for fighting techniques. One of the most striking observations was the extent to which the girls admitted to fear of losing or of being hurt. In many cases this led to an over-reaction, to initiating violence in an attempt to stun the prospective opponent before damage could be sustained by the girl herself. References to this fear appeared parenthetically throughout the discussion. Here are some examples:

- It frightened me. 'Cos that girl at United – I just seen the blood and I thought, 'You stupid bleeder,' like. And it frightened me.

- If someone else has got a weapon, the other person is bound to pick that up just to show they're not frightened.

- She started picking a fight and it went on for about six weeks, and I was trying to avoid it as much as I could, you know what I mean? 'Cos she might be dead rough, like. I was keeping out of her way, like.

- I just think to myself, make sure they don't do it. Give them everything you've got. And if you're being beat, leg it. If someone came up and I knew she was going to stick it in me, I'd try my hardest to get out her grips and leg it.

- I'd just say, 'Right, come on then. You wanted to fight, you start it.' And if I think they're going to start it, I'll just hit them because I think if you hit them, you finish the fight. That stuns them. I always try and hit people first.

- When I'm fighting with someone I'm always frightened, right, that I'm going to hit them but not hard enough.

- I'm frightened of getting beat.

- I fight dirty. If they fight dirty with me, I can fight dirtier with them.

- I says, 'Do what you want, I'm not scared of you,' and I thought it was really big of me to say, 'I'm not scared of you.'

Given the free-for-all nature of the fights that the girls described, this degree of fear is hardly surprising. Biting, weapon use and unannounced attacks from behind are all described by the girls as fairly common. Another common theme that emerged was that at a certain point of pain or anger during the fight all control is lost, and the girls' main aim *at that moment* is to 'kill'.

AC   When you're fighting do you feel in control?

–   I don't care – I don't know what I do.

–   If I fight for no particular reason, I know every move I make. But if I'm fighting and there's a real good reason for it, then I really lose control and really go mad.

–   Most of the fights I've had, I've tried to control myself. I've never really, really lost my temper.

–   I don't really lose my temper until she hurts me, but when she's hurt me, then I go mad. I don't even see her. I just grab and everything that I've got she gets, everything, and after the fight, I'm buggered.

AC   Do you think girls should find their own way of fighting, or should they try and fight like blokes?

–   In a fight, just do your own thing. Because if you're practising it, there's no way you're going to win. Because you don't know what the girl's going to do.

–   Everything goes blank. You don't know what you're doing.

–   You just see red, and you think, 'Kill.' Well, I do, anyway. I always go into a fight thinking, 'Kill him,' 'cos if I go in thinking, 'Give them a good going over, give them a slap,' I know I'm going to get beat.

–   I was really banging her and my mind just went blank, and all I could think of was really to kill her, and I really damaged her.

–   So I marched out of there, took her with me, marched back into the café, took her up to the counter, and says 'Did she tell you I emptied ashtrays all over the table?' She goes, 'Yes,' and I can't even remember what I done. All I can remember is that I banged the girl and I was supposed to have done some bad damage to her.

There were some implicit understandings about the basis of a fight. Girls were indignant about being attacked from behind or when they were off-guard. There was some indication that if weapons were introduced, they should not be used until both girls were armed. It was also understood that all those involved would conspire to keep it secret from any official authority.

When they were asked about what was and was not legitimate behaviour in a fight, the responses were contradictory. Here are some examples of reported behaviour during fights.

– I haven't had any really bad ones. I had a fight at school once. I didn't even feel in the mood for a fight, but this other girl, she wanted it. She had a weird sense of humour, and it used to get up people's noses a lot. She started and, like, all her mates were saying, 'Come on, do this.' But to me it wasn't a proper fight because she was pulling my hair and I was trying to hit her because I prefer punching and I don't like pulling or scratching. I don't like biting, I like punching, to me that's it. It weren't really a fight, it stopped – it only went on for about 15 minutes.

AC You know, people who scratch and bite – do you think most people who fight a lot learn to stop doing that, or do you think it's just a personal style?

– Some people do do that. If they've got nails, they will do it – scratch – because it's a graze that hurts more than a cut. A cut hurts, a scratch usually stings.

– Girls who fight a lot learn to lay in, you know?

AC Did you learn how to fight? Did you get better at it as you went on?

– I've only ever got hurt once in a fight, and that was when I was about 11 and I was at school. This girl was always fighting and we went in the bogs one time and she bit me there. She was really biting hard and it hurt, and I just went for her throat and I almost strangled her. I always go for the throat.

– I never go for the throat. I always just start a fight

punching in the face, giving them a good crack in the face.

– My brothers, if ever they had fights, it was always punch-ups till about four or five years ago. He [one of my brothers] came in the house one night, big scar on his face, he'd been to hospital, blood all over him. He'd got a glass in his face and ever since then my brother has never had a punch-up. If ever a fight starts in a pub, and I've been in once when he's done it, he glasses them straight away. Ever since then, he's just glassed them. Doesn't give a damn.

– In my class, one girl, like, stuck me with a knife.

– When I was younger, I used to poke forks in people's eyes.

– I still prefer paint brushes, because one time this girl stuck one in my eye and it really hurt. Ever since then, when I was at school I used to do it to them. If someone annoyed me, I used to go straight for their eyes because I knew it would hurt them.

Note that one of the girls openly admitted in a previous quotation to biting in a fight. Scratching too seems to be a question of personal style, although one girl suggests that you learn to 'lay in' more as you get better at fighting. No sanctions whatever are brought to bear against girls who admit freely to strangling and poking forks into eyes.

Among Borstal girls 'hardness' seems to be closely associated with vicious attacks, ungoverned by any limiting rules. Expressions of hate and the desire to kill were frequent. None of the girls boasted about damage that they had sustained, though many offered exaggerated accounts of the damage they themselves had inflicted. Rules were considered 'soft'. Most fights were about maintaining or establishing reputations or were connected with very intense emotional involvements. Fear of hurt or loss of reputation were common, and girls were often surprised at their own success in 'bluffing' hardness or beating opponents.

The extent of unconstrained aggression within the girls'

families was remarkable, and, as we have seen, most girls had been systematically encouraged to fight by their parents. In the subcultures from which these girls come fighting seems to have shed its ritual component. Interpersonal violence emerges as a vicious expression of hatred and resentment and is bound up more with establishing and maintaining a tough reputation than with settling disputes. Violence serves less a social function than a personal one; it enhances a feeling of self-worth at the expense of often considerable injury to others. While on one hand deploring it, the girls see no way of managing without it among the people they know. Sadly, their stay in Borstal is likely to have the worst possible effect, by increasing their tough reputation and giving them an even harder image to which they must live up. Often it is an image that they never wanted in the first place.

CHAPTER 6

Care Orders

During the 1960s the face of British juvenile justice altered drastically. The Ingelby Committee in 1963 stated clearly: 'It is the situation and the relationships with the family which seem to be responsible for many children being in trouble, whether the trouble is called delinquency or anything else' (see Ford, 1975, p. 22). This new concern with seeing children and young people in a family context and with rooting their misconduct in socialization rather than in some mysterious 'bad streak' provided the background to the Children and Young Persons Act 1969. A young person appearing at juvenile court may now be placed in the hands of the local authority if one of six conditions is met:

1. The child's development is being avoidably arrested or neglected, or his health is being avoidably impaired or neglected, or he is being ill-treated.
2. Conditions similar to those indicated above have been proved in respect of another child in the same household.
3. He is exposed to moral danger.
4. He is beyond the control of his parents or guardian.
5. He is truanting when of compulsory school age.
6. He is guilty of a civil or criminal offence, excluding homicide.

These first five points must be proved 'on the balance of probabilities', the last (as with adult criminal cases) 'beyond reasonable doubt'. The court must be further satisfied that a young person is in need of care or control that he is unlikely to receive unless the court makes an order in respect of him. Although the local authority, a police constable or some other 'authorized person' can bring a child to court, in real terms the decision about what action is to be taken against a young person lies chiefly with the social services. This is usually done through juvenile bureaux established by the police. In bringing a case the social services department will offer reports from social workers, probation officers, the police, education officers, doctors and psychiatrists to ensure that the fullest possible information on the young person is presented to the three magistrates. Having heard all the evidence from both the professionals and the young person and his family, the court may decide to make one of five types of order:

1   an order requiring the parent or guardian to enter into an undertaking, backed by a financial penalty, to exercise proper care and control over the young person;
2   a supervision order;
3   a care order;
4   a hospital order – this procedure is laid down in the Mental Health Act 1959, and such an order must be supported by two doctors;
5   a guardianship order, which has to have the same support as (4) above.

In the case of a young person over 14 years, the court may bind him over for up to £25 to be of good behaviour for up to one year and it may order that compensation be paid by him or his parents.

A supervision order corresponds roughly to placement on probation under the supervision of the probation service or the local authority. A care order places the local authority (Social Services Department) *in loco parentis* and it is for the authority, not the magistrates, to decide on the particular action to take. This may mean removal from home to a community home. In criminal proceedings the court has the same powers but, in addition, is free to grant an absolute or conditional discharge, to fine the offender or to order that he attend an intermediate treatment or detention centre. Whether the case is civil or criminal, the child and his parents are entitled to legal aid.

While the new legislation sought to separate adult crime quite clearly from juvenile misbehaviour, in a practical sense this is not always easy to achieve. Frequently, juvenile courts are held in ordinary magistrates' courts (although always on a different day from adult proceedings), and it is therefore difficult to avoid the starchy and intimidating atmosphere of a courtroom. Although in theory juvenile court magistrates are appointed by virtue of their expertise and interest in young people, the shortage of such people has meant that some magistrates are old and staunchly upper-class, with very little informal contact with young people, (Berlins and Wansell, 1974). Courtroom customs and language are quite unfamiliar to the defendants, and the large number of 'extras' (social workers, probation officers and so on) add to the general level of nervousness. The young persons themselves, often unaware of the benevolent function of the court, simply feel that they are on trial and in danger of 'going down'. Often the social worker, who has been an ally, appears to change sides in court, presenting evidence of the shortcomings of the child and of the family. All this, probably combined with a two- or three-hour wait in a draughty waiting-room before the case is heard, contribute to a formality that the Act itself sought to minimize. Ford (1975), in his excellent book on the juvenile court, cautions magistrates as follows:

> Those who work in court regularly, the magistrates, the clerks, the social workers and probation officers, the police and the lawyers, tend, almost unconsciously, to develop their own 'language network'. There are phrases and expressions which are a form of shorthand for them; these may be completely incomprehensible to the defendant and parents – and it may seem that things are being said and done from which they are excluded. At all times, in all these ways, the bench must be careful to see that the proceedings are not passing over the heads of those who have been summoned to the court. This is not only a requirement of the law, but also one of common decency – it is the barest minimum of courtesy at such a time. (pp. 61–2)

The court experience

Many magistrates have been concerned about the comprehensibility of the court proceedings. Younghusband (1959) and Cavanagh (1959) have both attested to the need for magistrates to clarify procedures and to avoid esoteric language. Recently psychologists have turned their attention to empirical studies of the juvenile court experience. Fears (1977) took Bernstein's analysis of spoken language as her starting point for such a study. Bernstein distinguishes between elaborated and restricted speech codes:

> An elaborated code is universalistic with reference to its meaning in as much as it summarizes general means and ends. A restricted code is particularistic with reference to its meaning in as much as it summarizes local means and ends.

A restricted code is used by many working-class adolescents; speaker and listener share implicit understandings that are utilized in conversation. Only sophisticated verbal training, available to the middle classes, can lead to the acquisition of the elaborated code with which speakers articulate the universals of their experience and can therefore manipulate them. These rather vague descriptions can be operationalized in terms of the usage of particular grammatical constructions. Fears collected court transcriptions from 297 children's appearances and began by simply counting the number of sentences spoken by magistrates, clerks, children and families. Expressed as percentages of the total volume of sentences spoken, they were respectively 60 per cent, 16 per cent, 8 per cent and 16 per cent. When the percentages of words spoken were indexed (see table 6.1), the results confirmed that even when children speak, they speak little and in very short sentences. Fears (1977, p. 138) offers a good example of a typical interchange:

Magistrate: What have you got to say about this? Who did it belong to, the motorbike? You have got no idea? You did not know the person concerned? What prompted you to do this? What did you want it for? Why did you give these things to your mates? Did they give you money? Why did you do it? Which café is this?

Child: The one on Elm Drive.

TABLE 6.1   *Proportion of words spoken in court by officials and defendants*

Speakers	Words spoken %
Magistrates	41
Clerks	9
Children	3
Parents	10
Other	37

SOURCE: Fears, 1977, p. 139.

The child answers not only the most concretely factual question, but also the one that has least bearing on the case. The child's reluctance to speak seems not only to be linguistically related but also to rest on his inability or unwillingness to consider motives and other private phenomena. Linguistic simplicity was investigated by examining the percentage of each speaker's sentences that contained no verb phrases. The results for city and county courts were remarkably consistent (see table 6.2).

Although magistrates and clerks use conversational or restricted code in the early stages of the hearing (when the facts are being established), they switch codes rapidly when they give and discuss the decision of the court. The crucial question is, of course, to what extent do the children and parents understand the whole court experience?

Davies's (1976) study of girls appearing before a juvenile court was conducted between 1967 and 1969 (before the implementation of the new Act) but can still provide useful information about the girl and her family's comprehension of the court

TABLE 6.2   *Analysis of sentence construction in city and county courts*

Area of jurisdiction of court	Proportion of sentences without verb phrases (%)					
	Magistrates	Clerks	Children	Family	χr^2	p
City	7.2	8.2	43.7	6.2	12.15	< .01
County	5.4	4.6	42.0	9.4	13.05	< .01

SOURCE: Fears, 1977, p. 140.

proceedings. Fifty-five girls and parents were interviewed after their cases had been heard, and the court proceedings were witnessed by the interviewer. Out of 36 cases for which information was available, 20 girls (56 per cent) recognized no one in the court room; 12 (33 per cent) recognized one person; and 4 (11 per cent) knew two or more people. Out of 48 girls, 20 (42 per cent) never understood what was happening; 6 (13 per cent) understood on one occasion; and 22 (46 per cent) claimed that they always understood. Twenty-eight girls said that their parents or guardians felt the same. Twenty-nine out of 35 mothers (83 per cent) used words like 'ashamed', 'upset', 'terrified', 'worried', 'hostile' or 'angry' to describe their feelings about their daughters' court appearance. Davies's assessment of behaviour displayed in court rated 32 out of 54 girls (59 per cent) as pathetic, upset, worried, hostile, annoyed or sullen. Thirty-six mothers out of 54 (67 per cent) were rated in these same categories. Yet court officials treated only 30 per cent of cases – 16 out of 54 – as distressing or serious. On almost all indices of reaction to the court experience, girls who appeared in court on grounds of civil action rather than criminal proceedings fared worse. Even the court officials found care proceedings to be more difficult, distressing or serious than criminal charges.

Perhaps this is not surprising. Officials, the police and social workers often do not take sufficient care to inform the girl of the attitude of the court and the law to various forms of misbehaviour. Instead of being aware of the court's concern and benevolence, the girl often feels she is being tried for noncriminal acts such as truancy, staying out late or having undesirable companions. She is unlikely to be familiar with the complexities of legal and penal philosophy. Being 'put away' is usually seen by the girl as a punishment, even when magistrates attempt to persuade her that it may be for her own good. Her fear and ignorance of the court proceedings usually result in a terrified or hostile silence. Even when explicitly asked about their feelings about their cases, the majority of girls say nothing. Nor is it widely known to them or to their parents that they are entitled to legal representation and legal aid. In the face of a barrage of adult 'experts', the girl often feels intimidated and betrayed. Since so many girls appear in court on civil rather than criminal grounds, the experience may be even worse. What appears to be on trial is not just a single (criminal) act but a girl's whole character and personality. Her IQ, mental stability, friends, school, sex life and social skills may be reviewed. Much of the 'evidence' is not factual but impressionistic and anecdotal. In the last decade much has been said about this discriminatory practice of judging boys' actions but girls' character. We shall turn now to a discussion of the philosophy behind such a practice and the data that have been gathered to attack and defend it.

Sex discrimination

Virtually every introductory textbook that deals with female delinquency and crime expresses the view that women are under-represented in crime statistics. As Reckless (1961) states:

> Citizens are willing to report the behaviour of males much more readily than that of females. The police are supposed to be much more lenient in their arrests of females. Judicial processes in America are supposed to be very much more lenient with women than men. Consequently, female offenders have a much better chance than male offenders of not being reported, of not being arrested and of dropping out of the judicial process, that is, of remaining uncommitted. (p. 37)

From this it seems that females have a relatively good deal. However, other writers (Campbell, 1977; Chesney-Lind, 1973; Cohn, 1970) have suggested that in one particular sense the system penalizes girls more harshly. In both the United States and Britain young people may appear in court for civil or status offences – that is, acts that would not be considered criminal if performed by an adult. Being 'in moral danger' is one such case. The argument is that proportionately more girls than boys face courts on these status offences and, because of this, are more likely to end up in juvenile institutions or in psychiatric care than are boys. Because status offences are fundamentally issues of sexual morality (although they may appear in various guises; such offences include being beyond parental control, running away, failing to come in at night), they are of particular concern in relation to girls in a society that continues to enforce sexual double standards for boys and girls. The issue has been named the 'sexualization of female crime' by Chesney-Lind and has given rise to heated and sometimes hysterical argument. To examine the extent of discriminatory practice, we will consider data derived from successive stages of the legal procedure – the arrest, pre-trial remand and detention, court reports and court disposal of boys and girls charged with criminal and status offences.

When a juvenile is apprehended, the police have the discretionary right simply to caution the offender and to take no further legal action. Few would argue in principle with this provision, since the booking and charging of every young suspect would result in a massive work overload for the police and in delinquent stigmatization, with all its attendant trauma, for many normal but 'naughty' teenagers. However, it is suggested that police selectively caution a greater proportion of girls than boys – a legacy perhaps from the days of male chivalry or, more pejoratively, from the days when girls' misbehaviours were so inconsequential as to warrant little concern and a great deal of paternalism (see Campbell, 1977). In Britain the crime statistics present information on the number of offenders cautioned as a percentage of all those cautioned and found guilty. These figures are presented in table 6.3. It is quite clear that for every offence in every age category a greater percentage of girls are cautioned than boys. This is most marked among young people under the age of 17. The highest cautioning rates for both males and females are for the two particularly 'female' offences of sex and theft. Sexual offences, of course, cover a multitude of behaviours, including soliciting (for girls) and rape (for boys). With increasing age, these offences are taken more seriously, although the highest discrepancy between males and females over 21 is probably related to the lax attitude taken towards adult female prostitutes and the much more punitive attitude adopted towards rape. For both sexes crime perpetrated at an older age (17-plus) is more likely to result in criminal procedings. In the younger age group crime is seen as indicative of some real disturbance of personality or home situation, but at 17 offenders are expected to have grown up and to

TABLE 6.3 *Offenders cautioned for indictable offences as a percentage of all those cautioned or found guilty, 1977*

Offence	All ages		10–13 years		14–16 years		17–20 years		21 + years	
	M	F	M	F	M	F	M	F	M	F
Violence against the person	8	20	56	61	24	35	2	7	4	11
Sexual offences	33	56	73	83	64	100	54	60	13	46
Burglary	15	29	47	63	18	31	1	3	1	4
Robbery	3	6	23	25	6	11	–	–	–	–
Theft and handling	24	34	76	87	43	63	3	5	4	11
Fraud and forgery	6	11	70	79	38	52	3	5	2	6
Criminal damage	16	19	60	69	29	38	2	5	2	6
Other offences	1	7	69	95	30	53	3	5	2	3
Total indictable offences	19	31	67	85	34	58	3	5	3	10

SOURCE: Home Office 1977, Criminal Statistics for England and Wales.

take responsibility for wilfully wrong acts. Between 14 and 16 the police still seem to view criminality as a transient, even natural, phase associated with adolescence and therefore caution a large proportion of offenders. This indulgence with 'children' seems to last slightly longer with girls, among whom 58 per cent of girls between 14 and 16 are still escaping with a caution. But at seventeen the law clamps down almost equally, with a drop in cautioning rate of 31 per cent for boys and a massive 53 per cent for girls. Table 6.4 shows cautioning rate trends over a 20-year period for boys and girls. The 1969 Act made its effects felt from 1970 onwards, resulting in more use of cautions for juveniles of both sexes. The same sharp disjunction can be seen at the watershed of 17 years old, when the police take a tougher line, and the advantages of being female sharply reduce. However, in the younger age group the sex difference in cautioning rates actually increases quite steadily over time. In 1957 the sex difference in cautioning was only 9 per cent; by 1977 it had risen to 23 per cent. With juveniles at least, a clear discrimination can be seen.

In the United States Terry (1962) reported an investigation of police procedures that showed that the sex of an offender bore a statistically significant relationship to the type of disposition accorded. In a study reported in 1970 by the same author, disposal by police, probation and courts in relation to sex was investigated. The correlations computed between 'maleness' and disposal were those that appeared after certain control variables

TABLE 6.4   *Cautions given for indictable offences as a proportion of all those cautioned and found guilty for selected years, 1957–77*

	Male		Female	
	10–16 years	17+ years	10–16 years	17+ years
1957	22	4	31	9
1960	21	4	33	9
1966	23	3	36	9
1970	35	3	52	10
1976	44	3	66	9
1977	47	3	70	9

SOURCE: Home Office, Criminal Statistics for England and Wales.

had been partialled out. Using four categories of police action (release, referral to welfare agency, referral to probation department, referral to Department of Public Welfare for institutionalization), Terry reports a very small negative correlation between maleness and disposal ($\tau = -0.05$). However, Terry himself notes in explaining this finding:

> While girls account for only 17.9 per cent of all offences, they represent nearly half of the sex offences and incorrigibility cases. Nearly 70 per cent of all referrals to social and welfare agencies are in this category. Thus the apparently greater severity in dealing with girls stems from their disproportionate commission of offences which result in referral to social and welfare agencies. (p. 86)

The reason why girls appear to be penalized, then, is associated with society's concern with female sexual behaviour. Presumably, precocious sex among girls is considered more serious than the minor misdemeanours of boys, and because of this fewer of them are released. It should be remembered that the English statistics deal with indictable offences only and say nothing of the status offences with which Terry deals. In recent years in Britain fewer girls have been charged in juvenile courts with status offences and more with criminal acts. Whether this reflects real changes in girls' criminality or simply a changing and more egalitarian attitude on the part of the police is unclear. May (1977), in a study of a Scottish juvenile court, found that only 10.5 per cent of girls who appeared were there for juvenile or sexual offences, and Hart (1975) suggests that 75 per cent of girls sent for assessment by the courts or the social services are now charged with indictable offences. However, Chesney-Lind (1973) quotes a study in Philadelphia dealing with law violations that showed that the police do release a larger proportion of girls than boys. Piliavin and Briar (1964) reported that the police gave an informal reprimand or straightforward release to 86.6 per cent of co-operative juvenile offenders. The same was true for only 9.6 of unco-operative suspects. This difference in attitude to authority may underlie some of the sex differences in prosecution rates. The evidence certainly suggests that in the United States, as in Britain, girl criminal offenders are more likely to be released. However, status offences among girls, particularly in the United States, are more likely to result in further action (see Chesney-Lind, 1973).

After being picked up by the police, young people can be detained in an institution prior to court appearance, sometimes for 'holding' purposes, sometimes because the home situation is critical at the time and sometimes for purposes of assessment and the preparation of court reports. Chesney-Lind (1974) draws attention to the double standard existing here too:

> A study of a Honolulu detention home in 1971 showed that 43 per cent of residents were girls while only 30 per cent of the juveniles arrested during that period were girls. And 46 per cent of the detention home population had been arrested for either running away or being incorrigible; most were girls. (p. 45)

She also quotes a Pennsylvania study showing that 46 per cent of girls charged with status offences were detained prior to trial, as compared with 24 per cent charged with misdemeanours and 35 per cent charged with felonies. Girls also spend twice as long as boys in pre-trial detention. This has been established in both New York and Honolulu. While there, they may have to undergo vaginal examinations to establish whether they are carrying veneral disease, even when they are not being charged with a sexual offence. Such a procedure is far from standard among male detainees. This is true in England also, and evidence of a girl's virginity is often given to the court to establish the extent to which she is in moral danger. Such procedures are bound to have an upsetting effect on a girl who is already under stress because of her removal from home and her future trial. Davies's (1976) investigation of girls appearing before a British juvenile court showed that 56 per cent of girls appearing in civil proceedings (for status offences) were remanded to detention centres prior to their court appearance, while only 16 per cent of offenders were remanded. Even if this were as a result of unfavourable home circumstances, the girls themselves certainly feel it to be a punishing and upsetting experience. If the rationale for detention is to ensure time to gather full social reports, it is still unclear why this is considered particularly vital for non-offender girls. For the 30 non-offenders a total of 105 reports were prepared for the court; for the 25 offenders there were only 51 reports. The discrepancy is particularly marked with respect to the number of psycho-medical reports (see table 6.5).

Girls who have committed no offence at all (except against sexual morality) are more likely to be regarded and labelled as psychiatrically or medically 'sick'. Medical examinations, as noted above, virtually always entail vaginal examination. Before turning to the probation officers' role in discriminatory practices, Davies noted the extent to which the magistrates accepted the recommendations of probation officers; in only 2 out of 55 cases were these reports *not* accepted. In influencing the magistrates, probation officers ranked much higher than psychologists, psychiatrists and children's departments.

Terry (1970) examined recommendations made by probation officers in relation to a number of demographic characteristics, including sex. Officers could select one of four dispositions ranked in increasing order of gravity – release, informal supervision, referral to juvenile court, referral to criminal court. Fewer females than males were released (27.7 per cent and 30 per cent respectively), but more females were given informal supervision (46.2 per cent and 28.6 per cent). The most telling difference appeared with respect to referral to criminal court – recommended for only 0.8 per cent of girls but for 8.5 per cent of boys. Once again, this provides a clue to the interpretation of the data; girls were rarely charged with crimes at all but were charged instead with sex offences and incorrigibility, for which informal supervision is most likely to be recommended. Unfortunately, a

TABLE 6.5 *Psycho-medical reports submitted in respect of offenders and non-offenders*

Type of report	Number of reports	
	Offenders (N = 25)	Non-offenders (N = 30)
Medical	4	14
Psychological	4	15
Psychiatric	4	16

SOURCE: Davies, 1976, p. 69.

complementary study by Cohn (1970) notes neither the proportion of girls charged with status offences nor the proportion of such girls who are recommended to informal supervision. Instead Cohn selected pre-sentence reports by probation officers on 175 young people, 50 of whom were recommended for probation, 50 for institutionalization, 50 for psychiatric examination and 25 for discharge. The sex distribution of Cohn's data is presented in table 6.6.

Of those who were brought before the courts, three times as many girls as boys were recommended for institutionalization. Cohn adds:

> Cross-tabulation of data for the 21 girls recommended to an institution reveals that most of them had committed delinquent acts against sexual taboos – acts which were generally considered decisive factors in arriving at the recommendation they received. (p. 193)

Since girls in this sample were predominantly status offenders, not criminal offenders, it is interesting to look at the disposition recommendation by type of offence. Of offenders charged with offences against life or property, only 35 per cent were recommended to an institution or a psychiatrist; the remainder were split equally between probation and discharge. Of all sexual taboo offenders (most of whom were girls), 67 per cent were recommended to an institution or a psychiatrist, and the same

TABLE 6.6 *Dispositions recommended by probation officers for young people awaiting trial*

Recommended disposition	Young people awaiting trial (N = 175)				
	Male	%	Female	%	Total
Probation	47	28	3	9	50
Institutionalization	29	18	21	60	50
Psychiatric examination	41	25	9	26	50
Discharge*	48	29	2	6	50
Total	165	100	35	101†	200

*Figures doubled to enable the comparison of data.
†Rounding up of decimals gives total > 100.

SOURCE: Cohn, 1970, p. 193.

was true of 77 per cent of those who had offended against parents. Although status-offence girls may be more likely to receive informal supervision, it is clear that in those cases that reach the courts a girl is more likely to be 'locked away' than either criminal girls or boys in general.

Having reached court, Terry's data clearly shows, girls receive harsher disposal than do boys. In his sample 76.7 per cent of girls were sent to institutions, as compared with 59.7 per cent of boys. Once again, most of the girls were committed for non-criminal acts, and females were treated more harshly, in spite of the fact that they had less extensive records of previous delinquent behaviour. In 1965 a US children's bureau reported that the average length of commitment for boys was 8.2 months, as compared with 10.7 months for girls (see Chesney-Lind, 1973).

The same observation has been made in Scotland by May (1977). Although only a small proportion of girls were brought to court for status offences, 52 per cent of these girls were placed on probation or sent to an institution. Data is also available on two samples of English girls in juvenile courts before the 1969 Children and Young Persons Act. Smith (1978) reports that 58.8 per cent of girls appearing as deemed to be in need of care and protection were given an approved school order. Approved school was prescribed only for 5.8 per cent of shoplifters and 11.8 per cent of girls who had committed larceny, breaking and entering and malicious damage. Of those charged with receiving, breach of probation, taking and driving away and violence, none received approved school orders. In Davies's (1976) London sample, she considered 25 offenders and 30 non-offenders (who appeared as beyond parental control or in need of care and protection). Seventeen of the 25 offenders (68 per cent) received an absolute or conditional discharge, costs or a fine. Court orders (probation, approved school or supervision) were made on only 8 girls (32 per cent), and in two cases these referred only to the continuation of an already existing order. The 30 status offenders did not get off so lightly; 26 (87 per cent) were made the subject of court orders.

In summary, evidence from both sides of the Atlantic points to discrimination in the juvenile justice system. Juvenile girls who commit criminal offences are more likely to be treated leniently by the police, probation officers and courts. They are less likely than status offenders to end up in institutions (whether sentenced or on remand). Girls who breach the code of sexual morals evoke a more positive response. Police are more likely to refer them to the social services; courts and probation officers are more likely to demand psychiatric and medical examination; and they are more likely to be committed to an institution. In the United States the Equal Rights Amendment may soon cause discriminatory laws to be abolished or modified (see Sarri, 1976). But the majority of these discriminations are not enshrined in legislation itself but occur in its implementation. Interpretations of the law are made by those who are as concerned with morals as with justice. Who decides what constitutes moral depravity or danger? To what extent does running away, having sexual relations or skipping school contribute to 'moral' decline? We shall examine each of these issues in more detail in the next sections.

Sexual behaviour

As we have seen, the juvenile law displays a disproportionate concern with female sexuality combined with a complete lack of attention to it among boys. Male sexual behaviour is sanctioned only when it is expressed through crimes of rape, indecent assault, living on immoral earnings or under-age homosexuality. Heterosexual sexual experiences in which the female partner is consenting remain unrecorded by the court except in relatively rare cases, when older males (21 years and over) are prosecuted for having intercourse with girls under 16 years of age. The fact that a boy of 16 may have had intercourse with more than one partner would most certainly not be considered reasonable grounds for locking him up. In the past medical records and testimony for social workers on girls have made implicit reference to sexual experience. Often this bias has been made explicit; for example, Cowie et al. (1968) bracket together care and protection orders, truancy and beyond-control cases as 'sexual misbehaviour'. While the girls' sexuality may have been at issue in some proportion of the cases, it is quite misleading to assume promiscuity where no direct evidence exists. In recent years, fewer girls have appeared in court on these status offences and more have been charged with criminal acts. However, such status cases are still much more frequently made against girls than against boys, and the assumptions behind such a practice should be examined. Richardson (1969) remarked of such sexually 'aberrant' girls:

> Those who were hardly touched emotionally were often disturbed much by the aftermath, and doubtless the subsequent inquiries, physical examinations (often physical treatment) and Court evidence served to magnify and distort experiences. (p. 219)

The academic literature has accepted unquestioningly that female delinquency is sexual delinquency. To chart the development of such a notion would be time-consuming, but it has been taken as axiomatic by psychoanalysts (Blos, 1957), sociologists and criminologists (A. K. Cohen, 1955; Morris, 1964), psychologists (Eysenck, 1964) and practitioners (Cowie et al., 1968; Konopka, 1966; Richardson, 1969). It is only recently that the double standard of court treatment with respect to 'sex offences' has been noted and, indeed, that the whole question of who defines delinquency has been opened up (Becker, 1973). Formerly girls' sexual experience was considered as legitimate a target for censure as any criminal act. Indeed Cowie et al. (1968) note that it was often considered more serious:

> Among the sexually delinquent group there are girls who are known to have stolen; but larceny, if it has occurred, has been regarded as of much less significance than aspects of the case calling for care or protection. (p. 68)

The literature on the subject, in just the same way as the courts, has noted among girls, but not boys, the incidence of venereal disease on admission, virginity or the lack of it, pregnancies, miscarriages and abortions. Putative unmarried fathers among approved school boys are not especially noted.

Some studies have attempted to establish the actual rate of under-age sexuality for girls, both in the community and in residential institutions. The somewhat scanty results are shown in table 6.7. The figures for 'normal' (that is, non-adjudicated delinquents) range from 12 per cent (1965) to 65 per cent (1978). Adjudicated delinquent girls show figures ranging from 70 to 83 per cent. Obviously, such figures are impossible to verify. A few notes of caution should be added. Both Richardson and the Approved School Association drew their figures not from the girls themselves but from social workers and court reports. Such reports are often based on informed (or uninformed) speculation. Secondly, even self-report studies are in doubt when the relationship between researcher and girls is fleeting. In my own study, for example, schoolgirls had a much higher motivation to keep up appearances than did assessment centre girls, who were well aware that they had been labelled as 'bad'. Out of the subset of schoolgirls with whom I talked in more depth, the percentage of sexually experienced girls was much higher, and I have every reason to believe that the subset was not untypical of the broader population. The much higher figure offered by Wilson (1978) seems the most reliable, since although her sample size was small (20 girls), her investigation was a sympathetic study of sexual norms, and she maintained close contact with the girls over a period of time. Their own statements about rules of sexual conduct also tallies well with those noted by McRobbie (1978b), although the latter did not perform any numerical analysis. Schofield's (1965) study is the only one to investigate boys as well – only 20 per cent (8 per cent more than girls) claimed to have experienced intercourse.

This preoccupation with sexual precocity was based, it was often claimed, on concern for the girls' own good. The concern was characterized as medical or psychological rather than sociological or political. Early sexual experience, especially in the 1950s and 1960s, was feared to result in venereal disease and pregnancy. Richardson notes that 23 per cent of girls were admitted to institutions with venereal infections, and Cowie et al. put their figure at 46 out of 322 girls (14 per cent). Chesney-Lind (1974) has suggested that this preoccupation stems from the view that girls, more than boys, are 'carriers' of the disease – a quite unfounded assumption. Venereal disease is seen as a 'dirty' disease, the consequence of a sexually promiscuous lifestyle, and for this reason carries with it a stigma far beyond

TABLE 6.7 *Experience of sexual intercourse among girls aged 16 years and younger*

	Approved School Association* 1954	Schofield 1965	Richardson 1969	Smith 1969	Campbell 1976	Wilson 1978
	%	%	%	%	%	%
'Normal' girls	–	12 (5)	–	13.3	15.2	65 (10)
Gang members	–	–	–	–	–	–
Assessment centre	–	–	–	73.3	82	–
Probation	–	–	–	70	–	–
Approved school	73.5	–	83 (79.6)	–	–	–

*Not based on self-report.
( ) Percentage who had had more than one sexual partner.

that of a mere illness. Richardson refers to the 'smells' of her approved school and brackets together as causes venereal infection, reluctance to bathe and dirty clothing. Thus venereal disease is classified less as a health risk than as an indicator of the girls' 'dirty' lifestyle. Unwanted pregnancy used to be a real hazard for many teenage girls. Not only did it prematurely abbreviate their adolescence, but it also caused concern among authorities who worried about starting 'cycles of deprivation', anticipating a future illegitimate generation of delinquents spawned by 'wayward' girls. At the turn of the century sterilization was even suggested for female criminals (Guibord, 1917). Even in the 1960s pregnancy was often held to be the 'punishment' for sexual misbehaviour. Lurking behind such ideas lay a common romanticization of the Mother Earth figure. Motherhood, in its Victorian sense, was seen as essentially separate from the mechanical necessity of sexual intercourse. Men characteristically viewed mothers as selfless, devoted, almost asexual in their transformation to caretaker. Note, for example, that breast feeding may be carried out in front of men without fear that any sexual stimulation will result from the sight of the female breast *in that context*. Authorities reacted not only with alarm but also with outrage to young mothers who were still sexually active with more than one partner and who did not see motherhood as necessarily the end of their sexuality. Pregnancy made manifest a truth that both parents and authorities attempted to ignore: girls *did* have intercourse before marriage. The availability of contraception, abortion and treatment for venereal infection began to alter prevailing sexual morals. Persuading teenage girls to avoid pre-marital sex could no longer be disguised by a concern for their health. The true basis of the sexual double standard became increasingly apparent.

Rowbotham (1973) has commented upon the societal role of sex, which at first sight seems to be an area of life untouched by political considerations. But sexuality has been regarded and controlled by the state in almost every culture for economic ends. Sexual activity is seen, on the one hand, as potentially distracting from the real business of labour. Sexual frustrations, as well as sexual excesses, are to be avoided. Both can lead to insubordination and dissatisfaction. A state that can ensure the provision of basic human needs and pleasures (housing, food, sex) forestalls unhappiness and disruption. The institution of marriage serves such an end, while also ensuring the continuation of the nuclear family. The dependence of wife and child on the man's income effectively restricts the limits of his industrial action. The nuclear form of the family makes mobility easier and ensures manpower availability where it is needed. The hinge of this political machinery is the exchange by women of sex for marriage. To secure such a bargain, sex must not be available by other means, and anyone who attempts to give sex away is severely sanctioned. This is the fate of those teenage girls who come before the courts for their promiscuous behaviour. The notion of 'morals' is introduced to justify the court and the community's attitude towards promiscuity. A similar fate awaits those who attempt to sell sex for material profit – prostitutes. McRobbie (1978b) captures this point in her discussion of 'cheapness':

> But the word which is richest in connotation is 'cheap'. The fear expressed in this descriptive term is that girls will cheapen themselves by dispensing with their 'sexual favours' in a free and indiscriminate way. To put it another way, as impressionable, vulnerable adolescents these girls could end up selling their sexuality below the 'market price', that is, outside marriage. And this cheapness is expressed in provocative clothing and heavy make-up. (p. 5)

Data gathered in the last ten years must serve as reassurance for sexual moralists, for the bulk of it suggests that the differential standards of sexual behaviour among boys and girls and the paramount importance of marriage are still strong. Schofield (1965) interviewed 934 boys and 939 girls aged 15–17 and 19 years about their sexual behaviour and attitudes. Only 1 per cent of girls and 6 per cent of boys said they did not want to marry. Thirty-eight per cent of the younger girls wanted to marry before 21, and more than a quarter of boys and girls agreed with the statement 'Girls believe today that if they are not married before they are 21, they are on the shelf.' At the same time, 28 per cent of boys and 27 per cent of girls agreed that 'It is best to have a good time before you are married because after that life is pretty dreary.' Far more girls (61 per cent) than boys (35 per cent) thought sex before marriage was wrong, and far more girls than boys endorsed the double standard – 42 per cent of girls but only 23 per cent of boys thought that sex before marriage was 'all right for boys but not girls'.

Although only 64 per cent of boys wanted to marry a virgin, 85 per cent of girls wanted to be a virgin when they married. Why did so many girls refuse to have sex before marriage? Perhaps the answer lies in the 'reputation' that girls believed they would acquire; 57 per cent of girls (but only 46 per cent of boys) thought a girl acquired a bad reputation if she indulged in pre-marital sex.

Since the time of that survey the women's liberation movement might have been expected to engender some radical changes in teenage girls' attitude to sex. In a more recent study Wilson (1978) revealed some liberalization of attitudes in a group of 20 urban teenage girls. Sex before marriage was acceptable and practised by 13 of the girls, but it was only permissible with one partner and in the context of love and possible future marriage. Any girl who deviated from this prescriptive code was sanctioned equally strongly by males and females:

> Within these groups of girls, expressions of sexuality could only receive support or be condoned when they maintained the triangular relationship of love, sexuality and marriage. . . . Any deviation by a girl from what Reich (1970) has called the repressive triangle resulted in a rejection by her peers. This effectively meant that access to her former social life was denied. . . . The boys also had their part to play in the maintenance of the sexual mores of the neighborhood (that is, in controlling the sexual behaviour of the girls). This was achieved in two ways; either by the boys appearing to support the ideal of romantic love in order to convince the girls to have sex with them without breaking their code of sexual conduct or by sanctioning those girls who freely admitted to believing in sex without love and who appeared to share the boys' instrumental attitude towards sex. (p. 71)

McRobbie (1978b) has also noted that girls censure 'tarts' and believe that their own reputation is in jeopardy simply by associating with them. The stigma may take the form not only of moral outrage but also of pity. Such girls are seen as paying the price for their 'fun' when marriage time arrives. So even today sexual behaviour is regulated quite successfully by the norms and rules of the peer group itself and the *status quo* remains firmly intact. The social dangers of heterosexual relationships has been suggested as a reason for girls' marginality in youth subcultures. As long as pubescent girls remain closeted in their bedrooms, dreaming of inaccessible rock stars, they do not run the risk of actual sexual encounters, with all their attendant rumours and possible stigma (McRobbie, 1978).

It seems unlikely that the court will succeed in controlling a girl's sexual behaviour when her peer group has failed. It will certainly not succeed by complementing her informal label as a 'slag' with a formal one that identifies her as being in 'moral danger'. Neither will placement in a single-sex home do anything other than temporarily curtail her activities. Whether or not girls should be sexually stigmatized where boys are not is at the moment an academic question only. Teenage girls themselves succeed admirably in maintaining the time-honoured distinction between the 'scrubber' and the 'nice girl'.

Running away

Being 'beyond parental control' covers not only precocious sexuality but other forms of misbehaviour as well. Running away from home is another reason why many girls and some boys may be made the subject of care orders. Running away does, of course, carry overtones of sexuality. The stereotypical picture is that of the young teenage girl who is picked up by pimps or drug dealers in the big city and introduced to a life of vice. A second reason for concern is related to compulsory school attendance. Young people under 16, by virtue of the fact that they are still of compulsory school age, are likely to encounter difficulty in finding legitimate employment and so be more likely to fall into criminal careers. As far as the juvenile court is concerned, they are also committing an offence in not being present at a full-time educational institution. Although a young person may be made the subject of a care order up to the age of 18, running away is considered a serious problem only when it occurs below the age of 16.

Like sexuality, running away is an enigmatic area from the point of view of research. Facts and figures are difficult to establish. Certainly, according to self-report figures, a substantial number of teenagers run away from home, if only for a few hours or days. Sometimes this may be done as a protest, either in anger or quite instrumentally in order to attend a party, club or date against the wishes of parents. It is only when the young person stays away for some time and his whereabouts are unknown that real concern is manifested by police, parents and social workers. Once again, girls are seen to be 'at risk' far more than boys and invite far more popular concern and media attention.

In London a number of centres deal with homeless young people. In spite of the pamphlets that they and the National Association of Youth Clubs issue, which warn teenagers not to come to London, thousands do arrive with no money, no jobs and no housing. Centrepoint runs both an emergency shelter and a smaller, longer-term hostel for young people of both sexes. In 1976, for example, the shelter accepted 4458 people and refused another 3188. Girls Alone in London Service (GALS) saw 708 girls in 1977. Not all of these were new customers; at Centrepoint 2173 (less than half) were first-timers, and GALS had 465 new girls. Some of the regular customers were certainly not at risk; many of them made use of the place as a stop-gap measure or even when they missed the last bus home. In spite of the media attention devoted to females, less than half of Centrepoint's annual clientele were female (1203).

The proportion of clients who were under 16 was surprisingly small – at Centrepoint 1.6 per cent of boys and 3.6 per cent of girls were under school-leaving age. GALS put the figure even lower, at 1.8 per cent of all customers (that is, only nine girls per year). At Centrepoint 84.9 per cent of males and 74.8 per cent of females were over 18, and at GALS 66.8 per cent were technically adult. In other words, the media representation of the teenage runaway girl in fact constitutes a relatively small proportion of all those who are young and homeless in London. GALS, in a breakdown of reasons given for homelessness, reports only 5.4 per cent of all its clients as runaways. The most common reason for homelessness was a bad relationship with parents, which had caused 38.4 per cent of girls to leave home and live elsewhere. Almost 20 per cent of the girls were or had been pregnant. All the girls were asked where they had spent the previous night. Only 10.9 per cent had actually slept rough. The majority had stayed with friends or family, in hotels or hostels or had been travelling. Virtually all clients were successfully passed on to more permanent accommodation or were sent home. Only those who refused to accept such help would find themselves homeless the next night.

I talked to some of the workers at Centrepoint. Most rejected the equation of running away with vice among girls. If anything, girls may be more aware of such dangers than boys. As one worker said:

> You can't put the problem on to specifically girls. It stretches right across the board. It depends on the person. I do find that the girls who do come in here tend to hold back more, tend to be a bit more frightened, that bit more wary of these kind of dangers and so will look at things perhaps that bit longer than will a boy. (Personal communication, Centrepoint worker 1978)

In general, girls tend to arrive in pairs or as one member of a heterosexual couple. It is rare to find a single girl wandering the streets alone. Some of the older ones do become involved in prostitution but often voluntarily and for economic reasons. Both the police and social workers accept that there is relatively little they can offer such girls. Their lifestyle, while perhaps widely unacceptable, has been chosen by them and offers particular attractions that a steady job does not.

> The girls who are on the streets are those who choose to. They are either unable to use the help agencies can offer them or they are attracted by the West End scene and what it can offer. But they know that if they come up, we are always here.

However, another member of the team (male) took a less charitable attitude. He related the story of a teenage girl who asked for shelter, claiming that she wanted to get out of prostitution:

What I in fact said to her, because I didn't particularly believe her story – I mean, girls' tears I treat with absolute distaste, in a sense – what I said to her in fact was if she was still stuck tomorrow night to come back at eight o'clock, which was a means of testing her. I did believe she was working in Piccadilly, but I didn't believe she was any more wanting to come out of it. More likely was the fact that she had had a bad night – the weather, wasn't much clientele around – and therefore she was stuck for a bed for a night. And in a sense to take her in on that basis would almost have been morally approving of her situation. As far as I am concerned, I don't give a damn what people do. To me, if people are working Piccadilly, that's fine. But if they have a bad night, they have to pay the price for that in a sense and to take them in is almost supporting what you consider to be a destructive lifestyle.

Had the girl been earning her living in a more acceptable way, her homelessness might have been more sympathetically treated. Similarly, anyone suspected of being on drugs or smelling of alcohol is not admitted. Help from agencies such as these is conditional upon demonstrating at least nominal adherence to conventional moral values.

The particular concern that surrounds girl runaways is related both to the traditional means of socializing girls and to an insistence on the passivity and sexual purity of women. Hagan et al. (1979) suggest that formal and informal social controls are inversely related, both in the community and with respect to individuals. The rise of dependence on the police and on judicial restraints accompanies a breakdown of reliance on the family as a control agency. Furthermore, these two methods of control are differentially applied to and by males and females. The authors contend that women are both the agents (mothers) and objects (daughters) of informal, family control, whereas men are the agents (police, magistrates) and objects (delinquents, criminals) of formal, societal control. They tested this hypothesis by taking measures of self-reported delinquency, degree of control exerted by mother and father and police contact among boys and girls. Maleness correlated positively with the extent of delinquency (+0.40) and police contact (+0.37) but negatively with paternal

(–0.25) and maternal (–0.36) control. This basic thesis certainly fits in with common-sense observation of socialization differences.

Hagan et al. also note that among males delinquent activity (embodying elements of independence, aggressiveness and assertiveness) connotes freedom or the absence of control. It is usually anticipated that teenage boys will struggle to liberate themselves from the control of the family (particularly the mother), and this is considered a healthy part of development toward autonomy. Girls, by contrast, are expected not to escape the informal control system but to change roles within it, moving from objects to agents. When childhood is behind them they traditionally adopt roles as older sisters and finally mothers in their own right. It is easy to see, then, why runaway girls cause such alarm. By breaking out of the informal control cycle, their future position as control agents comes into question, as does the whole system of home-based containment. The moral and sexual sanctions brought to bear on runaway girls are stigma under the guise of paternalistic concern. By viewing runaway girls as sexually cheap, society stigmatizes them. By expressing concern, it encourages them to move back into the security of family control. In the days when the only escape from the family was marriage the nuclear family remained intact, even though a substantial proportion of early marriages were economically and emotionally distressing. As girls come to see at least a part of their future (however transient) as economically autonomous, marriage is postponed until later in life. They escape to big cities, where they hope the chances of employment and anonymity are greater. In the search for this anonymity, such girls reject a purely role-defined identity. They are, at least temporarily, no longer someone's daughter, sister or wife.

While sexist aspects of concern over runaways are still prominent, the class factor remains important. As the director of Centrepoint says:

Society has to acknowledge that it is not just the middle-class group who have the right to leave home. Nobody expects students to go to university or college in their home town, yet when working-class kids want the same kind of independence, there are no facilities. (*The Guardian*, 18 August 1977)

The vast majority of young people in London shelters have a working-class background. Middle-class teenagers who do not leave home to go to college at least leave home armed with relatively well-paid employment, a better chance of getting adequate housing and the knowledge that, if all else fails, they can rely on parents for at least temporary economic support. Their knowledge of housing agencies, accommodation rights and rent tribunals, plus their general confidence and accent, put them at an immediate advantage. Most working-class teenagers come to London with only the vaguest idea of the cost of living and of employment opportunities, let alone geography. Many agencies issue pamphlets warning teenagers of the problems, and Centrepoint publishes a survival guide, offering information on shelters, cheap cafés, contraception and employment agencies. Such a booklet is aimed at those who have tried to survive and have failed. Better still would be help offered before such people become homeless. Independent teenagers have a right to do more than just survive. While they establish themselves, they deserve active help in finding employment and accommodation. They need better preparation at school for the realities of independent living. While university students are treated to three years of effortless food and housing before they must cope alone, society still expects working-class teenagers to struggle through or to remain at home until they are rescued by marriage.

Truancy

As with homelessness and sexual behaviour, it is hard to arrive at any accurate estimate of the magnitude of truancy. The Department of Education and Science's report on school attendance throughout Britain estimates that only 5 per cent of the school population is absent for any reason on any one school day. Tennent (1969), by contrast, quotes a figure of around 1,500,000 absentees out of 8 million schoolchildren every week as the average non-attendance rate (18.75 per cent). By no means all of these absences are accountable for in terms of truancy, however. Kahn and Nursten (1964) estimate that only about 1 per cent of absences are truants. In Manchester Medlicott (1973) found that in only 4–5 per cent of cases of absenteeism were the parents unaware of the child's absence from school.

Persistent absence from some form of full-time education is sufficient grounds for a child under 16 years to appear in juvenile court. In fact, Kahn and Nursten estimate that only 0.5 per cent of truants are taken to juvenile court. Tennent puts the figure even lower in the London borough that he studied – only two out of 1000 truants were actually taken to court (0.2 per cent). As Kahn and Nursten point out, there are many ways of dealing with truancy, only one of which is to bring the child to court. It may be treated as an educational problem, involving the child in a change of class or school, or as a medical or psychiatric one, approached through a local doctor, a psychiatric out-patients department or a child guidance clinic. The range of people who could potentially be involved in a treatment decision is very broad – they include teachers, parents, educational welfare officers, educational psychologists, social workers, probation officers, magistrates and psychiatrists. The action that will be taken depends on a number of factors, and the definition of the child's problem largely depends on which of the professionals is involved. In Manchester, for example, before the 1969 Children and Young Persons Act 350 children per annum appeared before juvenile courts for truancy. Since then the figure has dropped to about 50 per year, in line with the spirit of the new legislation, the aim of which was to decriminalize young peoples' 'problem' behaviour. This new latitude in treatment practices throws far more responsibility on those who are involved at a pre-court stage. It is they who define and treat the behaviour, and there is a body of evidence that strongly suggests that one crucial factor in their evaluation and treatment is social class.

Basic texts on school refusal (for example, Kahn and Nursten, 1964) make a primary distinction between truancy and school phobia. The truancy syndrome is described thus:

Although truants are often dull children, they seem robust, adventurous and crave constant change. They have few strong ties and have had a lack of warm relationships in early life. The homes are often broken. The parents have usually little energy left over for interest in the child's welfare, and they are able to provide little discipline. The children are often the victims of material and emotional poverty. Despite this picture, studies have shown that these children possess fairly normal emotional stability and have hardly any neurotic symptoms. (p. 4)

This contrasts markedly with the description of school phobia:

School phobia is very different from truancy and has its own pathology, manifestations and needs in treatment. ... The child with school phobia seems to come from a materially good home where the emotional climate is likely to be intense rather than lacking, and such children usually have above-average intelligence. (p. 6)

Having thus dismissed truancy as a working-class and therefore psychiatrically uninteresting condition, the book continues to discuss the etiology and treatment of phobia for a further 225 pages, even though school phobia accounts for only a fraction of school absences. Of all referrals to child guidance clinics in 1960, only 6.2 per cent were cases of school phobia, and a breakdown of school absences shows simple truancy to be twice as prevalent as phobia (11.2 per cent and 4.2 per cent respectively). If we include in the truancy figure those cases in which the parents do not insist on the child's return to school, even though there is no medical reason for absence, the truancy rate among absentees rises to 37.2 per cent. In Tennent's study of truants only 10.7 per cent displayed any symptoms that might be considered evidence of school phobia.

The class distinction implicit in these definitions is nowhere explicitly discussed, and the view of working-class children as essentially healthy but naughty and of middle-class children as sick but good is immediately reminiscent of the double-think attitude to sex differences in deliquency. Paternalism towards one faction, whether defined by sex or by class, expresses itself in the same manner: responsibility and accountability are removed from the subject to the family, which has caused the fundamentally 'good' child to become sick. Once the problem is so defined, it requires not punishment but treatment. Similarly, the view of working-class children as virtually immune to psychiatric disturbance is reminiscent of the paradoxical view of women as hardy survivors (see chapter 1), unlike the more sophisticated and therefore more dysfunction-prone male (or, in this case, the middle class). Studies by Hersov (1960) and Cooper (1966) both showed a highly significant effect of class in attempts to discriminate phobias from truants. Hersov considered three groups of children: One group that had been diagnosed as school phobic (Group N – neurotic); one group that had been truanting, but its members had not spent their time at home (Group T – truants); and a matched control group (Group C). The proportion of children in social classes 1 and 2 (that is, fathers in professional and intermediate occupations) was 32 per cent for Group N, 8 per cent for Group T and 14 per cent for the control group. Cooper investigated a group of school non-attenders who were referred to the school psychological service (Group A, school phobics), another group who were handled by school welfare (Group B, truants) and two control groups matched for age and sex. Group A came from families of significantly higher (p < .01) socio-economic status than Group B.

In Hersov's study a number of other variables showed significant differences between truants and phobics. Most of these were clearly related to class: truants more often had adverse school reports and a poor standard of school work, and they experienced frequent changes of school; they also suffered from the absence of father or mother from the home, maternal rejection and inconsistent home discipline. Exactly the same phenomena occurred in Cooper's study: Group A were more intelligent, more truthful, more anxious to respond to authority, more persistent, more fastidious and more affected by failure, and they stayed at home more often when not at school. Group B were significantly less cared-for in appearance. Cooper quite correctly concludes: 'The truants and phobics appear to occupy the opposite extreme ends of socio-economic status and the difference in family size and attitudes to education probably stemmed from this' (p. 228). Neither Hersov nor Cooper considers the possibility that the very allocation of children to these two groups may in itself be class-influenced, or that those two diagnostic categories may be nothing more than class artefacts tagged on to essentially identical behaviour. Tennent (1969) for example, experienced some difficulty in allocating his 65 absentee children to the diagnostic categories. He concluded that eight were school refusers and seven were phobics, although 13 other boys showing 'similar symptoms' were not so adjudicated. It is hardly surprising that such difficulties are encountered. Even directors of child guidance clinics and school psychological services when approached by Cooper were unable to provide breakdowns of phobics and truants. Only 21 per cent of those contacted were able to help. Others called the whole syndrome of school phobia a 'psychiatric fad'.

In principle, any diagnostic label should apply exclusively to a single, specifiable checklist of 'symptoms' or behavioural manifestations. Once two phenomena have been established as separate and discrete problems, it becomes appropriate to search for different etiologies or causes. In the case of school non-attendance, no such diagnostic criterion has been established. Children refuse to attend school, and subsequently, on the basis of social class, they are deemed to have one of two independent problems, one legal and one psychiatric. Cooper has pointed out the practical repercussions of such a class-based dichotomy; school phobias are treated much more sympathetically by teachers and local authorities. Rather than being suspended or sent to juvenile court, phobics are seen by school psychologists or receive psychiatric help from child guidance clinics. A simple scan of any basic bibliography on school absenteeism (for example, that of Kahn and Nursten, 1964) quickly reveals that it is the middle-class phobics who receive the bulk of attention in terms of research and theory. Truancy, on the other hand, is seen as one manifestation of delinquency and therefore receives little consideration as a specific phenomenon.

Psychoanalytical explanations of school phobia are presented in terms of the early relationship between mother and child as it affects the child's development of his own identity at puberty. Although one might imagine this pubescent conflict to be common to all children, apparently it is not. Bolman (1967) investigated several cases of school refusal and found that it was only middle-class children who were capable of suffering from such subtle disturbances:

> Work with children in these disordered slum communities by Parenstedt, Deutsch and others suggests that these children are so massively constricted and over-defended by compulsory school-attendance age that they are incapable of showing the acute separation anxiety type of school refusal and may be better classed as proto-phobic or pre-school phobic. (pp. 1348–9)

A reasonable paraphrase would be that working-class mothers are so inadequate that their children are too damaged psychologically to be able to experience anxiety at leaving them.

Both Coolidge et al. (1957) and Harrington and Hassan (1958) worked with female phobics and were largely in agreement on the etiology of the disturbance. Coolidge et al. suggested that mother and child enter a tacit conspiracy to reject development and eventual adulthood. The mother encourages her daughter's dependency upon her, and this results in the child's inability to pass the Oedipal phase, in which the child must recognize and accept her own sex role, with all its appropriate libidinal direction. Harrington and Hassan similarly blamed the mother but suggested that the sharing of mothering functions with others (often the maternal grandmother) lead to a poor affectional bond between mother and daughter. This in turn hindered the formation of strong feminine identification. They also noted that the first realization of being female is bound to be a depressing experience:

> The issue which throws this system [projective defences] into relief is, in normal development, the first recognition of sex differences, a crisis which leads to a more or less transitory depreciation of herself. (p. 47)

Most females manage to come to terms with themselves eventually. The phobic girl refuses to accept her femininity, however, and regresses to babyhood.

It would be wrong to imply that this infantilized view of phobics is peculiar to girls. Adams et al. (1966) took a similar line with boys (as well as girls). They saw both separation anxiety and sex-role anxiety as functionally similar 'resistances to individuation'. In order to avoid seeing the self as a separate, autonomous being, the child at puberty refuses to leave the mother, to go to school or to accept his or her own sex role. To test this hypothesis, they studied seven male and 14 female school phobics, comparing them on a number of variables. There were no significant sex differences in the proportion showing parental conflict, bisexual conflict and separation anxiety, though boys did score higher on antisocial behaviour. The important figure is the size of correlation between bisexuality and separation anxiety, which for all girls was +0.49 and for all boys −0.26. Puzzled by the negative relation for boys, Adams et al. divided their sample by age. The results are shown in table 6.8. The effect was due to the older boys, who showed separation anxiety but normal heterosexual development. This type of boy was immediately dismissed as fundamentally 'delinquent' and therefore not phobic at all.

> He stands a good chance of ranking high on anti-social behaviour. ... It is conceivable that we were treating these older boys as lower-class characterological disorders with heavy admixtures of anti-social behaviour. (p. 545)

Any subject who fails to confirm the theory is then reclassified as a truant and is of no further interest to psychiatrists.

The question still remains of the link between other forms of delinquency and truancy. Many writers take it as axiomatic that truancy is the first step on the road to crime. Fitzherbert (1977), for example, suggests that for most boys school refusal 'puts

TABLE 6.8 *Correlation between bisexuality and separation anxiety among schoolchildren, by age*

	Boys	Girls
Under 10 years	+0.19	+0.38
Over 10 years	−0.81	+0.52

SOURCE: Adams et al., 1966, pp. 545–6.

[them] in danger of delinquency, drugs or mental illness in later life'. But is there evidence to support such dramatic claims? Studies in Britain by Essex–Carter (1961), McLintoch and Bagot (1952) and Scott (1965) suggest that between 43 and 73 per cent of all adjudicated delinquents have a history of irregular school attendance. In looking at such figures it should be remembered that self-report figures among ordinary schoolchildren show that between 26 and 81 per cent truant from school occasionally. A study of Glasgow school-leavers in 1947 (Ferguson, 1952) produced the results shown in table 6.9. Certainly, truants did commit more detected crimes than regular school attenders, but at least 71.8 per cent of them did not become involved in crime. Tennent (1969) did a more recent follow-up study of a group of boys who were at Stamford House Remand Centre between 1965 and 1968 for breaches of Section 5.40 of the 1944 Education Act. Between 12 and 18 months after their juvenile court appearance only 19 of the 65 had made a court appearance for any criminal offence. Of these 19, 10 had already been previously convicted of crimes and four of the remaining nine appearances were for minor offences. Hersov's (1960) study of 50 school phobics and 50 truants show the latter to lie more often, to wander from home and to steal. However, these behaviours were evaluated by the psychiatrist in charge of the study, who may have been influenced by his knowledge of which groups the boys belonged to. Social-class differences, acknowledged in passing by the author, are not partialled out

TABLE 6.9   *Relationships between school attendance levels and criminality*

| | Number of school-children | Convictions | |
		While at school %	After leaving %
Regular attendance	986	4.1	6.6
Irregular attendance	362	8.5	10.2
Absence through illness	165	7.3	5.5
Absence for domestic reasons	149	6.0	10.7
Truancy	46	28.2	19.5

SOURCE: Ferguson, 1952.

and may be more important than truancy in predicting these behaviours.

Tennent compared his truant boys with a group of boys in detention for theft offences, who were matched for age, class, loss of parents and number and criminality of siblings. There were no differences in the subjects' relationships with other boys or general attitude to school. Property offenders were significantly more likely to have a criminal record and a larger number of convictions. Truants were more likely to have a previous court appearance for truancy and to be remanded at their first prosecution. The disposal of the two types of cases by the court was similar, except that truants were never fined or sent to attendance centres. When a child is categorized as a truant rather than a phobic, he is likely to be dealt with as harshly as any other type of delinquent, even though he has committed no criminal offence. Berg et al. (1978) studied the effects on the subsequent behaviour of truants of various forms of court action. Half of the young people appearing before a juvenile court received supervision orders (to be carried out by Social Services Departments), and the other half had their cases adjourned. Allocation to treatment condition was carried out randomly. Subsequently, the supervised group was absent more frequently than the adjourned group. Although the groups were matched for previous criminal offences, in the follow-up period the supervised group committed more crimes than those who had had no action taken against them. The evidence certainly suggests that treating truants as criminals helps to ensure that they will become criminals.

Increasingly, attention is being focused on the school itself. If young people refuse to attend school it may be because they gain little satisfaction from what the school is offering. Power et al. (1967) found that within one London borough some schools were responsible for more than their share of adjudicated delinquents. The most obvious explanation is clearly that some schools take their pupils from particularly criminogenic neighbourhoods. To test this hypothesis, the authors divided the borough into the 301 enumeration districts used for the 1961 census and looked at the relative delinquency rates per 100 boys aged 11 to 14. In this way they were able to define high- and low-delinquency districts and to look at the interaction between

TABLE 6.10 *Delinquency rates: interaction between district and school in a London borough*

| Secondary schools in Tower Hamlets | Delinquency rates per 100 boys | | |
	All districts	High-delinquency district	Low-delinquency district
School B	3	3	4
School D	4	6	3
School K	7	9	5
School C	11	13	9
School Q	25	25	25

SOURCE: Power et al., 1967, p. 543.

the area in which the boys lived and the schools they attended. The results are shown in table 6.10. These data show clearly that the school contributes more to the likelihood of a boy's delinquency than does the area in which he lives. A boy living in a low-delinquency district is six times more likely to be delinquent if he attends school Q than if he attends school B.

A similar study of truancy would be valuable. Instead of providing therapy for the middle classes and punishment for the working class – and who can say which causes more damage? – we should turn our attention to the schools, which may be as much to blame as the parents or the children.

CHAPTER 7

Epilogue: the Politics of Subjectivity

As the quantity of work on female crime grows, so does the diversity of its subject matter. Studies are now looking beyond the old concerns with women as the perpetrators of prostitution and shoplifting and as the victims of rape and wife-beating. Cross-cultural analyses have begun (Adler, 1977), as well as longitudinal studies (Gora, 1979). Research is beginning to look at 'male' factors, such as friendship groups (Giordano, 1978), career opportunities (Datesman et al., 1975) and education (Jensen and Eve, 1976). But very many of the studies display in their introductory notes a continuing concern with two major problems. The first is the link between the women's movement and the increase in female crime. The second is the future direction in which the study of female crime should proceed.

In both cases the issues are political and polemic. In both cases they reflect predominantly middle-class concerns. Over the last decade the women's movement has oscillated uncertainly between personal and legislative liberation for women. Consciousness-raising, assertiveness training, medical self-help groups and the destigmatization of lesbianism have been the visible manifestations of the first. Abortion availability, the Equal Rights Amendment and sex discrimination laws are instances of the second. Ultimately, legal changes will improve the lifestyle of all women, regardless of race or class, but personal liberation has been almost exclusively the privilege of the middle class. Indeed, it has taken on an importance far in excess of its true role in bringing equality to women in general. The extent to which such women have sunk into privileged self-absorption is illustrated by their refusal to acknowledge the real importance of societal and structural changes. Adler (1975), for example, states:

234

Nor is it in the factories or universities or legislature that the most consequential events are occurring. The Rubicons which women must cross, the sex barriers which they must breach are ultimately those that exist in their own minds. (p. 250)

By reducing the issue to a personal and intellectual one, the material basis of women's position is ignored. By 'sorting out her head', it is claimed, woman can overcome the problem. Self-analysis may, in fact, be the answer for university-educated professionals, but it is unlikely to cut much ice among factory workers.

This detachment from the real world is equally evident in the main concerns of those criminologists who study women. The role of the movement in crime or the place of female criminality in the study of sociology are of little more than 'academic' interest, an indulgence of those whose future lies in perpetuating such questions. To sit in offices and worry about intellectual abstractions may be a more comfortable choice than going out into the street or prison to gather data, but if female criminology is to be more than a branch of the philosophy of knowledge, that is what must be done. And that is why in this book I have chosen to spend more time on research results than on fruitless speculation. Unfortunately, changes in the implementation of law and the future of research and practice are more likely to result from the publicity given to these kinds of questions than from the body of research that has been produced to date. Television, newspapers, magazines, novels and government reports have all reflected a fascination with the women's move-ment and crime. The old guard accuses women of having brought about their own downfall. Feminists deny that any link exists. Sex, crime and controversy form a very marketable com-modity.

In my opinion, the question of whether women's liberation has had a causal effect on the increase in the number of females arrested is an unanswerable one. In the first place, reliable statistics are not available to prove or disprove the proposition. Crime statistics from early in the century can be interpreted only with reference to the general willingness of the police and the courts to prosecute women at that time. This we have no way of knowing. Second, changes in legislation mean that many offences are not comparable over time. Third, these statistics are affected by fluctuations in such factors as the size of the police force, the concentration of police in a given area or on a certain crime and the relative size of the female population within specified age categories. In addition to this, there is the problem of operationalizing female liberation. Economic arguments in terms of employment and wages would not satisfy those who maintain that liberation is 'in the head'. Legislative changes would not satisfy those who maintain that liberation lies in personal relationships. Self-reports of attitudes or surveys of contemporary literature would not be acceptable to those who demand 'scientific' data. Nevertheless, Gora (1979) has made an attempt to address the issue of whether the seriousness of women's crime is related to recent social changes. By analysing sex differences in crime seriousness between 1939 and 1976, she was able to compare the effects of the age of the offender, periodicity (the years in which most serious crime was committed) and cohort (whether certain birth cohorts had particularly serious crime rates). The liberation argument would favour a periodicity hypothesis, contending that the effects of the women's movement should have been evident in the last ten years. However, sex differences were best predicted by cohort and were unrelated to recent social changes. These cohort effects were almost certainly the result of the particular *economic* periods during which these women lived.

It should come as no surprise that sex differences in crime (as in many other spheres) are ultimately dictated by economic factors. Unemployment and inflation have their greatest impact on low wage earners, so that it is all the more surprising how often studies of female criminality show little concern with social class. Some of the better studies at least attempt to partial it out as a variable or hold it constant in the control group. But virtually no studies look at social class directly as a critical variable in determining the parameters of 'femininity' and 'criminality'. Such studies have been done among males and have produced some of the most clear-sighted analyses (see Miller, 1958). A joint focus on gender and class from an economic and criminal viewpoint would seem an obvious next step, since for years sociologists and feminists have noted the change in 'acceptable' female behaviour as a function of the economic climate. Under conditions of high unemployment women are squeezed out of the work force and back into the home: the psychological pressure exerted on women in the post-war years is exemplified by Bowlby (1953). Similarly, when birth rates drop access to abortion is made more difficult, just as when it rises contraception and even homosexuality are encouraged by the law. The interplay between economics, class and sex role is far more likely to account for fluctuations in crime than are genetic differences or child-rearing practices.

It is evident that many proponents of liberation have become preoccupied more with middle-class female public relations than with empirical research. While always ready to take credit for any positive steps they may achieve, they show no interest at all in working-class women, who are the casualties of the economic system in which they live. For example, at the National Conference on Women and Crime in Washington, DC, in 1976 one feminist expressed her anger at the fact that women criminals were even being discussed:

> You can tell a lot of us are upset. I think the reason is because we came to talk about *what we see as women who are victims*, victims of law like prostitution, victims of criminal justice system such as the kind of treatment they get in prison and victims of crime such as rape and battered women. (Loving and Olson, 1976, p. 10, present author's emphasis)

What she saw as a victim was the victim of *men* rather than of the whole economic system. This has been a recurring theme of the American women's movement. Without a more radical change in the *status quo*, we shall succeed only in liberating women into poverty, alienation, despair and crime – along with the men who are there already. As Jock Young has pointed out, the time has come for women to move out of the 'politics of subjectivity into a fully socialist analysis' (Taylor et al., 1975). The movement in America, however, seems to favour leaving intact the capitalist structure. This predominant concern with getting women into the higher echelons of business and professional life makes this clear. By setting up the male sex as the enemy, energy is diverted into a relatively harmless personal and subjective struggle that leaves the economic system unchallenged. If these women succeed, they will replace a male-dominated repressive system with a female-dominated one. Working-class men and women will remain in the same old situation, and the crime rate will reflect this.

In Britain Smart (1977) has posed the question of the academic future of female criminology. Should the study of women constitute a separate and distinct branch of psychology or sociology, or should it be integrated into the general study of people in society? The first alternative, Smart suggests, may result in a 'ghetto' effect, as a result of which the study of women by women may become a low-status enterprise. The second alternative presents the danger that male scientists might take over and treat women 'analytically in ways similar to any other subject of study', (p. 179). Such paranoia does women a great disservice. In the world towards which we are working, why should we assume that women as researchers or as subjects of study should be second-rate? Such a view seems to support the very state of affairs from which we are trying to escape. Rather than perpetuating well-worn catechisms about our own academic inferiority, surely we should begin the task of doing such research and doing it well. Smart's objections to the integration of women's studies into the mainstream of social science clearly reflects the subjective politics of which the women's movement has been accused. She fears that the study of women will become 'just another area of social science, like education, industry or race' (p. 179). But unless we admit that issues such as these are just as important as sex in determining social injustice, the study of women will sink into a morass of impotent and egocentric self-pity. The poorly educated, the production-line worker, blacks – these are people we should not be ashamed to stand next to in terms of academic study or political action.

It is a truism to say that social science cannot be apolitical; but there are also considerations to be made in terms of interpretative parsimony. According to common sense and scientific practice, a phenomenon requires separate and distinct study in so far as it is unique. If reasoning, memory, learning and so on were shown to operate according to totally different laws in men and women, we should need a separate psychology of women. If economic forces of supply and demand no longer

applied when females ran the economy, we should need a whole
new economic theory. If women did not respond to unemployment and marginal status with alienation, we should need a new
sociology. We do not appear to need a second set of theories for
women. We do, however, need empirical studies that document
the particular nature of social and psychological effects among
different races, classes and sexes. The laws apply equally, but
their effect is specific to the social and historical background of
any given group.

Smart's contention that women as a topic have been ignored
as much by radical criminologists as by everyone else is
manifestly true. But we should not let our disappointment turn
into disillusionment. We do indeed need studies of women (as
Smart concludes) to increase their visibility as a legitimate topic
of research, to document the position in which women find
themselves and ultimately to improve their position. Whether
such research is performed by men or women matters less than
the quality of the research. Women are people too – people
divided by opportunity, class and wealth. Unless we realize the
paramount importance of these factors, we shall succeed only in
setting up an artificial battle between men and women rather
than addressing the real struggle between those who have and
those who have nothing.

Bibliography

Adams, P. L., McDonald, N. F. and Huey, W. P. (1966), School phobia and bi-sexual conflict: a report of 21 cases, *American Journal of Psychiatry*, 123, 541–7.

Adler, F. (1975), *Sisters in Crime*, New York: McGraw-Hill.

Adler, F. (1977), The interaction between women's emancipation and female criminality: a cross-cultural perspective, *International Journal of Criminology and Penology*, 5, 101–12.

Anderson, V. V. (1917), The criminal woman as seen in court, *Journal of the American Institute for Criminal Law and Criminology*, 8, 902–10.

Andry, R. G. (1960), *Delinquency and Parental Pathology*, London: Methuen.

Arboleda-Florez, J., Durie, H., and Costello, J. (1977), Shoplifting – an ordinary crime?, *International Journal of Offender Therapy and Comparative Criminology*, 21, 201–7.

Ardrey, R. (1976), *The Hunting Hypothesis*, London: Collins.

Argyle, M., Graham, J. A., Campbell, A., and White, P. (1979), The rules of different situations, *New Zealand Psychologist*, 8, 13–22.

Argyle, M., and Little, B. B. (1972), Do personality traits apply to social behaviour?, *Journal for the Theory of Social Behaviour*, 2, 1–35.

Armstrong, G. (1977), Females under the law – 'protected' but unequal, *Crime and Delinquency*, 23, 109–20.

Ashley-Montagu, M. F. (1976), *The Nature of Human Aggression*, New York: Oxford University Press.

Bandura, A., Ross, D., and Ross, S. A. (1961), Transmission of aggression through imitation of aggressive models, *Journal of Abnormal and Social Psychology*, 63, 575–82.

Bandura, A., and Walters, R. (1959), *Adolescent Aggression*, New York: Ronald Press.

Barack, L., and Widom, C. S. (1977), Levels of extraversion, neuroticism and psychoticism in women awaiting trial, Harvard University: unpublished manuscript.

240

Beall, H. S., and Panton, J. S. (1956), Use of the MMPI as an index of escapism, *Journal of Clinical Psychology*, 12, 392–4.

Becker, H. S. (1973) *Outsiders: Studies in the Sociology of Deviance*, New York and London: The Free Press.

Berg, I., Constardine, M., Hullin, R., McGuire, R., and Tyver, S. (1978), The effect of two randomly allocated court procedures on truancy, *British Journal of Criminology*, 18, 232–44.

Berlins, M., and Wansell, G. (1974), *Caught in the Act*, Harmondsworth: Penguin.

Bhagat, M., and Fraser, W. I. (1970), Young offenders' images of self and surroundings: a semantic enquiry, *British Journal of Psychiatry*, 117, 381–7.

Blackburn, R. (1974a), *Personality and the Classification of Psychopathic Disorders*, London: Special Hospitals Research Reports.

Blackburn, R. (1974b), MMPI dimensions of sociability and impulse control, *Journal of Consulting and Clinical Psychology*, 37, 166.

Blos, P. (1957), Preoedipal factors in the etiology of female delinquency, *Psychoanalytic Studies of the Child*, 12, 229–42.

Bolman, W. M. (1967), A behavior systems analysis of the school refusal syndrome. *American Journal of Orthopsychiatry*, 37, 348–9.

Bowlby, J. (1953), *Child Care and the Growth of Love*, Harmondsworth: Penguin.

Boyle, J. (1977), *A Sense of Freedom*, Harmondsworth: Penguin.

Broverman, I. K., Broverman, D. M., Clarkson, E. E., Rosengrantz, P. S., and Vogel, S. R. (1970), Sex role stereotypes and clinical judgements of health, *Journal of Consulting and Clinical Psychology*, 34, 1–7.

Broverman, D. M., Klaiber, E. L., Kobayashi, Y., and Vogel, W. (1968), Roles of activation and inhibition in sex differences in cognitive abilities, *Psychological Review*, 75, 23–50.

Brown, W. K. (1977), Black female gangs in Philadelphia, *International Journal of Offender Therapy and Comparative Criminology*, 21, 221–8.

Buss, A. H. (1961), *The Psychology of Aggression*, New York: Wiley.

Butcher, H., Coward, R., Evarish, M., Garber, J., Harrison, R., and Winship, J. (1974), *Images of Women in the Media*, Birmingham: Centre for Contemporary Cultural Studies.

Cameron, M. O. (1964), *The Booster and the Snitch*, New York: The Free Press.

Campbell, A. (1976), The Role of the Peer Group in Female Delinquency, Oxford University: unpublished D.Phil. thesis.

Campbell, A. (1977), What makes a girl turn to crime?, *New Society*, 39, 172–3.

Campbell, A. (1978), *Female Aggression*, paper delivered to the Contemporary Violence Research Centre Conference, Oxford, September, 1978.

Campbell, A. and Marsh, P. (1979), *Aspects of Violence and Aggression in Community Contexts*, Oxford: Report to the Whitbread Foundation.

Cavanagh, W. E. (1959), *The Child and the Court*, London: Gollancz.

Chesney-Lind, M. (1973), Judicial enforcement of the female sex-role: the family court and the female delinquent, *Issues in Criminology*, 8, 51–69.

Chesney-Lind, M. (1974), Juvenile delinquency: the sexualisation of female crime, *Psychology Today*, 8, 43–6.

Chesney-Lind, M. (1977), Judicial paternalism and the female status offender: training women to know their place, *Crime and Delinquency*, 23, 121–9.

Cicourel, A. V. (1968), *The Social Organisation of Juvenile Justice*, New York: Wiley.

Clark, J. P., and Tifft, L. L. (1966), Polygraph and interview validation of self-reported deviant behaviour, *American Sociological Review*, 31, 516–23.

Cleckley, H. (1964), *The Mask of Sanity*, St Louis: Mosby.

Cloninger, C. R., and Guze, S. B. (1970), Psychiatric illness and female criminality: the role of sociopathy and hysteria in the anti-social woman, *American Journal of Psychiatry*, 127, 301–11.

Cloward, R. A., and Ohlin, L. E. (1960), *Delinquency and Opportunity*, Glencoe: The Free Press.

Cochrane, R. (1971), Personality and value in delinquent boys and girls and among high school students in Michigan (unpublished paper).

Cohen, A. K. (1955), *Delinquent Boys: The Culture of the Gang*, Glencoe: The Free Press.

Cohen, A. K., and Short, J. F. (1958), Research in delinquent subcultures, *Journal of Social Issues*, 14, 20–37.

Cohen, S. (1972), *Folk Devils and Moral Panic*, London: MacGibbon and Kee.

Cohn, Y. (1970), Criteria for the probation officer's recommendation to the juvenile court judge, in P. G. Garabedian and D. C. Gibbons (eds.), *Becoming Delinquent*, Chicago: Aldine.

Conner, H. L., and Levine, S. (1969), Hormonal influences on aggressive behavior, in S. Garattini and E. B. Segg (eds.), *Aggressive Behavior*, Amsterdam: Excerpta Medica Foundation.

Coolidge, J. C., Hahn, P. B., and Peck, A. L. (1957), School phobia: neurotic crisis or way of life?, *American Journal of Orthopsychiatry*, 27, 296–306.

Cooper, M. G. (1966), School refusal: an enquiry into the part played by school and home, *Education Research*, 8, 223–9.

Cowie, J., Cowie, B., and Slater, E. (1968), *Delinquency in Girls*, London: Heinemann.

Dalton, K. (1961), Menstruation and crime, *British Medical Journal*, 2, 1752–3.

Daniel, S., and McGuire, P. (eds) (1972), *The Paint House*, Harmondsworth: Penguin.

Datesman, S. K., Scarpitti, F. R., and Stephenson, R. M. (1975), Female delinquency: an application of self and opportunity theories, *Journal of Research in Crime and Delinquency*, 12, 107–22.

Davies, R. (1976), Girls appearing before a juvenile court, in Home Office Research Unit, *Further Studies of Female Offenders*, London: HMSO.

Debuyst, C., Leiour, G., and Racine, A. (1960), *Petits voleurs de grands magasins*, Brussels: CEDI.

Deutsch, R., Esser, A. H., and Sossin, K. M. (1978), Dominance, aggression and the functional use of space in institutionalized female adolescents, *Aggressive Behavior*, 4, 313–29.

Dickens, B. M. (1969), Shops, shoplifting and law enforcement, *Criminal Law Review*, 464–71.

Downes, D. M. (1966), *The Delinquent Solution*, London: Routledge and Kegan Paul.

Durkheim, E. (1951), *Suicide: A Study in Sociology*, Glencoe: The Free Press.

Efran, M. G. (1974), The effect of physical appearance on judgement of guilt, interpersonal attraction and severity of recommended punishment in a simulated jury task, *Journal of Research in Personality*, 8, 45–54.

Ellis, D. P., and Austin, P. (1971), Menstruation and aggressive behavior in a correctional center for women. *Journal of Criminal Law, Criminology and Police Science*, 62, 388–95.

Epps, P. (1961), Women shoplifters in Holloway, in T. C. N. Gibbens and J. Prince, *Shoplifting*, London: Institute for the Study and Treatment of Delinquency.

Epps, P., and Parnell, R. W. (1952), Physique and temperament of women delinquents compared with women undergraduates, *British Journal of Medical Psychology*, 25, 249–55.

Erhardt, A. A., and Baker, S. W. (1974), Fetal androgens, human central nervous system differentiation and behavior sex differences, in R. C. Friedman, R. W. Richart and R. L. Vande Wiele, *Sex Differences in Behavior*, New York: Wiley.

Erickson, M. L. (1971), The group context of delinquent behavior, *Social Problems*, 19, 114–29.

Essex-Carter, A. (1961), Boys on remand – a study of 367 cases, *British Journal of Criminology*, 2, 132–49.

Eysenck, H. J. (1964), *Crime and Personality*, London: Routledge and Kegan Paul.

Farrington, D. P. (1973), Self-reports of deviant behaviour: Predictive and stable?, *Journal of Criminal Law and Criminology*, 64, 99–110.

Fears, D. (1977), Communication in English juvenile courts, *The Sociological Review*, 25, 131–45.

Felice, M., and Offord, D. R. (1971), Girl delinquents: a review, *Corrective Psychiatry and Journal of Social Therapy*, 17, 18–33.

Ferguson, T. (1952), *The Young Delinquent in his Social Setting*, London: Oxford University Press.

Fesbach, N. D. (1969), Sex differences in children's modes of aggressive responses toward outsiders, *Palmer Quarterly*, 15, 249–58.

Figes, E. (1975), Guilty men and sick women, *Psychology Today*, 9, 13–17.

Fitzherbert, K. (1977), Going unwillingly to school, *New Society*, 39, 332–4.

Ford, D. (1975), *Children, Courts and Caring*, London: Constable.

Fox, R. (1977), The inherent rules of violence, in P. Collett (ed.), *Social Rules and Social Behaviour*, Oxford: Blackwell.

Freeman, D. (1964), Human aggression in anthropological perspective, in J. D. Carthy and F. J. Ebling (eds.), *The Natural History of Aggression*, London: Academic Press.

Freud, S. (1973), Femininity, in *New Introductory Lectures on Psychoanalysis*, J. Strachey and A. Richards (eds.), Harmondsworth: Penguin; taken from papers originally written in 1925 and 1931.

Fulker, D. (1979), *Genetic factors in aggression*, paper delivered to Contemporary Violence Research Centre conference, Perspectives on Aggression and Violence, Oxford, September 1979.

Fyvel, T. R. (1963), *The Insecure Offenders*, Harmondsworth: Penguin.

Gannon, T. M. (1966), Emergence of the defensive gang, *Federal Probation*, 30, 44–8.

Gardner, R., and Heider, K. G. (1968), *Gardens of War*, New York: Random House.

Gibbens, T. C. N. (1959), Supervision and probation of adolescent girls, *British Journal of Delinquency*, 10, 84–103.

Gibbens, T. C. N. (1971), Female offenders, *British Journal of Hospital Medicine*, 6, 279–86.

Gibbens, T. C. N., Palmer, C., and Prince, J. (1971), Mental health aspects of shoplifting, *British Medical Journal*, 3, 612–15.

Gibbens, T. C. N., and Prince, J. (1962), *Shoplifting*, London: Institute for the Study and Treatment of Delinquency.

Gibson, H. B., Morrison, S., and West, D. J. (1970), The confession of known offences in response to a self-reported delinquency schedule, *British Journal of Criminology*, 10, 277–80.

Giordano, P. (1978), Girls, guys and gangs: the changing social context of female delinquency, *Journal of Criminal Law and Criminology*, 69, 126–32.

Glueck, S., and Glueck, E. T. (1934), *Five Hundred Delinquent Women*, New York: Knopf.

Gold, M. (1966), Undetected delinquent behavior, *Journal of Research in Crime and Delinquency*, 3, 27–46.

Gold, M. (1970), *Delinquent Behavior in an American City*, California: Wadsworth.

Gora, J. G. (1979), *A cohort analysis of trends in crime seriousness 1929–1976*, paper delivered to the 31st meeting of the American Society of Criminology, Philadelphia, November.

Goy, R. W. (1968), Organising effects of androgens on the behaviour of rhesus monkeys, in R. P. Michael (ed.), *Endocrinology and Human behaviour*, London: Oxford University Press.

Gray, J. A. (1971), Sex differences in emotional behaviour in mammals including man: endocrine bases, *Acta Psychologica*, 35, 29–46.

Gray, J. A., and Drewett, R. F. (1977), The genetics and development of sex differences, in R. B. Cattell and R. M. Dreger (eds.), *Handbook of Modern Personality Theory*, London: Wiley.

Guibord, A. S. B. (1917), Physical states of criminal women, *Journal of the American Institute of Criminal Law and Criminology*, 8, 82–95.

Hagan, J., Simpson, J. H., and Gillis, A. R. (1979), The sexual stratification of social control, *British Journal of Sociology*, 30, 25–38.

Hamburg, D. A. (1971), Psychobiological studies of aggressive behavior, *Nature*, 230, 19–23.

Hannum, T. E., and Warman, R. E. (1964), The MMPI

characteristics of incarcerated females, *Journal of Research in Crime and Delinquency*, 1, 119–26.

Hanson, K. (1964), *Rebels in the Streets: The Story of New York's Girl Gangs*, Englewood Cliffs: NJ: Prentice-Hall.

Hardt, R. H., and Peterson-Hardt, S. (1977), On determining the quality of the self-report delinquency method, *Journal of Research in Crime and Delinquency*, 14, 247–61.

Hare, R. (1970), *Psychopathy: Theory and Research*, New York: Wiley.

Hare, R., and Shalling, D. (eds.) (1978), *Psychopathic Behaviour: Approaches to Research*, London: Wiley.

Harlow, H. F., and Harlow, M. (1962), Social deprivation in monkeys, *Scientific American*, 207, 136–46.

Harré, R., and Secord, P. (1972), *The Explanation of Social Behaviour*, Oxford: Blackwell.

Harrington, M., and Hassan, J. (1958), Depression in girls during latency, *British Journal of Medical Psychology*, 31, 43–50.

Harris, M. (1974), *Cows, Pigs, Wars and Witches*, London: Hutchinson.

Hart, T. (1975), *The New Adolescent Offender*, paper delivered to The Institute for the Study and Treatment of Delinquency, Spring conference.

Hatfield, J. S., Ferguson, L. R., and Alpert, R. (1967), Mother–child interaction and the socialisation process, *Child Development*, 38, 365–414.

Healy, W. (1925), A review of some studies of delinquents and delinquency, *Archives of Neurology and Psychiatry*, 14, 25–30.

Healy, W., and Bronner, A. F. (1936), *New Light on Delinquency and its Treatment*, London: Oxford University Press.

Heidensohn, F. (1968), The deviance of women: a critique and an enquiry, *British Journal of Sociology*, 19, 160–75.

Hersov, L. A. (1960), Refusal to go to school, *Journal of Child Psychology and Psychiatry*, 1, 137–45.

Hindelang, M. J. (1971), Age, sex and the versatility of delinquent involvements, *Social Problems*, 18, 522–35.

Hindelang, M. J. (1976), With a little help from their friends: group participation in reported delinquent behaviour, *British Journal of Criminology*, 16, 109–25.

Hirschi, T. (1969), *Causes of Delinquency*, Berkeley and Los Angeles: University of California Press.

Hoffman-Bustamante, D. (1973), The nature of female criminality, *Issues in Criminology*, 8, 117–36.

Hoggart, R. (1958), *The Uses of Literacy*, Harmondsworth: Penguin.

Hoghughi, M., and Nethercott, S. (1977), *Troubled and Troublesome:*

A Comparative Study of Boys and Girls Under Conditions of Security, Durham: Aycliffe Studies of Problem Children.

Home Office (1973), *Shoplifting and Thefts by Shop Staff*, Report of a Working Party on Internal Shop Security, London: HMSO.

Home Office (1978), *Criminal Statistics for England and Wales*, London: HMSO.

Hull, C. L. (1952), *A Behavior System: An Introduction to Behavior Theory Concerning the Individual Organism*, New Haven: Yale University Press.

Hutt, C. (1972), *Males and Females*, Harmondsworth: Penguin.

Jamison, R. N. (1977), *Personality, anti-social behaviour and risk perception in adolescents*, paper delivered to the British Psychological Society, London.

Jefferson, T. (ed.) (1975), *Resistance Through Rituals*, London: Hutchinson/Birmingham Centre for Contemporary Cultural Studies.

Jensen, G. J., and Eve, R. (1976), Sex differences in delinquency: an examination of popular sociological explanations, *Criminology*, 13, 427–48.

Jolly, A. (1972), *The Evolution of Primate Behavior*, New York: Macmillan.

Kahn, J. H., and Nursten, J. P. (1964), *Unwillingly to School*, London: Pergamon.

Kaplan, A. F. (1971), cited in N. M. Ferdon, Chromosomal abnormalities and anti-social behaviour, *Journal of Genetic Psychology*, 118, 281–92.

Klein, D. (1973), The etiology of female crime: A review of the literature, *Issues in Criminology*, 8, 3–30.

Klein, M. W., and Crawford, L. Y. (1967), Groups, gangs and cohesiveness, *Journal of Research in Crime and Delinquency*, 4, 63–75.

Klüver, H., and Bucy, P. C. (1939), Preliminary analysis of functions of temporal lobes in monkeys, *Archives of Neurology and Psychiatry*, 42, 979–1000.

Koller, K. M. (1971), Parental deprivation, family background and female delinquency, *British Journal of Psychiatry*, 118, 319–27.

Konopka, G. (1966), *The Adolescent Girl in Conflict*, Englewood Cliffs, NJ: Prentice-Hall.

Kretschmer, E. (1925), *Physique and Character*, New York: Harcourt, Brace and Co.

Krohn, M., Waldo, G. P., and Chiricos, T. G. (1975), Self reported delinquency: a comparison of structured interviews and self administered checklists, *Journal of Criminal Law and Criminology*, 65, 543–53.

Kulik, J. A., Stein, K. B., and Sarbin, T. R. (1968), Disclosure of delinquent behavior under conditions of anonymity and non-anonymity, *Journal of Consulting and Clinical Psychology*, 32, 506–9.

Kvaraceus, W. C., and Miller, W. B. (1959), *Delinquent Behavior Culture and the Individual*, Washington: National Education Association.

Lagerspetz, K. M. J. (1969), Aggression and aggressiveness in laboratory mice, in S. Garattini and E. B. Segg (eds.), *Aggressive Behavior*, Amsterdam: Excerpta Medica Foundation.

Lemert, E. M. (1951), *Social Pathology*, New York: McGraw-Hill.

Lombroso, C., and Ferrero, W. (1959), *The Female Offender*, New York: Peter Owen Ltd.; originally published in 1895.

Lorenz, K. (1966), *On Aggression*, London: Methuen.

Loving, N., and Olson, L. (1976), *Proceedings of the National Conference on Women and Crime*, Washington, D.C.: National League of Cities/US Conference of Mayors.

Maccoby, E., and Jacklin, C. N. (1974), *The Psychology of Sex Differences*, Stanford: Stanford University Press.

McIntyre, A. (1972), Sex differences in children's aggression, *Proceedings of the 80th Annual Convention of the American Psychological Association*, 7, 93–4.

McLintoch, F. H., and Bagot, J. H. (1952), *Detention in Remand Homes*, London: Macmillan.

McRobbie, A. (1978a), *Jackie: An Ideology of Adolescent Femininity*, Birmingham: Centre for Contemporary Cultural Studies.

McRobbie, A. (1978b), Working class girls and the culture of femininity, Birmingham University: unpublished MA thesis.

McRobbie, A., and Garber, J. (1975), Girls and subcultures: an exploration, in T. Jefferson (ed.), *Resistance Through Rituals*, London: Hutchinson/Birmingham Centre for Contemporary Cultural Studies.

Mark, V. H., and Ervin, F. R. (1970), *Violence and the Brain*, New York: Harper and Row.

Marsh, P. (1978), *Aggro: The Illusion of Violence*, London: Dent and Son.

Marsh, P., and Campbell, A. (1978a), The youth gangs of New York go into business, *New Society*, 46, 67–9.

Marsh, P., and Campbell, A. (1978b), The Sex Boys on their own turf, *New Society*, 46, 133–6.

Marsh, P., Rosser, E., and Harré, R. (1978), *The Rules of Disorder*, London: Routledge and Kegan Paul.

Marx, K., and Engels, F. (1977), *Manifesto of the Communist Party*, Peking: Foreign Language Press; first published 1848.

May, D. (1977), Delinquent girls before the courts, *Medicine, Science and the Law*, 17, 203–12.

May, D. (1978), Juvenile shoplifters and the organisation of store security: a case study in the social construction of delinquency, *International Journal of Criminology and Penology*, 6, 137–60.

Medlicott, P. (1973), Is truancy really a problem?, *New Society*, 25, 768–70.

Merrick, B. (1970), Shoplifting – a microcosm, *Criminologist*, 5, 68–81.

Merton, R. K. (1957), *Social Theory and Social Structure*, Glencoe: The Free Press.

Miller, W. B. (1958), Lower class culture as a generating milieu of gang delinquency, *Journal of Social Issues*, 14, 5–19.

Miller, W. B. (1975), *Violence by Youth Gangs as a Crime Problem in Major American Cities*, Washington, DC: United States Government Printing Office.

Mischel, W. (1966), A social learning view of sex differences in behavior, in E. Maccoby (ed.), *The Development of Sex Differences*, Stanford: Stanford University Press.

Mischel, W. (1968), *Personality and Assessment*, New York: Wiley.

Money, J. (1965), Influences of hormones on sexual behavior, *American Review of Medicine*, 16, 67–82.

Money, J., and Erhardt, A. A. (1972), *Man and Woman, Boy and Girl*, Baltimore and London: Johns Hopkins University Press.

Morris, R. (1964), Female delinquents and relational problems, *Social Forces*, 43, 82–9.

Morris, R. (1966), Attitudes towards delinquency by delinquents, non-delinquents and their friends, *British Journal of Criminology*, 5, 249–65.

Moynihan, D. P. (1965), *The Negro Family: A Case for National Action*, Washington, DC: United States Government Printing Office.

Neustatter, W. L. (1953), *Psychological Disorder and Crime*, London: Johnson.

Nye, F. I. (1958), *Family Relationships and Delinquent Behavior*, New York: Wiley.

O'Kelly, E. (1955), Some observations on relationships between delinquent girls and their parents, *British Journal of Medical Psychology*, 28, 59–66.

Oakley, A. (1972), *Sex, Gender and Society*, London: Maurice Temple Smith.

Omark, D. R., Omark, M., and Edelman, M. (1973), *Peer group interactions from an evolutionary perspective*, paper presented to the Society for Research in Child Development Conference, Philadelphia.

Panton, J. H. (1974), Personality differences between male and female prison inmates (measured by the MMPI), *Criminal Justice and Behaviour*, 1, 40–7.

Parker, H. J. (1974), *View from the Boys*, Plymouth: Latimer Trend Co.

Patrick, J. (1973), *A Glasgow Gang Observed*, Bristol: Eyre Methuen.

Patterson, G. R., Littman, R. A., and Bricker, W. (1967), Assertive behavior in children: a step toward a theory of aggression, *Monographs of the Society for Research in Child Development*, 32, 13.

Persky, H., Smith, K. D., and Basu, G. K. (1971), Relation of psychologic measures of aggression and hostility to testosterone production in man, *Psychosomatic Medicine*, 33, 265–77.

Peterson, D. R., and Becker, W. C. (1965), Family interaction and delinquency, in H. C. Quay (ed.), *Juvenile Delinquency: Research and Theory*, Princeton, N.J.: Van Nostrand.

Peterson, D. R., Quay, H. C., and Cameron, G. R. (1959), Personality and background factors in juvenile delinquency as inferred from questionnaire responses, *Journal of Consulting Psychology*, 23, 395–9.

Phillips, D. L., and Segal, B. E. (1969), Sexual status and psychiatric symptoms, *American Sociological Review*, 34, 58–72.

Piliavin, I., and Briar, S. (1964), Police encounters with juveniles, *American Journal of Sociology*, 70, 206–14.

Pollak, O. (1961), *The Criminality of Women*, New York: A. S. Barnes and Co.; originally published in 1950, Philadelphia: University of Pennsylvania Press.

Powell, R., and Clarke, J. (1975), A note on marginality, in T. Jefferson (ed.), *Resistance Through Rituals*, London: Hutchinson/Birmingham Centre for Contemporary Cultural Studies.

Power, M. J., Alderson, M. R., Phillipson, C. M., Schoenberg, E., and Morris, J. N. (1967), Delinquent schools?, *New Society*, 10, 542–3.

Price, J. B. (1968), Some results of the Maudsley Personality Inventory from a sample of girls in Borstal, *British Journal of Criminology*, 8, 383–401.

Quadagno, D. M., Briscoe, R., and Quadagno, J. S. (1977), Effects of perinatal hormones on selected nonsexual behavior patterns: a critical assessment of the literature, *Psychological Bulletin*, 84, 63–80.

Raisman, G., and Feld, P. M. (1971), Anatomical considerations relevant to the interpretation of neuroendocrine experiments, in L. Martini and W. F. Ganong (eds.), *Frontiers in Neuroendocrinology*, New York: Academic Press.

Reckless, W. C. (1961), *The Crime Problem*, 3rd edn., New York: Appleton-Century-Crofts.

Reckless, W. C., and Dinitz, S. (1967), Pioneering self-concept as a vulnerability factor in delinquency, *Journal of Criminal Law, Criminology and Police Science*, 58, 515–23.

Reich, W. (1970), *The Mass Psychology of Fascism*, New York: Farrar, Straus and Giroux.

Reiss, A. J. (1967), *Studies in Crime and Law Enforcement in Major Metropolitan Areas: Field Surveys I–III*, Washington, DC: United States Government Printing Office.

Richardson, H. J. (1969), *Adolescent Girls in Approved Schools*, London: Routledge and Kegan Paul.

Riege, M. (1972), Parental affection and juvenile delinquency in girls, *British Journal of Criminology*, 12, 55–73.

Robin, G. D. (1963), Patterns of department store shoplifting, *Crime and Delinquency*, 9, 163–72.

Rohner, R. P. (1976), Sex differences in aggression: phylogenetic and enculturation perspectives, *Ethos*, 4, 57–72.

Rosanoff, A. J., Handy, L. M., and Plessett, I. R. (1941), The etiology of child behaviour difficulties, juvenile delinquency and adult criminality with special reference to their occurrence in twins, *Psychiatric Monographs*, no. 1, Sacramento: Department of Institutions.

Rose, R. H., Holaday, J. W., and Bernstein, I. S. (1971), Plasma testosterone, dominance, rank and aggressive behavior in male rhesus monkeys, *Nature*, 231, 366–8.

Rosenblatt, E., and Greenland, C. (1974), Female crimes of violence, *Canadian Journal of Criminology and Corrections*, 16, 173–80.

Rosenhan, D. L. (1973), On being sane in insane places, *Science*, 79, 250–8.

Rothaus, P., and Worchel, P. (1964), Ego-support, communication, catharsis and hostility, *Journal of Personality*, 32, 293–312.

Rowbotham, S. (1973), *Women's Consciousness, Man's World*, Harmondsworth: Penguin.

Rutter, M. (1972), *Maternal Deprivation Reassessed*, Harmondsworth: Penguin.

Sandhu, H. S., and Allen, D. E. (1969), Female delinquency, goal obstruction and anomie, *Canadian Review of Sociology and Anthropology*, 6, 107–10.

Sarri, R. C. (1976), Juvenile law: how it penalises females, in L. Crites (ed.), *The Female Offender*, Lexington: D. C. Heath and Co.

Schofield, P. (1965), *The Sexual Behaviour of Young People*, Harmondsworth: Penguin.

Scott, P. (1956), Gangs and delinquent groups in London, *British Journal of Delinquency*, 7, 4–24.

Scott, P. (1965), *Memorandum to the Royal Commission on the Penal System from the Institute of Psychiatry*, London: Maudsley and Bethlem Royal Hospitals.

Sears, R. R. (1961), Relation of early socialisation experiences to aggression in middle childhood, *Journal of Abnormal and Social Psychology*, 63, 466–92.

Sears, R. R., Maccoby, E. E., and Levin, H. (1957), *Patterns of Child Rearing*, New York: Row Peterson.

Sears, R. R., Rau, L., and Alpert, R. (1965), *Identification and Child Rearing*, Stanford: Stanford University Press.

Sellin, T. (1937) Research memorandum on crime in the Depression, *Social Science Research Council Reports*, 27, New York.

Shapland, J. M. (1975), Behaviour and personality in delinquent children, Oxford University: unpublished D.Phil. thesis.

Sharpe, S. (1976), *Just Like A Girl*, Harmondsworth: Penguin.

Sheldon, W. H., Hartt, E. M., and McDermott, G. (1949), *Varieties of Delinquent Youths*, New York: Harper.

Sherif, M., and Sherif, C. (1967), Group processes and collective interaction in delinquent activities, *Journal of Research in Crime and Delinquency*, 4, 43–62.

Short, J. F., and Nye, F. I. (1958), Extent of unrecorded juvenile delinquency, *Journal of Criminal Law, Criminology, and Police Science*, 49, 296–302.

Short, J. F., and Strodtbeck, F. L. (1965), *Group Process and Gang Delinquency*, Chicago: University of Chicago Press.

Shortell, J. R., and Biller, H. B. (1970), Aggression in children as a function of sex of subject and sex of opponent, *Developmental Psychology*, 3, 143–4.

Simon, R. J. (1975), *The Contemporary Woman and Crime*, Maryland: NIMH.

Skinner, B. F. (1953), *Science and Human Behavior*, London: Collins.

Smart, C. (1977), *Women, Crime and Criminology: A Feminist Critique*, London: Routledge and Kegan Paul.

Smith, L. S. (1978), Sexist assumptions and female delinquency: an empirical investigation, in C. Smart and B. Smart (eds.), *Women, Sexuality and Social Control*, London: Routledge and Kegan Paul.

Sohier, J. (1969), A rather ordinary crime: shoplifting, *International Criminal Police Review*, 24, 161–6.

Spaulding, E. R. (1914), The results of mental and physical examinations of 400 women offenders – with particular reference to their treatment during commitment, *Journal of the American Institute of Criminal Law and Criminology*, 5, 704–17.

Spencer, J. C. (1964), *Stress and Release in an Urban Estate*, London: Tavistock.

Sykes, G. M., and Matza, D. (1957), Techniques of neutralisation: a theory of delinquency, *American Sociological Review*, 22, 667–89.

Tax, M. (1970), *Woman and her Mind: The Story of Daily Life*, London: Bread and Roses.

Taylor, I., Walton, P., and Young, J. (1973), *The New Criminology: For a Social Theory of Deviance*, London: Routledge and Kegan Paul.

Taylor, I., Walton, P., and Young, J. (1975), *Critical Criminology*, London: Routledge and Kegan Paul.

Taylor, S. P., and Epstein, S. (1967), Aggression as a function of the interaction of the sex of the aggressor and the sex of the victim, *Journal of Personality*, 35, 474–96.

Tennent, T. G. (1969), School non-attendance and delinquency, Oxford University: unpublished MD thesis.

Terry, R. M. (1962), Criterion utilized by the police in the screening of juvenile offenders, University of Wisconsin: unpublished Masters thesis.

Terry, R. M. (1970), Discrimination in the handling of juvenile offenders by social control agencies, in P. G. Garabedian and D. C. Gibbons (eds.), *Becoming Delinquent*, Chicago: Aldine.

Thomas, W. I. (1967), *The Unadjusted Girl*, New York: Harper and Row; first published 1923, New York: Little, Brown and Co.

Thompson, H. S. (1967), *Hells Angels*, New York: Random House.

Tiger, L. (1969), *Men in Groups*, New York: Random House.

Tollman, J., and King, J. A. (1956), The effects of testosterone propinate on aggression in male and female C57BL/10 mice, *British Journal of Animal Behaviour*, 4, 147–9.

United States Department of Labor, Women's Bureau (1972), *Statistical Report*, Washington DC: United States Government Printing Office.

United States President's Commission on Law Enforcement and the Administration of Justice (1967), *Field Surveys I*, Washington, DC: United States Government Printing Office.

Van Lawick-Goodall, J. (1968), The behaviour of free-living chimpanzees on the Gombe Stream Reserve, *Animal Behaviour Monographs*, I, 161–241.

Versele, S. C. (1969), Study of female shoplifters in department stores, *International Criminal Police Review*, 24, 66–70.

Walker, N. (1977), *Behaviour and Misbehaviour: Explanations and Non-Explanations*, Oxford: Blackwell.

Ward, D. A., Jackson, M., and Ward, R. E. (1968), Crimes of violence by women, in D. J. Mulvihill and M. M. Tumin (eds.), *Crimes of Violence*, vol. 13, Washington, DC: United States Government Printing Office.

Washburn, S. L. (1959), Speculations of the inter-relations of the history of tools and biological evolution, in J. N. Spuhler (ed.), *The Evolution of Man's Capacity for Culture*, Detroit: Wayne State University Press.

Weitz, S. (1977), *Sex Roles*, New York: Oxford University Press.

West, D., and Farrington, D. P. (1973), *Who Becomes Delinquent?*, London: Heinemann.

White, D. (1971), Brum's Mobs, *New Society*, 18, 760–3.

Whiting, B., and Pope, C. (1974), cited in E. Maccoby and C. Jacklin, *The Psychology of Sex Differences*, Stanford: Stanford University Press.

Widom, C. S. (1977), Self-esteem, sex-role identity and feminism in female offenders, Paper presented to the 85th Annual Convention of the American Psychological Association, San Francisco.

Widom, C. S. (1978), Toward an understanding of female criminality, *Progress in Experimental Personality Research*, 8, 245–308.

Wilkins, L. T. (1964), *Social Deviance: Social Policy, Action and Research*, London: Tavistock Publications.

Williams, J. R., and Gold, M. (1972), From delinquent behavior to official delinquency, *Social Problems*, 20, 209–29.

Willis, P. (1975), *How Working Class Kids Get Working Class Jobs*, Birmingham: Centre for Contemporary Cultural Studies.

Willis, P. (1978), *Profane Culture*, London: Routledge and Kegan Paul.

Wilson, D. (1978), Sexual codes and conduct: a study of teenage girls, in C. Smart and B. Smart (eds.), *Women, Sexuality and Social Control*, London: Routledge and Kegan Paul.

Wise, N. (1967), Juvenile delinquency among middle class girls, in E. Vaz (ed.), *Middle Class Juvenile Delinquency*, New York: Harper and Row.

Woodside, M. (1962), Instability in women prisoners, *Lancet*, 2 (1962), 928–30.

Yablonsky, L. (1962), *The Violent Gang*, New York: Macmillan.

Young, M., and Willmott, P. (1957), *Family and Kinship in East London*, Harmondsworth: Penguin.

Younghusband, E. (1959), The juvenile court and the child, *British Journal of Delinquency*, 7, 181–95.

Author Index

257

Subject Index

261